KU-675-362

Contents

1114

CUNARD

THE MOST FAMOUS OCEAN LINERS IN THE WORLD™

24 Hour Loan Only

Library Services by Ocean Books

Credits

Footprint credits

Editor: Alan Murphy
Production and layout: Angus Dawson, Emma Bryers, Elysia Alim, Danielle Bricker
Maps: Kevin Feeney

Managing Director: Andy Riddle
Commercial Director: Patrick Dawson
Publisher: Alan Murphy
Publishing Managers: Felicity Laughton, Nicola Gibbs.
Digital Editors: Jo Williams, Tom Mellors
Marketing and PR: Liz Harper
Sales: Diane McEntee
Advertising: Renu Sibal
Finance and Administration: Elizabeth Taylor

Photography credits

Front cover: AndreD/Shutterstock
Back cover: Wendy Townrow/Shutterstock

Printed in Great Britain by CPI Antony Rowe, Chippenham, Wiltshire

Publishing information

Footprint *Focus Brisbane & Queensland*
1st edition
© Footprint Handbooks Ltd
November 2011

ISBN: 978 1 908206 46 6
CIP DATA: A catalogue record for this book is available from the British Library

® Footprint Handbooks and the Footprint mark are a registered trademark of Footprint Handbooks Ltd

Published by Footprint
6 Riverside Court
Lower Bristol Road
Bath BA2 3DZ, UK
T +44 (0)1225 469141
F +44 (0)1225 469461
footprinttravelguides.com

Distributed in the USA by Globe Pequot Press, Guilford, Connecticut

The content of Footprint *Focus Brisbane & Queensland* has been taken directly from Footprint's *East Coast Australia Handbook* which was researched and written by Darroch Donald.

Queensland's capital, Brisbane, has enjoyed phenomenal growth in recent years and along with the Gold Coast is the fastest developing region in Australia. The reason for this is very simple and revolves almost entirely around its greatest assets – climate and lifestyle. What the Gold Coast is to glitz and theme parks and Far North Queensland to the Barrier Reef and rainforests, the Sunshine and Fraser Coasts are to sand, surf and sunshine. Off the coast lies Fraser Island, the largest coastal sand island in the world. With its unique range of habitats, natural features and rich biodiversity, all of which can only be fully explored by 4WD, Fraser presents the opportunity for a truly memorable eco-experience.

For many, the Central and North Coasts of Queensland are the raison d'être of an Australian holiday. Here are the sublime Whitsunday Islands, the effortlessly appealing Magnetic Island, heart-achingly beautiful Hinchinbrook and luscious Lizard Island. But it's not all about beaches, coral reef and tropical islands. Eungella National Park boasts slopes draped in lush rainforest and cloaked in rain-bearing clouds that in turn give rise to wonderful waterfalls and unusual wildlife, while inland from Townsville, the historic gold-mining town of Charters Towers gives many their first taste of Queensland outback.

Cairns is the region's tourist heart and gateway to the Great Barrier Reef and Wet Tropics Rainforest. Nowhere else on earth do two World Heritage-listed ecosystems meet. North of Cairns is the small and sophisticated resort of Port Douglas, gateway to the wonderful Daintree National Park and the exhilarating route north to the wilds of Cape Tribulation. West of Cairns the lush, green plateau known as the Atherton Tablelands offers relief from the heat and humidity of the coast and a dramatic change in landscape.

Planning your trip

When to go

Broadly speaking, the far north from October to April is extremely hot, humid and monsoonal. Cairns still gets visitors who want to see the Great Barrier Reef, but most people will want to enjoy the glorious summer weather in the southern regions and avoid the humidity up north. A visit during May to September not only opens up the north, but also allows an itinerary to range almost anywhere within the two states.

The peak season between Sydney and Brisbane is from mid-December to the end of January. Conversely autumn to spring (March to October) is considered the peak season north of Rockhampton (Tropic of Capricorn), when dry, warm weather is the norm. The 'stinger season' between October and May also presents its own dangers. Generally, accommodation and tourist sites in all three states stay open year round, the main exceptions being in the far north in midsummer (December to March).

Watch out for school holidays and peak seasons, when some areas get completely booked out months in advance (particularly between Sydney and Brisbane). School holidays tend to take place from mid-December to late January, a week or two around Easter, a couple of weeks in June and July and another couple during September and October. If planning a long trip, say three months or more, try to make spring or autumn the core of your time. ▸▸ See Public holidays, page 18.

Getting there

Air
There are international flights direct to Melbourne, Sydney, Brisbane and Cairns and it is quite possible to have different points of arrival and departure that complement your intended itinerary. If there is not a direct flight to your primary choice there will usually be a same-day connection from Sydney or Melbourne. It is usually possible to book internal Australian flights when booking your international ticket, at lower prices than on arrival. Some do not even require a stated departure and arrival point. If you have any plans to fly within New South Wales or Queensland check this out prior to booking.

Fares depend on the season, with prices higher during December and January unless booked well in advance. Mid-year sees the cheapest fares. **Qantas**, www.qantas.com.au, is Australia's main international and domestic airline and flies from most international capitals and major cities. That said, with the advent of the global financial crisis, competition is fiercer than ever, and Qantas is struggling in international and domestic markets against other airlines like Emirates, V Australia and Tiger Airways. Most other international major airlines have flights to Australia from their home countries.

Departure tax
There are currently a number of departure taxes levied by individual airports (such as noise tax) and the government. All taxes are included in the cost of a ticket.

Don't miss ...

Numbers relate to numbers on map on page 4.

Getting around

Public transport is generally good and efficient and often easier than driving. Most cities have good metropolitan bus services, though some are curiously unaware of tourist traffic and there is many an important outlying attraction poorly served by public transport, or even missed off the bus routes completely. Some cities are compact enough for this to be a minor irritation, others are so spread out that the visitor must invest in an expensive tourist bus service or taxis. In such places staying at a hostel or B&B with free or low-cost bike hire can save a lot of money. Bear in mind that when it comes to public transport in the major centres, Australia is hardly comparable to Japan or to a lesser extent Europe or North America.

By far the best way of seeing the East Coast is under your own steam, or with a tour operator with an in-depth itinerary. See individual town and city sections for details. The further from the cities you go, the more patchy and irregular public transport becomes. All the states have networks based on a combination of air, bus and train. Some of these services connect up at border towns but check first. If you are short on time and long on funds, flying can save a lot of time, money and effort, both interstate and within New South Wales and Queensland. In some cases it is the only real option. Most other interstate options involve long-distance buses, and on a few routes, trains. Train fares and domestic air travel can be considerably cheaper if booked in advance and on the net. For flights within Australia, try www.webjet.com.au.

Air

Qantas, T131313, www.qantas.com.au, **Tiger Airways**, T03-9335 3033, www. tigerairways.com, **Jetstar**, T131538, www.jetstar.com.au, and **Virgin Blue**, T136789, www.virginblue.com.au, link most state capitals to each other and to many of the larger towns and main tourist destinations. There are also several regional airways operating smaller planes on specialist routes including **Regional Express (REX)**, T131713, www. regionalexpress.com.au. Domestic fares have dropped dramatically in recent years. But bear in mind with budget airlines this does not take into account cargo baggage, for which you will pay significantly more. For up-to-date information on whether a destination is served by scheduled or charter flights, contact your destination's tourist office or each airline direct.

Bear in mind that many provincial airports may not be staffed when you arrive. Check with the local tourist office regarding transport from the airport to the town.

Rail

Train travel up and down the East Coast is a viable mode of transport and can be a delightful way to get from A to B, especially if you are short of time. Given the distances between the main centres, Australia lends itself to rail travel and you may find routes with such evocative names as *Sunlander* and *Spirit of the Outback* irresistible. That said, a car or coach is a better option if you wish to explore or get off the beaten track. The East Coast offers endless beaches and numerous national parks that are well away from any railway stations. Also bear in mind that track gauges differ in NSW and Queensland, so the crossing between the two takes in an intriguing transition by road. Also, note that overnight travel by rail is possible, though often expensive, if you wish to have the comfort of your own compartment and to do it in style. Well worth considering is a jaunt into the outback from Brisbane to Longreach on board the **Spirit of the Outback**.

In New South Wales, **Countrylink**, T132232 (within Australia), www.countrylink .nsw. gov.au, offers rail and rail/coach services state-wide and to Brisbane. There are several **Countrylink travel centres** at principal stations in Sydney including the Sydney Central Railway Station, T02-99379 3800. A useful website for travel throughout New South Wales is www.webwombat.com.au/transport/nsw.htm.

In Queensland, **Queensland Rail**, T131617, www.qr.com.au, offers a range of rail services up and down the coast and into the outback. Brisbane (Roma Street) Transit Centre in Brisbane, T07-3236 2528, hosts offices for most major coach and rail service providers and is a fine source of general travel information. Outback Queensland is also well served by all of the above but stopovers and less frequent travel schedules are obviously the norm.

In Victoria state, **V-Line**, T136196, www.vline.com.au, is the principal service provider.

Road

Bus State and interstate bus services offer the most cost-effective way of constructing an itinerary for a single traveller. A large selection of bus services can be found at www. buslines.com.au. Always check the journey duration and time of arrival, as some routes can take days, with just a couple of short meal stops. Many coaches are equipped with videos but you may also want something to read. It's also a good idea to take warm clothing, socks, a pillow, toothbrush and earplugs. There's a good chance you'll arrive in the late evening or the early hours of the morning. If so, book accommodation ahead and, if possible, transfer transportation.

The main operator throughout New South Wales and Queensland is **Greyhound Pioneer**, T1300 473946, www.greyhound.com.au (referred to simply as Greyhound throughout this guide), while in Victoria the principal service provider is **V-Line**, T136196, www.vline.com.au. Their networks follow all the main interstate highways up and down the coast with offshoots including the Blue Mountains, New England (Hunter Valley), Armidale, Charters Towers, the Atherton Tablelands and so on. As well as scheduled routes, they offer a range of passes. There are also many other smaller regional companies. Most are listed under the relevant destinations. **Countrylink**, T132232, www.countrylink.info, also offers coach services to some centres in conjunction with rail schedules between New South Wales and Queensland.

Greyhound offer a wide variety of passes with several jump-on, jump-off options. The **Day Passes** system has three options: the **Standard Day Pass** allows you to travel anywhere on the Greyhound network for the number of consecutive days you choose with a pre-set kilometre limit. You can buy a pass for three days (1000 km limit, $154), five days (1500 km limit, $223), seven days (2000 km limit, $286), 10 days (3000 km limit, $398), 20 days (6000 km limit, $755), 30 days (10,000 km, $1030). The **Flexi Day Pass** gives you total flexibility without a kilometre restriction. Customers purchase the number of days' travel required (10, 15 or 21) and have up to 60 days to use the travelling days purchased, while The **Fixed Day Pass** gives you freedom to travel for a consecutive number of days (10, 15 and 21) without a kilometre restriction.

The **Explorer Pass** commits you to a set one-way or circular route and is valid for between 30 and 365 days. There are a couple of dozen options including **Best of the East**, which takes in Cairns to Melbourne and the Red Centre at around $1451, and an **All Australian** at $2988.

Other passes include the **Mini Traveller**, which provides travel between two popular destinations; in between you can hop on and hop off as much as you like in the one direction, over 45 days. From Cairns to Sydney will cost around $408.

Backpacker buses There are now several operators who make the assumption that the most important part of your trip is the journey. These companies combine the roles of travel operator and tour guide, taking from two to five times longer than scheduled services (a good indicator of just how much they get off the highway). They are worth considering, especially if you are travelling alone. In terms of style, price ($95-175 per day) and what is included, they vary greatly and it is important to clarify this prior to booking. Some offer transport and commentary only, others include accommodation and some meals, a few specialize in 4WD and bush camping. A few, including **Oz Experience** (see below) offer jump-on, jump-off packages and are priced more on distance. The popular option of flying Sydney to Cairns independently and then returning by bus (or vice versa) is also worth considering and would cost about $675. The main backpacker bus company in NSW and Queensland is **Oz Experience**, T1300 300028, www.ozexperience.com.

Car If you live in a small and populous country, travelling by car in Australia will be an enlightening experience, as well as an enervating one. Distances are huge and travelling times between the major cities, towns and sights can seem endless, so put on some tunes and make driving part of the whole holiday experience.

You should consider buying a car if you are travelling for more than three months. Consider a campervan if hiring or buying. Traffic congestion is rarely an issue on the East Coast route – only Sydney has anything like the traffic of many other countries, so driving itineraries can be based on covering a planned distance each day, up to, say, 100 km for each solid hour's driving. The key factor in planning is distance. It is pretty stress-free and as the distances can be huge, drivers can get bored and sleepy. There are a lot of single-vehicle accidents in Australia, many the result of driver fatigue.

The other major factor when planning is the type of roads you may need to use. Almost all the main interstate highways between Sydney and Cairns are 'sealed', though there are a few exceptions. Many country roads are unsealed, usually meaning a stony or sand surface. When recently graded (levelled and compacted) they can be almost as pleasant to drive on as sealed roads, but even then there are reduced levels of handling. After grading, unsealed roads deteriorate over time. Potholes form, they can become impassable when wet and corrugations usually develop, especially on national park roads, with heavy usage. These are regular ripples in the road surface, at right angles to the road direction, that can go on for tens of kilometres. Small ones simply cause an irritating judder, large ones can reduce tolerable driving speeds to 10-20 kph. Generally, the bigger the wheel size and the longer the wheel base, the more comfortable the journey over corrugations will be. Many unsealed roads can be negotiated with a two wheel-drive (2WD) low-clearance vehicle but the ride will be a lot more comfortable, and safer, in a 4WD high-clearance one. Most

2WD hire cars are uninsured if driven on unsealed roads. Some unsealed roads (especially in the outback) are designated as 4WD-only or tracks, though individual definitions can differ according to the map or authority you consult. If in doubt, stick to the roads you are certain are safe for your vehicle and you are sufficiently prepared for. With careful preparation, however, and the right vehicles (convoys are recommended), traversing the major outback tracks is an awesome experience.

If you stray far from the coast, and certainly anywhere outback, prepare carefully. Carry essential spares and tools such as fan belts, hoses, gaffer tape, a tyre repair kit, extra car jack, extra spare wheel and tyre, spade, decent tool kit, oil and coolant and a fuel can. Membership of the NRMA (NSW) or the RACQ (QLD) is recommended (see below), as is informing someone of your intended itinerary. Above all carry plenty of spare water, at least 10 litres per person, 20 if possible. As far as the best make of vehicle for the outback, in Australia it is the iconic Toyota Landcruiser every time. Break down in a cruiser and the chances are spare parts can be sourced quite easily, without waiting days for foreign hard-to-come-by items. Break down in a Mitsubishi Delica and you may as well look for a job and get married to a local.

Rules and regulations To drive in Australia you must have a current driving licence. Foreign nationals also need an international driving licence, available from your national motoring organization. In Australia you drive on the left. Speed limits vary between states, with maximum urban limits of 50-60 kph and maximum country limits of 100-120 kph. Speeding penalties include a fine and police allow little leeway. Seatbelts are compulsory for drivers and passengers. Driving under the influence of alcohol is illegal over certain (very small) limits and penalties are severe.

Petrol costs Fuel costs are approximately half that in Britain and twice that in the US, but due to the recent increase in the price of crude are following the global trend and rising rapidly. In mid-2011 they were fluctuating between $1.20 and $1.30 a litre in city centres and marginally more in the outback. Diesel was traditionally more expensive than unleaded at about $1.35, but it's less prone to price fluctuations and in recent times can actually beat unleaded at a more consistent $1.20. When budgeting, allow at least $15 for every estimated 100 km. A trip around the eastern circuit can easily involve driving 20,000 km. Picking an economical vehicle and conserving fuel can save hundreds of dollars.

Motoring organizations Every state has a breakdown service that is affiliated to the **Australian Automobile Association (AAA)**, www.aaa.asn.au, with which your home country organization may have a reciprocal link. You need to join one of the state associations: in New South Wales **NRMA**, T132132, www.nrma.com.au, in Victoria **RACV**, T131329, www.racv.com.au, and in Queensland **RACQ**, T131905, www.racq.com.au. Note also that you may be covered for only about 100 km (depending on the scheme) of towing distance and that without cover towing services are very expensive. Given the sheer distances you are likely to cover by car, joining an automobile organization is highly recommended but read the fine print with regard to levels of membership in relation to coverage outside metropolitan areas and in the outback.

Vehicle hire Car rental costs vary considerably according to where you hire from (it's cheaper in the big cities, though small local companies can have good deals), what you hire and the mileage/insurance terms. You may be better off making arrangements in your own country for a fly/drive deal. Watch out for kilometre caps: some can be as low as 100 km per day. The minimum you can expect to pay in Australia is around $250 a week for a small car. Drivers need to be over 21. At peak times it can be impossible to get a car at short notice and some companies may dispose of a booked car within as little as half an hour of you not showing up for an agreed pick-up time. If you've booked a car but are going to be late, ensure that you let them know before the pick-up time.

Cycling
Long-term bicycle hire is rarely available and touring cyclists should plan to bring their own bike or buy in Australia. Bicycle hire is available in most towns and cities and companies are listed in the relevant sections of this book. If you do plan on touring the coast by bicycle, the website www.cycling.org.au is recommended.

Hitchhiking
Hitchhiking, while not strictly illegal in New South Wales and Queensland, is not advised by anyone. The tragic events near Barrow Creek in 2001 demonstrate that there will always be twisted souls who will assault or abduct people for their own evil ends. This is not to say that hitching is more dangerous in Australia than elsewhere else.

Sleeping

East Coast Australia presents a diverse and attractive range of accommodation options, from cheap national park campsites to luxurious Great Barrier Reef island retreats. The real beauty here, given the weather and the environment, is that travelling on a budget does not detract from the enjoyment of the trip. On the contrary, this is a place where a night under canvas in any of the national parks is an absolute delight.

Booking accommodation in advance is highly recommended, especially in peak seasons. Booking online will usually secure the best rates. Especially beyond the Queensland border, check if your accommodation has air conditioning (a/c) when booking. Rooms without air conditioning are almost impossible to sleep in during hot weather. Note that single rooms are relatively scarce. Twin or double rooms let to a single occupant are rarely half the price and you may even be charged the full cost for two people.

Hotels, lodges, motels and resorts
At the top end of the scale, especially in the state capitals, the Gold Coast, Moreton Bay Islands, Fraser Island, Whitsunday Islands, Cairns and the Great Barrier Reef Islands there are some impressive international-standard hotels, lodges and resorts, with luxurious surroundings and facilities, attentive service and often outstanding locations. For examples refer to the Kingfisher Bay Resort, www.kingfisherbay.com; the Daintree Eco-lodge and Spa, www.daintree-ecolodge.com.au; or the Park Hyatt in Sydney, www.hyatt.com.au.

Rooms in hotels and lodges will typically start in our $$$$ range. In the main cities are a few less expensive hotels in the $$$ range. Most 'hotels' outside of the major towns are pubs with upstairs or external accommodation. If upstairs, a room is likely to have access to shared bathroom facilities, while external rooms are usually standard en suite motel units. The quality of pub-hotel accommodation varies considerably but is usually a budget option ($$). Linen is almost always supplied.

Motels in Australia are usually depressingly anonymous but dependably clean and safe and offer the cheapest en suite rooms. Most have dining facilities and free, secure parking. Some fall into our $$ range, most will be a $$$. Linen is always supplied.

Sleeping and eating price codes

Sleeping

$$$$ over $200 $$$ $111-200 $$ $50-110

$ under $50

Prices are in Australian dollars include taxes and service charge, but not meals. They are based on a double room, except in the $ range, where prices are almost always per person.

Eating

$$$ over $35 $$ $25-35 $ under $25

Prices refer to the cost of a two-course meal, not including drinks.

B&Bs and self-catering

Bed and breakfast (B&B) is in some ways quite different from the British model. Not expensive, but rarely a budget option, most fall into our **$$$-$$** ranges. They offer very comfortable accommodation in usually upmarket, sometimes historic houses. Rooms are usually en suite or have access to a private bathroom. Most hosts are friendly and informative. Some B&Bs are actually semi or fully self-contained cottages or cabins with breakfast provisions supplied. Larger ones may have full kitchens. As well as private houses, caravan parks and hostels and some resorts and motels provide self-contained, self-catering options with apartment-style units. Linen may not be supplied in self-catering accommodation.

A couple of good websites are www.bedandbreakfast.com.au, www.bbbook.com.au and www.bedandbreakfastnsw.com (NSW).

National parks, farms and stations

Some national parks and rural cattle and sheep stations have old settlers' or workers' homes that have been converted into tourist accommodation, which is usually self-contained. They are often magical places to stay and include many old lighthouse keepers' cottages and shearers' quarters. Stations may also invite guests to watch, or even get involved in, the day's activities. Transport to them can be difficult if you don't have your own vehicle. Linen is often not supplied in this sort of accommodation.

Hostels

For those travelling on a tight budget there is a large network of hostels offering cheap accommodation (**$$-$**). These are also popular centres for backpackers and provide great opportunities for meeting fellow travellers. All hostels have kitchen and common room facilities, almost all now have internet and some have considerably more. A few, particularly in cities, will offer freebies including breakfast and pick-ups. Many are now open 24 hours, even if the front desk is closed at night. Standards vary considerably and it's well worth asking the opinions of other travellers. Most are effectively independent – even most **YHAs** are simply affiliates – but the best tend to be those that are owner-managed. Of several hostel associations, **YHA**, www.yha.org.au, and **NOMADS**, T02-9299 7710, www.nomadsworld.com, no membership fee, seem to keep the closest eye on their hostels, ensuring a consistency of quality. The **YMCA**, T03-9699 7655, www.ymca.org.au, and **YWCA**, T02-6230 5150, www.ywca.org.au, are usually a clean and quiet choice in the major cities. International visitors can obtain a **Hostelling International Card** (HIC) from any **YHA** hostel or travel centre: it's valid for one year and costs $32. For this you get a handbook of **YHA** hostels nationwide and around $3 off every night's accommodation. Some transport and tourist establishments also offer discounts to HIC holders. For more information, see www.hihostels.com.

Caravan and tourist parks

Almost every town will have at least one caravan park, with unpowered and powered sites varying from $25-40 (for two) for campers, caravans and campervans, an ablutions block and usually a camp kitchen or barbecues. Some will have permanently sited caravans (onsite vans) and cabins. Onsite vans are usually the cheapest option (**$**) for families or small groups wanting to self-cater. Cabins are usually more expensive (**$$**). Some will have televisions, en suite bathrooms, separate bedrooms with linen and well-equipped kitchens. Power is rated at the domestic level (240/250v AC), which is very convenient for budget travellers. Some useful organizations are: **Big 4**, T0300-738044 / T03-9811 9300, www.big4.com.au; **Family Parks of Australia**, T02-6021 0977, www.familyparks.com.au; and **Top Tourist Parks**, T08-8363 1901, www.toptourist.contact.com.au. Joining a park association will get you a discount in all parks that are association members.

If you intend to use motor parks, get hold of the latest editions of the tourist park guides published by the NMRA, RACV and RACQ. They are an essential resource.

Camping

Bush camping is the best way to experience the natural environment. Some national parks allow camping, mostly in designated areas only, with a few allowing limited bush camping. Facilities are usually minimal, with basic toilets, fireplaces and perhaps tank water; a few have barbecues and shower blocks. Payment is often by self-registration (around $6-15 per person) and barbecues often require $0.20, $0.50 or $1 coins, so have small notes and change ready. In many parks you will need a gas stove. If there are fireplaces you must bring your own wood as collecting wood within parks is prohibited. No fires may be lit, even stoves, during a total fire ban. Even if water is supposedly available it is not guaranteed so take a supply, as well as your own toilet paper. Camping in the national parks is strictly regulated. For details of the various rules, contact the National Parks Wildlife Service (NPWS) and Queensland Parks and Wildlife Service (QPWS) or Parks Victoria.

Campervans

A popular choice for many visitors is to hire or buy a vehicle that can be slept in, combining the costs of accommodation and transport (although you will still need to book into caravan parks for power and ablutions). Ranging from the popular VW Kombi to enormous vans with integral bathrooms, they can be hired from as little as $60 per day to a de luxe 4WD model for as much as $800. A van for two people at around $130 per day compares well with hiring a car and staying in hostels and allows greater freedom. High-clearance, 4WD campervans are also available and increase travel possibilities yet further. Kombis can usually be bought from about $2500. An even cheaper, though less comfortable, alternative is to buy a van or station wagon (estate car) from around $2000 that is big enough to lay out a sleeping mat and bag in.

Sales outlets Apollo, T+800 3260 5466, www.apollocarrentals.com.au; **Backpacker**, T03-8379 8893, www.backpackercampervans.com; **Britz**, T03-8379 8890, www.britz.com.au;

Getabout, T02-9380 5536, www.getaboutoz.com; **Maui**, T03-8379 8891 (T800 2008 0801), www.maui.com.au; **Wicked**, T07-3634 9000, www.wickedcampers.com.au. The latter are proving immensely popular with the backpacker set and you will see their vivid, arty vans everywhere. However, they may not suit everybody (you'll see what we mean).

Eating and drinking

The quintessential image of Australian cooking may be of throwing some meat on the barbie but Australia actually has a dynamic and vibrant cuisine all its own. Freed from the bland English 'meat and two veg' straitjacket in the 1980s by the skills and cuisines of Chinese, Thai, Vietnamese, Italian, Greek, Lebanese and other immigrants, Australia has developed a fusion cuisine that takes elements from their cultures and mixes them into something new and original.

Asian ingredients are easily found in major cities because of the country's large Asian population. Australia makes its own dairy products so cheese or cream may come from Tasmania's King Island, Western Australia's Margaret River or the Atherton Tablelands in Far North Queensland. There is plenty of seafood, including some unfamiliar creatures such as the delicious Moreton bugs (crabs), yabbies and crayfish. Mussels, oysters and abalone are all also harvested locally. Fish is a treat too: snapper, dhufish, coral trout and red emperor or the dense, flavoursome flesh of freshwater fish such as barramundi and Murray cod. Freshness is a major feature of modern Australian cuisine, using local produce and cooking it simply to preserve the intrinsic flavour. Native animals are used, such as kangaroo, emu and crocodile, and native plants that Aboriginal people have been eating for thousands of years such as quandong, wattle seed or lemon myrtle leaf. A word of warning, however: this gourmet experience is mostly restricted to cities and large towns. There are pockets of foodie heaven in the country but these are usually associated with wine regions and are the exception rather than the rule.

Eating out
Eating habits in Australia are essentially the same as in most Western countries and are of course affected by the climate. The barbecue on the beach or in the back garden is an Aussie classic but you will find that most eating out during daylight hours takes place outdoors. Weekend brunch is hugely popular, especially in the cities, and often takes up the whole morning. Sydney and Melbourne are the undisputed gourmet capitals, where you will find the very best of modern Australian cuisine as well as everything from Mexican to Mongolian, Jamaican to Japanese. Brisbane also boasts some fine eateries. Restaurants are common even in the smallest towns, but the smaller the town the lower the quality, though not usually the price. Chinese and Thai restaurants are very common, with most other cuisines appearing only in the larger towns and cities. Corporate hotels and motels almost all have attached restaurants, as do traditional pubs, which also serve counter meals. Some may have a more imaginative menu or better quality fare than the local restaurants. Most restaurants are licensed, others BYO only, in which case you provide wine or beer and the restaurant provides glasses. Despite the corkage fee this still makes for a better deal than paying the huge mark-up on alcohol. Sadly, Australians have taken to fast food as enthusiastically as anywhere else in the world. Alongside these are food courts, found in the shopping malls of cities and larger towns. Also in the budget bracket are the delis and milk bars, serving hot takeaways together with sandwiches, cakes and snacks.

Drinks

Australian **wine** will need no introduction to most readers. Many of the best-known labels, including **Penfolds** and **Jacob's Creek**, are produced in South Australia but there are dozens of recognized wine regions right across the southern third of Australia, where the climate is favourable for grape growing and the soil sufficient to produce high-standard grapes. The industry has a creditable history in such a young country, with several wineries boasting a tradition of a century or more, but it is only in the last 25 years that Australia has become one of the major players on the international scene, due in part to its variety and quality. There are no restrictions, as there are in parts of Europe, on what grape varieties are grown where, when they are harvested and how they are blended.

Visiting a winery is an essential part of any visit to the country, and a day or two's tasting expedition is a scenic and cultural as well as an epicurean delight. Cellar doors range from modern marble and glass temples to venerable, century-old former barns of stone and wood, often boasting some of the best restaurants in the country. In New South Wales the Hunter Valley provides one of the best vineyard experiences in the world with more than a 100 wineries, world-class B&Bs and tours ranging from cycling to horse-drawn carriage.

Australians themselves drink more and more wine and less beer. The average rate of consumption is now 20 litres per person per year, compared to eight litres in 1970. Beer has dropped from an annual 135 litres per person in 1980 to 95 litres now. The price of wine, however, is unexpectedly high given the relatively low cost of food and beer. Visitors from Britain will find Australian wines hardly any cheaper at the cellar door than back home in the supermarket.

The vast majority of **beer** drunk by Australians is lager, despite often being called 'ale' or 'bitter'. The big brands such as **VB** (Victoria), **Tooheys** (NSW) and **Castlemaine XXXX** (QLD) are fairly homogenous but refreshing on a hot day. If your palate is just a touch more refined, hunt out some of the imported beers on tap that are predominantly found in the pseudo-Irish pubs in almost all the main coastal towns. Beer tends to be around 4-5% alcohol, with the popular and surprisingly pleasant-tasting 'mid' varieties about 3.5%, and 'light' beers about 2-2.5%. Drink driving laws are strict and the best bet is to not drink alcohol at all if you are driving. As well as being available on draught in pubs, beer can also be bought from bottleshops (bottle-o's) in cases (slabs) of 24-36 cans (tinnies or tubes) or bottles (stubbies) of 375 ml each. This is by far the cheapest way of buying beer (often under $4 per can or bottle).

Essentials A-Z

Accident & emergency

Dial 000 for the emergency services. The 3 main professional emergency services are supported by several others, including the **State Emergency Service (SES)**, **Country Fire Service (CFS)**, **Surf Life Saving Australia (SLSA)**, **Sea-search and Rescue** and **St John's Ambulance**. The SES is prominent in coordinating search and rescue operations. The CFS provides invaluable support in fighting and controlling bush fires. These services, though professionally trained, are mostly provided by volunteers.

Electricity

The current in Australia is 240/250v AC. Plugs have 2- or 3-blade pins and adaptors are widely available.

Embassies and high commissions

For a list of Australian embassies and high commissions worldwide, see www.embassy.gov.au.

Health
Before you go

Ideally, you should see your GP or travelclinic at least 6 weeks before your departure for general advice on travel risks, malariaand vaccinations. No vaccinations are required or recommended for travel to Australia unless travelling from a yellow fever-infected country in Africa or South America. Check with your local Australian Embassy for further advice. A tetanus booster is advisable, however, if you have one due. Make sure you have travel insurance, get a dental check (especially if you are going to be away for more than a month), know your own blood group and, if you suffer a long-term condition such as diabetes or epilepsy, make sure someone knows or that you have a Medic Alert bracelet/necklace with this information on it.

A-Z of health risks

There are three main threats to health in Australia: the powerful sun, dengue fever and poisonous snakes and spiders.

For **sun protection**, a decent wide-brimmed hat and factor 30 suncream (cheap in Australian supermarkets) are essential. Follow the Australians with their Slip, Slap, Slop campaign: slip on a shirt, slap on a hat and slop on the sunscreen.

Dengue can be contracted throughout Australia. In travellers this can cause a severe flu-like illness, which includes symptoms of fever, lethargy, enlarged lymph glands and muscle pains. It starts suddenly, lasts for 2-3 days, seems to get better for 2-3 days and then kicks in again for another 2-3 days. It is usually all over in an unpleasant week. The mosquitoes that carry the dengue virus bite during the day, unlike the malaria mosquitoes, which sadly means that repellent application and covered limbs are a 24-hr issue. Check your accommodation for flower pots and shallow pools of water since these are where the dengue-carrying mosquitoes breed.

In the case of **snakes and spiders**, check loo seats, boots and the area around you if you're visiting the bush. A bite itself does not mean that anything has been injected into you. However, a commonsense approach is to clean the area of the bite (never have it sutured early on) and get someone to take you to a medical facility fast. The most common poisonous spider is the tiny, shy redback, which has a shiny black body with distinct red markings. It regularly hides under rocks or in garden sheds and garages. Outside toilets are also a favourite. Far more dangerous, though restricted to the Sydney area only, is the Sydney funnel-web, a larger and more aggressive customer, often found in outdoor loos. There are dozens of venomous snake species in Australia. Few are actively aggressive and even those only during certain key times of year, such as mating seasons, but all are easily provoked and for many an untreated bite can be fatal (see box opposite).

Australia has reciprocal arrangements with a few countries allowing citizens of those countries to receive free emergency treatment under the **Medicare** scheme. Citizens of New Zealand and the Republic of Ireland are entitled to free care as public patients in public hospitals and to subsidized medicines under the Pharmaceutical Benefits Scheme. Visitors from Finland, Italy, Malta, the Netherlands, Sweden and the UK also enjoy subsidized out-of-hospital treatment (ie visiting a doctor). If you qualify, contact your own national health scheme to check what documents you will require in Australia to claim **Medicare**. All visitors are, however, strongly advised to take out medical insurance for the duration of their visit.

For safety tips in the water, see box above.

Money
All dollars quoted in this guide are Australian unless specified otherwise. The Australian dollar ($) is divided into 100 cents (c). Coins come in denominations of 5c, 10c, 20c, 50c, $1 and $2. Banknotes come in denominations of $5, $10, $20, $50 and $100. **Exchange rates** as of September 2011 were as follows: US$1 = A$0.94; £1 = A$1.52; €1 = A$1.35.

Banks, ATMs, credit and cash cards
The four major banks, the **ANZ**, **Challenge/Westpac**, **Commonwealth** and **NAB (National Australia Bank)** are usually the best places to change money and traveller's cheques, though bureaux de change tend to have slightly longer opening hours and often open at weekends. You can withdraw cash from ATMs with a cash card or credit card issued by most international banks and they can also be used at banks, post offices and bureaux de change. Most hotels, shops, tourist operators and restaurants in Australia

accept the major credit cards, though some places may charge for using them. When booking always check if an operator accepts them. **EFTPOS** (the equivalent of Switch in the UK) is a way of paying for goods and services with a cash card. Unfortunately EFTPOS only works with cards linked directly to an Australian bank account. Bank opening hours are Mon-Fri, from around 0930 to 1630.

Traveller's cheques
The safest way to carry money is in traveller's cheques, though they are fast becoming superseded by the prevalence of credit cards and ATMs. **American Express**, **Thomas Cook** and **Visa** are the cheques most commonly accepted. Remember to keep a record of the cheque numbers and the cheques you've cashed separate from the cheques themselves. Traveller's cheques are accepted for exchange in banks, large hotels, post offices and large gift shops. Some insist that at least a portion of the amount be in exchange for goods or services. Commission when cashing traveller's cheques is usually 1% or a flat rate. Avoid changing money or cheques in hotels as rates are often poor.

Money transfers
If you need money urgently, the quickest way to have it sent is to have it wired tothe nearest bank via **Western Union**,T1800 337377, www.travelex.com.au. Charges apply but on a sliding scale.Money can also be wired by **Amex** or **Thomas Cook**, though this may take a dayor two, or transferred direct from bank to bank, but this again can take several days. Within Australia use money orders to send money. See www.auspost.com.au.

Cost of travelling
By European, North American and Japanese standards Australia is an inexpensive place to visit. Accommodation, particularly outside the main centres, is good value, though prices can rise uncomfortably in

peak seasons. Transport varies considerably in price and can be a major factor in your travelling budget. Eating out can be indecently cheap. There are some restaurants in Sydney comparable with the world's best where $175 is enough to cover dinner for 2 people. The bill at many excellent establishments can be half that. Australian beer is about $4-8 and imported about $6-8 in most pubs and bars, as is a neat spirit or glass of wine. Wine will generally be around 1½ times to double the price in restaurants than it would be from a bottleshop. The minimum budget required, if staying in hostels or campsites, cooking for yourself, not drinking much and travelling relatively slowly, is about $80 per person per day, but this isn't going to be a lot of fun. Going on the odd tour, travelling faster and eating out occasionally will raise this to a more realistic $100-130. Those staying in modest B&Bs, hotels and motels as couples, eating out most nights and taking a few tours will need to reckon on about $220 per person per day. Costs in the major cities will be 20-50% higher. Non-hostelling single travellers should budget on spending around 60-70% of what a couple would spend.

Opening hours
Generally Mon-Fri 0830-1700. Many convenience stores and supermarkets are open daily. Late night shopping is generally either Thu or Fri. For banks, see above.

Public holidays
New Years Day; **Australia Day** (26 Jan 2011); **Good Friday** (22 April 2011); **Easter Monday** (25 April 2011); **Anzac Day** (25 Apr 2011); **Queen's Birthday** (13 Jun 2011); **Labour Day** (3 Oct 2011 in NSW, 2 May 2011 in QLD); **Christmas Day** (25 Dec); **Boxing (Proclamation) Day** (26 Dec).

Safety
Australia certainly has its dangers, but with a little common sense and basic precautions

they are relatively easy to minimize. The most basic but important are the effects of the **sun**, see Health, page 16. In **urban areas**, as in almost any city in the world, there is always the possibility of muggings, alcohol-induced harassment or worse. The usual simple precautions apply, like keeping a careful eye and hand on belongings, not venturing out alone at night and avoiding dark, lonely areas. For information on road safety see page 10, or contact one of the AAA associations, see page 9.

Smoking
This is not permitted in restaurants, cafés or pubs where eating is a primary activity, or on any public transport.

Taxes
Most goods are subject to a **Goods and Services Tax** (GST) of 10%. Some shops can deduct the GST if you have a valid departure ticket. GST on goods over $300 purchased (per store) within 30 days before you leave are refundable on presentation of receipts and purchases at the GST refund booth at Sydney International Airport (boarding pass and passport are also required). For more information, T1300 363263.

Telephone
Most public payphones are operatedby nationally owned **Telstra**, www.telstra. com. au. Some take phonecards, available from newsagents and post offices, and credit cards. A payphone call within Australia requires $0.40 or $0.50. If you are calling locally (within approximately 50 km) this lasts indefinitely but only a few seconds , outside the local area. Well worth considering if you are in Australia for any length of time is a pre-paid mobile phone. Telstra and **Vodafone** give the best coverage and their phones are widely available from as little as $150, including some call time. There are also some smaller companies like '**3**' and **Optus** offering attractive deals. By far the cheapest way of calling overseas is

to use an international pre-paid phone card (though they cannot be used from a mobile phone, or some of the blue and orange public phones). Available from city post offices and newsagents, every call made with them may initially cost about $1 (a local call plus connection) but subsequent per-minute costs are a fraction of Telstra or mobile phone charges.

There are no area phone codes. Use a state code if calling outside the state you are in. These are: 02 for ACT/ NSW (08 for Broken Hill), 03 for VIC and 07 for QLD. To call Eastern Australia from overseas, dial the international prefix followed by 61, then the state phone code minus the first 0, then the 8-digit number. To call overseas from Australia dial 0011 followed by the country code. Country codes include: Republic of Ireland 353; New Zealand 64; South Africa 27; the USA and Canada 1; the UK 44. Directory enquiries: 1223. International directory enquiries: 1225.

Telephones numbers starting with 1300 or 1800 are toll free within Australia. Where 2 telephone numbers are listed in this guide, this toll-free number appears in brackets.

Time

Australia covers 3 time zones: Queensland and New South Wales are in Eastern Standard GMT+10 hrs. NSW and Victoria operate daylight saving, which means that clocks go forward 1 hr from Oct and Mar.

Tipping

Tipping is not the norm in Australia, but a discretionary 5-10% tip for particularly good service will be appreciated.

Visas and immigration

Visas are subject to change, so check with your local Australian Embassy or High Commission. For a list of these, see www.embassy.gov.au. All travellers to Australia, except New Zealand citizens, must have a valid visa to enter Australia. These must be arranged prior to travel (allow 2 months) and cannot be organized at Australian airports. Tourist visas are free and are available from your local Australian Embassy or High Commission, or in some countries, in electronic format (an Electronic Travel Authority or ETA) from their websites and from selected travel agents and airlines. Passport holders eligible to apply for an ETA include those from Austria, Belgium, Canada, Denmark, France, Germany, the Irish Republic, Italy, Japan, Netherlands, Norway, Spain, Sweden, Switzerland, the UK and the USA. Tourist visas allow visits of up to 3 months within the year after the visa is issued. Multiple-entry 6-month tourist visas are also available to visitors from certain countries. Application forms can be downloaded from the embassy website or from www.immi.gov.au. Tourist visas do not allow the holder to work in Australia. See also www.immi.gov.au/visitors.

Weights and measures

The metric system is universally used.

Contents

Footprint features

Brisbane & South Coast Queensland

Gold Coast

With almost five million visitors a year the 'Coast with the Most' is Australia's most popular domestic holiday destination and for some inexplicable reason is seen by some native Australians as the perfect piece of real estate. Like any place that is bold and brash, the Gold Coast's reputation precedes it and no doubt those who have never been will already have formed a strong opinion. Sure it's a concrete jungle and a womb of artificiality, but for lovers of the laid-back beach lifestyle, socialites seeking a hectic nightlife, theme park and thrill ride junkies and shopaholics, it can promise more than just a surfers' paradise. For those of you just itching to scratch the mighty Gold Coast from your travelling agenda at the mere prospect of such a place, think again. Even for the greatest cynic, the worst (or the best) of the Gold Coast can prove utterly infectious and lead to a thoroughly enjoyable experience. Turning your back on the coast, only an hour away is one of the Gold Coast's greatest assets and the 'Green behind the Gold', in the form of the Springbrook and Lamington National Parks, two of Queensland's best, and perfect retreats from all the chaos.

Currumbin to Surfers Paradise

Just off the Gold Coast Highway is **Currumbin Wildlife Sanctuary** ① *T5534 1266, www. currumbin-sanctuary.org.au, 0800-1700, $40, children $24*, one of the most popular parks in the area. A small train takes you into the heart of the park where you can investigate the various animal enclosures housing everything from Tasmanian devils to tree kangaroos. But the highlight is the rainbow lorikeet feeding. To either partake or be a spectator at this highly colourful and entertaining 'avian-human interaction spectacular' is truly memorable and thoroughly recommended. Just before feeding time the air fills with the excited screeching of the birds and the trees are painted in their radiant hues, while the human participants below are each given a small bowl of liquid feed. Given that 80% of Australia's native wildlife is nocturnal, the Wildnight tour programme (1920-2145, from $71) is well worth considering. It includes an Aboriginal dance display.

Burleigh Heads, an ancient volcano, forms one of the few breaks in the seemingly endless swathe of golden sand and offers fine views back towards Surfers. There are also world-class surf breaks and several good walking tracks through the Burleigh Heads National Park. West of Burleigh Heads, **David Fleay Wildlife Park** ① *signposted 3 km west* *of Gold Coast Highway on Burleigh Heads Rd, T5576 2411, 0900-1700, $17, children $8*, is home to all the usual suspects (koalas, crocs, kangaroos and cassowaries), and some less well-known species, like bilbies, brolgas and dunnarts. Overall it offers a fine introduction to Australia's native species. The park is especially well known for its nocturnal platypus displays, breeding successes and care of sick and injured wildlife.

Surfers Paradise → *For listings, see pages 29-33.*

From its humble beginnings as a single hotel four decades ago, Surfers Paradise has mushroomed and now epitomizes all the worst aspects of the Gold Coast. An endless line of high-rise apartment blocks towers over shopping malls and exclusive real estate properties, and a thousand and one tourist attractions, many of them planted firmly and unashamedly at the kitsch end of the market, provide round-the-clock entertainment.

Ins and outs
Getting there and around As the transport hub of the Gold Coast, there are frequent links with all major towns and cities. The airport is at Coolangatta, 22 km south, with regular shuttles to Surfers, which is a small place with most of the action focused in and around the Cavill Avenue Mall and adjacent nightclub strip, Orchid Avenue. ▸▸ *See Transport, page 32.*

State phone codes and time difference

There are no area phone codes. Use a state code if calling outside the state you are in. These are: 02 for ACT/NSW (08 for Broken Hill), 03 for VIC and 07 for QLD.

Note that NSW operates daylight saving, which means that clocks go forward one hour from October to March.

Tourist information VIC ① *2 Cavill Av Mall, T5538 4419, www.goldcoasttourism.com.au, Mon-Fri 0830-1700, Sat 0830-1700, Sun 0900-1600*, is an incredibly small affair. Try to get a copy of the official *Gold Coast Holiday Guide*.

Sights

Surfers Paradise Beach is, of course, the big draw. If you can, take a stroll at sunrise along the 500-m sand-pumping jetty at the end of The Spit, north of Sea World. It opens at 0600 and for $1 you can walk out to the end and take in the memorable view of the entire beach and the glistening high-rises disappearing into the haze, all the way down to Tweed Heads.

One high-rise building stands out above the rest: **Q1** ① *Paradise Blvd, T5582 2700, Fri-Sat 0900-midnight, Sun-Thu 0900-2100, from $19, children $11 (day and night pass $29/$16.50)*. It's marketed as the world's highest residential building. As you might expect you can of course take in the elevated views from its 77th floor observation deck both day and night, which is well worth a look. On Friday and Saturday nights its swish QBar serves up cocktails, live music and the odd high-altitude DJ to enhance the view.

Gold Coast City Art Centre ① *135 Bundall Rd, 3 km west of Surfers, T5581 6500, www. gcac.com.au, Mon-Fri 1000-1700, Sat-Sun 1100-1700, free*, presents a dynamic programme of local contemporary work as well as a more wide-ranging historical collection. It is also home to one of Australia's longest running art prizes, now titled the Conrad Jupiters Art Prize, which has provided an exciting overview of contemporary Australian Art since 1968. The outdoor sculpture walk is also worth looking at.

Between Surfers Paradise and The Spit, **Main Beach** fringes the southern shores of Broadwater Bay and the Nerang River Inlet. The Marina Mirage shopping complex contains some of the best restaurants in the region, most of which offer alfresco dining overlooking Mariners Cove, the departure point for scenic cruises and helicopter flights.

The Gold Coast is often labelled as Australia's **Theme Park** capital, with millions visiting annually. The stalwarts are Sea World, Dreamworld and Movie World, with other less high-profile parks like Wet'n'Wild and the Australian Outback Spectacular providing back-up. Entry for each is expensive, from $72 (children $47), but that usually includes all the rides and attractions. Note also there are any number of combination passes with which to make life easier, or indeed, more complicated. To visit three parks over five days will cost around $150. And you thought this was a holiday? The VIC can help secure the latest complex discounts, or you can contact Myfun direct on T133386. For cheaper online bookings (and to complete your organizational odyssey) see www.myfun.com.au.

Sea World ① *Main Beach (1 km), T5588 2205, www.seaworld.com.au, 1000-1700, $72, children $47,* has been successfully developing its sea-based attractions for over 30 years, picking up numerous awards and earning a reputation as one of the world's best theme parks. The main attractions are the dolphin and seal shows, thrill rides and water ski stunts, resident polar bears (!) and multi-million dollar Shark Bay, which guarantees to get you up close and personal with the beasts. You can also go on whale and dolphin cruises or helicopter scenic flights.

Gold Coast detail

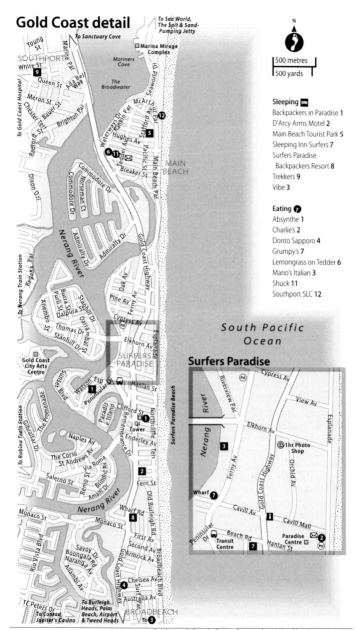

To Sea World,
The Spit & Sand-
Pumping Jetty

To Sanctuary Cove

Marina Mirage Complex

Mariners Cove

The Broadwater

MAIN BEACH

Nerang River

SURFERS PARADISE

Gold Coast City Arts Centre

South Pacific Ocean

Nerang River

BROADBEACH

To Burleigh Heads, Palm Beach, Airport & Tweed Heads

To Conrad Jupiter's Casino

N

500 metres
500 yards

Sleeping
Backpackers in Paradise **1**
D'Arcy Arms Motel **2**
Main Beach Tourist Park **5**
Sleeping Inn Surfers **7**
Surfers Paradise
  Backpackers Resort **8**
Trekkers **9**
Vibe **3**

Eating
Absynthe **1**
Charlie's **2**
Donto Sapporo **4**
Grumpy's **7**
Lemongrass on Tedder **6**
Mario's Italian **3**
Shuck **11**
Southport SLC **12**

Surfers Paradise

Nerang River

Wharf

Transit Centre

Paradise Centre

Movie World ① *Pacific Highway, T133386, www.movieworld.com.au, 1000-1730, $72, children $47,* is perhaps the most popular of all the theme parks. Even if you are not a great fan of Scooby Doo and co, cartoons or science fiction generally, a peek at the sets, props and costumes from the latest big release will certainly impress. Aside from the special effects of the main exhibits, thrill seekers can hit the water on the Wild West Adventure Ride, or even risk the rollercoaster.

As the name suggests, the **Australian Outback Spectacular** ① *Entertainment Road at Oxenford, T133386, www.outbackspectacular.myfun.com.au, Tue-Sun 1930, show and dinner $100, children $70,* is all 'yee haw' horses, Akubra hats and cracking whips. Although both commercial and expensive it is certainly highly entertaining and dinner is included. However, what a crusty ol' station owner in Tittybong or Mount Buggery would have to say about all the hyperbole is an entirely different matter…mate.

Coolangatta and Tweed Heads → *For listings, see pages 29-33.*

What Surfers Paradise is to rollercoasters and shopping malls, Coolangatta is to sand and surf. Its greatest attraction is undoubtedly its beaches and the mighty surf that breaks upon them. The coast around Coolangatta and Tweed Heads is not only renowned as one of the world's premier surf spots, it has also produced many world-class surfers such as the legendary Michael Peterson 'MP', and ex-world champions Peter Townend 'PT' and Wayne 'Rabbit' Bartholomew. Such a reputation has led to something of a population boom in the Coolangatta region and this, coupled with an increase in the popularity of surfing, has caused a massive increase in the numbers of surfers in the water on any good day.

Ins and outs
Getting there and around The airport is 2 km from Coolangatta. Major bus companies have services to the town, which is small enough to navigate on foot, with local bus services to surrounding sights. ▸▸ *See Transport, page 32.*

Tourist information Gold Coast (Coolangatta) VIC ① *Shop 22, Showcase on the Beach, Griffith St, T5569 3380, www.goldcoasttourism.com.au, Mon-Fri 0800-1700, Sat 0900-1500.* **Tweed Heads VIC** ① *corner of Bay St and Wharf St, Tweed Heads, T5536 6737, www. tweedcoolangatta.com.au, Mon-Sat 0900-1630, Sun 0930-1600.* There is a town map in the useful, free brochure *Tweed-Coolangatta Visitor's Guide.*

Sights
Coolangatta is fringed with superb beaches that surround the small peninsula known as Tweed Heads. The tip of the peninsula, named **Point Danger** by Captain Cook in 1770, provides a fine starting point from which to survey the scene. Below and to the right is **Duranbah Beach**, which flanks the sea wall at the mouth of the Tweed River. Like all the beaches around the heads it is a popular surf spot, and Point Danger provides a good vantage point if you want to watch.

To the left is **Snapper Rocks**, one of the most popular surf spots on the southern Gold Coast. It's a great place to watch the surfers as you can literally sit on the rocks beside the 'launch zone' only metres away from all the action. Just to the west of Snapper Rocks is the pretty little beach called **Rainbow Bay**, which is the first of the beaches that combines good surfing with safe swimming. Continuing west, Rainbow Bay is then separated from **Greenmount Beach** by a small headland that offers fine views from **Pat Fagan Park**.

Making waves

Between Snapper Rocks and Kirra Point is the so-called **Superbank**, a man-made phenomenon that has created one of the world's greatest point breaks and most incredible surfing experiences. In the early 1990s a scheme was proposed to remove sand from the mouth of the Tweed and relocate it to the northerly points. This was finished in 2001 and sand is now pumped from the mouth of the river, underground, to spots at Froggies Beach – just to the south of Snapper – Rainbow Bay and Kirra. However, no one expected the scheme to produce such an amazing sandbank or to have such a profound effect on the surf. On a perfect day, machine-like waves roll along the shallow sandbank in one unending steam-train. The Superbank is capable of producing rides of 2 km in length and multiple 10-second barrel rides, making it one of the most popular breaks on the entire Australian East Coast.

Greenmount Beach then merges with Coolangatta Beach, both of which are idyllic, excellent for swimming and enormously popular with families. At the western end of Coolangatta Beach, **Kirra Point** also provides great views back down Greenmount and Coolangatta beaches and north, beyond **North Kirra Beach**, to Surfers Paradise. Between Snapper Rocks and Kirra Point is the famed surfers' Superbank, see box opposite.

Gold Coast hinterland → For listings, see pages 29-33.

Less than an hour's drive from the Gold Coast are its greatest inland attractions, the national parks of Lamington, Springbrook and Mount Tamborine. Labelled 'the Green Behind the Gold', they provide their own natural wonderland of pristine subtropical rainforest, waterfalls, walking tracks and stunning views. The weather here can also be dramatically different from that on the coast with much more rain and the coolest temperatures in the state.

Ins and outs

Tourist information The principal QPWS offices are located within the parks ⓘ *Springbrook, T5533 5147, and Lamington, T5544 0634, www.derm.qld.gov.au*. Walking track guides with maps and details are available from each office. For vineyard information, visit www.goldcoastwinecountry.com.au. ►► *See Transport, page 32.*

Springbrook National Park

This 2954-ha park, 29 km south from Mudgeeraba on the Pacific Highway, is the most accessible for the coast and sits on the northern rim of what was once a huge volcano centred on Mount Warning. The park is split into three sections: **Springbrook Plateau**, **Natural Bridge** and the **Cougals**. The Natural Bridge section of the park is accessed from the Nerang to Murwillumbah Road.

Springbrook offers a rich subtropical rainforest habitat of ancient trees and gorges, interspersed with creeks, waterfalls and an extensive system of walking tracks. In addition, the park is well known for its many spectacular views including **Canyon**, **Wunburra**, **Goomoolahara** and the aptly named **Best of All**. Other attractions include the **Natural Arch** (1-km walk), a cavernous rock archway that spans **Cave Creek**, and the 190-m **Purling Brook Falls** (4-km walk). Natural Arch also plays host to a colony of glow worms. See Tour operators, page 32, if you don't have your own transport.

Mount Tamborine

Mount Tamborine is a name used loosely to describe the 17-section **Tamborine National Park** and the picturesque settlements of **Mount Tamborine**, **Tamborine Village** and **Eagle Heights**. Combined, they offer an attractive escape from the coast with fine coastal views, walking tracks, vineyards, B&Bs, teahouses and arts and crafts galleries. One of the most popular sections is the **Witches Falls**, first designated a national park in 1908, making it Queensland's oldest. Other popular spots include **Cedar Creek** section, with its pleasant 3-km walk to some pretty waterfalls, or the **Joalah** section, where, if you are lucky, you may see – or more probably hear – one of its best-known residents, the mimicking lyrebird.

Mount Tamborine is accessed via the Oxenford-Tamborine Road (Oxenford turn-off) or the Nerang-Tamborine Road (Nerang turn-off) both on the Pacific Highway. There is no public transport to Mount Tamborine but various tours are available.

The biggest attraction here is the new **Tamborine Rainforest Skywalk** ① *333 Geissmann Drive, North Tamborine, T5545 2222, www.rainforestskywalk.com.au, daily 0930-1600, $18.50, children $9.50.* This attraction aims to echo the success of other elevated forest walkways in The Otways in Victoria and in Tahune Forest in Tasmania. The idea is identical in that you can experience the forest and its many inhabitants from a unique viewpoint high above the forest floor. The walk takes about 45 minutes and there is an interpretative centre, shop and café.

Bushwacker Eco Tours ① *T1300 559355, www.bushwacker-ecotours.com.au*, and **JPT Day Tours** ① *T1300 363436, www.daytours.com.au*, both offer package deals from Brisbane.

The VICs can supply information on other attractions in the area, while the **Doughty Park Information Centre** ① *off Main Western Rd, North Tamborine, T5545 3200, www.tamborinemtncc.org.au*, stocks walks and parks information. There are no QPWS campsites in the park.

Lamington National Park

The 20,500-ha Lamington National Park sits on the border of Queensland and New South Wales and comprises densely forested valleys, peaks straddling the **McPherson Range** and an ancient volcanic area known as the **Scenic Rim**, about 60 km inland from the Gold Coast. The park is essentially split into two sections: the **Binna Burra** to the east and the **Green Mountains** (O'Reilly's) to the west. Combined, they offer a wealth of superb natural features and a rich biodiversity that can be experienced on over 100 km of walking tracks. The Green Mountains were first settled in 1911 by the O'Reilly family, who established a number of small dairy farms before consolidating their assets in 1915 with the opening of their now internationally famous guesthouse (see page 30). Other than the sense of escape and surrounding beauty, its most popular draw is the treetop canopy walkway: an ideal way to see the rainforest habitat. There are also some excellent walking tracks offering spectacular views and numerous waterfalls. Guided tours are available, along with a broad range of places to stay. The Green Mountains (O'Reilly's) section is accessed from Canungra.

The most accessible section is Binna Burra, 35 km south west of Nerang on the Pacific Highway. From Brisbane you can travel south via Nerang or via Mount Tamborine and Canungra. If you don't have your own transport, there are numerous tour operators, see page 32. Like the Green Mountains, Binna Burra offers a wealth of excellent rainforest walking opportunities and plays host to another historic guesthouse (see page 30). Guided tours are available from the lodge and there is a QPWS centre and campsite.

Gold Coast listings

▣ Sleeping

Surfers Paradise *p23, map p25*
The Gold Coast has accommodation of all types to suit all budgets. But even with the 60,000 odd beds currently available you are advised to book in advance. Prices fluctuate wildly between peak and off-peak seasons. Standby deals and packages are always on offer so you are advised to shop around and research thoroughly. Booking at least 7 days in advance will usually work out cheaper.

Here we list a small selection. For a much greater choice pick up the free Qantas and Sunlover Gold Coast brochures available from travel agents. Accommodation agents include the **Gold Coast Accommodation Service**, Shop 1, 1 Beach Rd, Surfers, T5592 0067, www.goldcoastaccommodation service.com.au. The Gold Coast City Council operates a number of excellent facilities up and down the coast. Look out for their free *Gold Coast City Council Holiday Parks* brochure or visit www.gctp.com.au.
$$$$ Vibe Hotel, 42 Ferny Av, Surfers Paradise, T5539 0444, www.vibehotels.com. au. Quality contemporary boutique hotel in a central location. Plenty of style and a good choice if you want to indulge.
$$$ Main Beach Tourist Park, Main Beach Pde, T5581 7722, www.gctp.com.au. This park offers cabins, en suite/standard powered and non-powered sites, with good facilities and camp kitchens, all nestled quietly amongst the high-rise blocks and across the road from the main beach.
$$ Backpackers in Paradise, 40 Peninsular Drive, just west of the Transit Centre, T5538 4344, www.backpackers in-paradise.com. Lively, colourful, friendly and well equipped. Dorms and 3 spacious doubles (en suite), café, bar, pool, excellent kitchen, broadband internet, tour desk and a comfy TV lounge with a huge screen.
$$ D'Arcy Arms Motel, 2923 Gold Coast Highway, corner of Frederick St, Surfers,

T5592 0882, www.darcyarms.com.au. Fine Irish hospitality, good value modern units and a good pub/restaurant (see page 30).
$$ Sleeping Inn Surfers Hostel and Apartments, 26 Peninsular Drive, T5592 4455, www.sleepinginn.com.au. Modern facilities with a wider choice of room options than most: from dorms and singles to doubles, twins and self-contained units with TV and living room. It can also throw a good party. They also have a modern apartment complex (**$$$$**) consisting of 1, 2 and 3 bedroom, twin or double rooms at 2963 Surfers Paradise Blvd, T5539 0090.
$$ Surfers Paradise Backpackers Resort, 2837 Gold Coast Highway, T5592 4677, www.surfersparadisebackpackers.com. au. Lively and popular purpose-built place on the border of Surfers and Broadbeach. It offers tidy en suite dorms, units (some self-contained with TV) and good facilities, including well-equipped kitchen, bar, free laundry, pool, sauna, gym, volleyball pitch, cable TV/games room, internet, party and activity tours, pick-ups and off-street parking.
$$ Trekkers, 22 White St, Southport, 2 km north of Surfers, T5591 5616, www. trekkersbackpackers.com.au. The best backpackers in the region. Small traditional suburban Queenslander, offering cosy, well-appointed rooms including en suite doubles with TV, good pool and garden. Great atmosphere, friendly, family-run business with the emphasis on looking after each guest rather than the turnover.

Coolangatta and Tweed Heads *p26*
$$$$ Kirra Beach Tourist Park, Charlotte St, off Coolangatta Rd, T5667 2740, www .gctp.com.au. Spacious, with good facilities, offering powered and non-powered sites, cabins, camp kitchen and saltwater pool.
$$$ Sunset Strip Budget Resort, 199-203 Boundary St, T5599 5517, www.sunsetstrip.

com.au. Much closer to the beach and the town centre, this is an old, spacious hotel with unit-style singles, doubles, twins, quads and family rooms with shared bathrooms, excellent kitchen facilities, large pool and within metres of the beach. Basic but spacious, good value. Fully self-contained 1- and 2-bedroom holiday flats also available.

$$ Coolangatta/Kirra Beach YHA,230 Coolangatta Rd, T5536 7644, booking@ coolangattayha.com. Near the airport and facing the busy Pacific Highway, offers tidy dorms, doubles/twins, pool, bike and surfboard hire, internet. Free shuttle to the beaches and Greyhound bus terminal.

Gold Coast Hinterland *p27*
$$$$ Binna Burra Mountain Lodge, Binna Burra Rd, Beechmont (via Nerang), Lamington National Park, T5533 3622, www.binnaburralodge.com.au. The most accessible of the Lamington National Park medium to luxury options. Well-appointed en suite cabins with fireplace (some with spa), activities, meals included.

$$$$ O'Reilly's Rainforest Guesthouse, Lamington National Park Rd (via Canungra), Lamington National Park, T5544 0644, www. oreillys.com.au. A range of room options from luxury suites to standard, pool, sauna, spa and restaurant. Package includes meals and some tours.

$$$$ The Mouses House, 2807 Springbrook Rd, Springbrook, T5533 5192, www.mouses house.com.au. Characterful luxury eco-resort with themed bush chalets with spa. Very romantic and cosy. Recommended.

QPWS campsites for Lamington National Park at both Binna Burra, T5533 3584, and Green Mountains (200 m from **O'Reilly's**) with water, hot showers and toilets. Fees apply, book ahead with the ranger or information centres at each location. Also at Purling Brook Falls, Springbook National Park, T5533 5147.

🍴 Eating

Surfers Paradise *p23, map p25*
There are too many good restaurants to list here; it's best to browse the menus at your leisure. The Marina Mirage in Main Beach is a favourite haunt, but don't expect a cheap deal. Further north, Sanctuary Cove is a fine spot for lunch but is also expensive. To the south, Burleigh Heads has superb views, while the many surf lifesaving clubs offer great value as do the dinner cruises.

$$$ Absynthe, ground floor, Q1, Hamilton Av, T5504 6466, www.absynthe.com.au. Chic new French/Australian restaurant where award-winning Chef Meyjitte Boughenout gets creative. Try the degustation menu.

$$$ Lemongrass on Tedder, 6/26 Tedder Av, T5528 0289. Of the many Thai options, this one stands out for quality and value for money, but book ahead.

$$ D'Arcy Arms Irish Pub and Motel, see page 29. Mon-Sat from 1800. Offers traditional wholesome pub food at reasonable prices.

$$ Donto Sapporo, 2763 Gold Coast Highway, T5539 9933. Considered one of the best Japanese restaurants in the city.

$$ Grumpy's, at the river end of Cavill Mall (Tiki Village), T5531 6177. Well known for its affordable seafood, casual atmosphere and pleasant views.

$$ Mario's Italian, Oasis Shopping Mall, Broadbeach, T5592 1899. A fine reputation and good value takeaway pizza.

$$ Shuck, Shop 1-4/20 Tedder Av, T5528 4286. Daily from 1200. Award-winning seafood restaurant with an imaginative and wide-ranging menu, good service and chic, contemporary decor. Try the signature dish: sand crab lasagne.

$ Charlie's, Cavill Mall, T5538 5285. Decent meals 24 hrs a day and good breakfast.

$ Southport SLC, McArthur Pde, Main Beach, T5591 5083, and the **Palm Beach SLC**, 7th Av and Jefferson Lane, Palm Beach, T5534 2180, are two of many surf lifesaving clubs (SLCs) along the coast, with great value meals.

Coolangatta and Tweed Heads *p26*
$$ Cooli Steak and Seafood Restaurant,
Shop 1, Blue C Resort, 3 McLean Street,
northern end of Marine Pde , T5536 8808.
Breakfast Sat-Sun from 0700; lunch Fri-Sun
1200-1400; dinner daily from 1730. Best
option for affordable steak and seafood. Tue
specials: buy one main meal and get one of
equal value free.
$$ Fisherman's Cove Seafood Taverna, at
Oaks Calypso Resort, Griffith St, T5536 1646.
Affordable and fine fishy fare.
$ Coffee Club, 120 Marine Pde, T5599
4755. Value light meals and quality coffee
overlooking the beach.

🎷 Bars and clubs

Surfers Paradise *p23, map p25*
If you are staying at any of the hostels you
will be well looked after by the staff and
will only need to go with the flow. If not,
Orchid Av, off Cavill Mall, is the main focus
for clubbing, with most places staying open
until about 0300. Dress is smart casual, carry
ID and be prepared to kiss your money
goodbye. Entry ranges from $12-20, which is
manageable, but drinks are expensive. For a
more sophisticated night out, try the **QBar**,
at the top of the Q1 tower; see page 24.

🎭 Entertainment

Surfers Paradise *p23, map p25*
Conrad Jupiter's Casino, off Hooker Blvd,
Gold Coast Highway, Broadbeach, T5592
8100, www.conrad.com.au. 2 floors of gaming
tables and pokies (slot machines). Open 24
hrs. There is a cinema and theatre at the **Arts
Centre**, 135 Blundall Rd, T5588 4008, and
other mainstream cinemas in the malls.

🎉 Festivals and events

Surfers Paradise *p23, map p25*
The Gold Coast hosts a number of exciting
annual events most of which involve lots of
money, fireworks and parties, festivals, races

and sporting spectaculars. Although listed
under Surfers, many of these are spread out
along the coast. For a detailed calendar, visit
www.verygoldcoast.com.au.
Feb kicks off with **Conrad Jupiter's Magic
Millions**, a 10-day horseracing event with a
very popular fashion event.
Mar The beach is the main focus for the
Australian Surf Life Saving Championships,
arguably the Gold Coast's most famous
event. It attracts over 7000 national and
international competitors, all trying to out
swim, run and row each other, to win the
prestigious Iron Man or Iron Woman trophy.
Jul Gold Coast Marathon is considered to
be Australia's premier long-distance running
event.
Oct It's green for go with the ever-popular
Nitro Super GP, when the streets of Surfers
are alive to the sound of racing cars and, in
the evenings, to the heady beat of parties,
parades and the mardi gras.
Numerous food festivals are also held
throughout the year, including the **Gold
Coast Food Festival** in **Sep**, the **Broadbeach
Festival** in **Oct** and the **Gold Coast
Signature Dish Competition** in **Dec**.

🛍 Shopping

Surfers Paradise *p23, map p25*
The Gold Coast offers a healthy dose of
retail therapy with some 3500 shops, all of
which contribute to over $3 billion of visitor
spending per annum.
Marina Mirage, Main Beach and Sanctuary
Cove. More upmarket than the **Paradise
Centre** but lacking atmosphere.
Paradise Centre, Cavill Av. A focus for
mainly tourist-based products and more
bikinis than an episode of *Baywatch*.

⛰ Activities and tours

Surfers Paradise *p23, map p25*
Other than the beach, shopping and the
theme parks, Surfers presents a mind-
blowing array of additional activities way

beyond the scope of this guide. Visit the VIC for the full list. If anything is to be recommended, it has to be a rainforest tour to the stunning Lamington and Springbrook national parks (see below), an hour's drive inland. The resorts on South Stradbroke Island offer a suitable coastal escape (see Moreton Bay, page 38).

Tour operators
Tour Gold Coast, T5532 8687, www.tourgc. com.au. Specialist eco-operator offering trips to see the Natural Bridge and its glow-worm tours in the Springbrook National Park and whale watching cruises.
Bushwacker Ecotours, T3720 9020 , www. bushwacker-ecotours.com.au. Day walking tours and overnight camping trips to Lamington and Moreton Island from $249.

Water sports
For anything water based, including self-hire, shop around at the Cruise Terminal, at Mariners Cove (Main Beach) or the wharf at the western end of Cavill Av.
For surfing lessons try **Cheyne Horan**, T1800 227873, www.cheynehoran.com.au.

Gold Coast Hinterland *p27*
Tour operators
Several tour operators offer day trips to Springbrook from both Brisbane and the Gold Coast including **Bushwackers Ecotours** (day and night tours, see above), and **Scenic Hinterland Tours**, T5531 5536, www.hinter landtours.com.au, from $75. The VIC has full listings.

⊖ Transport

Getting around the Gold Coast is generally very easy, with 24-hr local bus transport, numerous companies offering theme park/ airport transfers and car, moped, and bike hire. **Surfside Buslines Tourist Shuttle**, T5574 5111, www.gcshuttle.com.au, is the principal local operator and sells a Freedom Pass of 3-14 days, from $67 (children $34). Surfside also

offers airport (Coolangatta) transfers from $21.
Note for regular local use Surfside Buslines use Translink's GoCard Ticketless system. GoCard is a travel card that stores up to $200 so you can travel seamlessly on all TransLink buses.
Airtrain, T1800 119091, www.airtrain.com. au, operates suburban rail services and theme park and airport transfers ($45) from Robina and Nerang, 0830-2245 (main trunk services from Coolangatta to Southport 24 hrs).

Surfers Paradise *p23, map p25*
Bus
Active Tours, T5527 4144; **Coachtrans**,T3358 9700 (T1300 664700), www.coachtrans.com. au, and **Con-X-ions**, T5556 9888, www.con-x-ion.com, offer regular shuttles to and from **Brisbane** city, Brisbane and Coolangatta airports and the theme parks.
The long-distance terminal is on the corner of Beach Rd and Remembrance Drive. Most of the major coach companies have offices within the complex (0600-2200). **Premier Motor Services**, T133410, www.premierms.com.au, and **Greyhound**, T1300 473946, www.greyhound.com.au, offer daily interstate services. **Coachtrans**, T1300 664700, www.coach trans.com.au, are recommended for **Brisbane** city and airport transfers. **Kirklands**, T1300 367077, www. kirklands.com.au, and **Suncoast Pacific**, T131230, and several Byron Bay-based local operators offer regular services to **Byron Bay** and the **NSW coast**.

Cycling
Bike hire is available from **Red Rocket Rent-A-Car**, 16 Orchid Av, T5538 9074, www. redrocketrentals.com.au.

Mopeds/jeeps
Rent-A-Jeep, corner Ferny Av and Ocean Av, Surfers Paradise, T1800 228085. Small jeeps and microscopic Smart cars, starting from about $75 per day.
Yahoo, 88 Ferny Av, T5592 0227. From $50 for mopeds.

Train

Both Robina and Nerang train stations (15 km and 10 km southwest and west of Surfers respectively) are served by **Airtrain**, T1800 119091, www.airtrain.com.au, from **Brisbane** (with connections to Brisbane airport), from $45, children $22. **Airtrain Connect**, T1800 119091, and **Surfside Buslines** T5571 6555 (Nos 2 and 11), then offer road transport to the coast.

Coolangatta and Tweed Heads *p26*
Air

Gold Coast Airport is near Coolangatta,22 km south of Surfers, T5589 1100, www. goldcoastairport.com.au. **Jet Star**, T131538, www.jetstar.com.au; **Qantas**, T131313, www.qantas.com.au; **Tiger**, T03-9355 3033, www.tigerairways.com.au; and **Virgin Blue**, T136789, www.virgin blue.com.au, all offer domestic services (and/or international connections). **Con-X-ions**, T5556 9888, www.con-x-ion.com, and **Surfside Buses**, T5571 6555, offer local transfers, from $15, children $7.

Bus

Premier Motor Services, T133410, and **Greyhound**, T5531 6677, operate daily interstate services, while **Coachtrans**, T1300 664700, www.coachtrans.com.au, runs regular shuttles up and down the coast, to **Brisbane** and to/from the airport. **Kirklands**, T1300 367077, www.kirklands.com.au, and **Suncoast Pacific**, T131230, have regular services to **Byron Bay** and the **NSW coast**.

Surfside Buslines, T131230, www. gcshuttle.com.au, is the main suburban bus company with regular links north to **Surfers**.

Taxi

For a taxi, T5536 1144.

Gold Coast Hinterland *p27*
Coolangatta Coachlines Mountain Coach, T1300 762665, www.mountaincoach.com. au, run transportation to and from the**Gold Coast** (via Mount Tamborine) to **Tamborine Mountain** and **O'Reilly's Resort** in the Lamington National Park.

Binna Burra Mountain Lodge (Binna Burra section) uses Limousine Hire from both the Gold Coast and Brisbane,T1300 249622.

❶ Directory

Surfers Paradise *p23, map p25*
Banks All major branches with ATMs and currency exchange are around the Cavill Mall-Gold Coast Highway intersection.
Hospitals Gold Coast Hospital, 108 Nerang St, Southport, T5571 8211. **Paradise Medical Centre**, Shop 135 Hanlan Street, Surfers Paradise, T5538 8099 (24-hr).
Internet widely available including **The Chat Room Café** , Shop 37, 3240 Gold Coast Highway, T5539 0062. **Pharmacy Day and Night**, Piazza on the Boulevard (ANA Hotel), 3221 Gold Coast Highway, Surfers, T5592 2299, open 0700-2200. **Post** Centro Shopping Centre, Shop 165. Postcode 4217. Mon-Fri 0830-1730, Sat 0900-1230. **Useful numbers Police**, 68 Ferny Av, T5570 7888. **Surfers**, T5581 2900. **RACQ**, 239 Nerang St, Southport, T5588 7777.

Brisbane and Moreton Bay

Brisbane has come an awfully long way since its days as a penal settlement. A lot of money was pumped into the city for its Expo 88 and Brizzie has never looked back. South Bank, especially, represents the very essence of modern-day Brisbane with numerous cultural attractions and even its own inner-city beach. Australia's only true tropical city also enjoys a near-perfect climate. Wherever you go, alfresco restaurants, cafés and outdoor activities dominate. Nearby, the sand islands of Moreton Bay offer a wonderful opportunity to enjoy some peace and quiet.

Ins and outs ▸ *For listings, see pages 40-47.*

Getting there Trains and buses connect the CBD with both airport terminals: **Airtrain**, T3216 3308, www.airtrain.com.au, departs from Central (top end of Edward Street), Roma (Transit Centre) and Brunswick Street (Fortitude Valley) four times per hour from $14.50, children free. **Coachtrans** (SkyTrans service), T1300 664700, www.coachtrans.com.au, departs from Roma Street Transit Centre every 30 minutes (0500-2100) from $15. Accommodation pick-ups cost $2 extra. A taxi to the airport costs about $45. There are frequent long-distance buses and trains to the city from major centres and cities. ▸ *See Transport, page 45.*

Getting around There is an efficient transport system with the river playing a large part in navigating the city. The main centre is within walking distance. The city tours, see page 44, are a great way to get around and see the sights, especially if short of time.

Tourist information **Brisbane VIC** ① *Queen Street Mall, Albert St and Edward St, T3006 6290, www.experiencebrisbanetourism.com, Mon-Thu, 0900-1730, Fri 0900-1900, Sat 0900-1700, Sun 0930-1630*, offers free city maps and assists with tours and accommodation. **QPWS main office** ① *3rd floor, 400 George St, T1300 130372, Mon-Fri 0830-1700.*

Sights

Central Brisbane

A number of historical buildings stand out amidst the glistening high-rise blocks. At the top end of Albert Street is **City Hall** ① *T3403 8888, 0800-1700 guided tours available, lift free, Mon-Fri 1000-1500*, with its 92-m Italian renaissance clock tower. Built in 1930, it became known as the 'Million Pound Town Hall' due to its huge and controversial construction cost. The ride in the old lift to the top for the views is a highlight but the interior of the building is also worth a look. On the ground floor is the **Museum of Brisbane (MoB)** ① *daily 0900-1700, free*, which showcases the various aspects of contemporary social history and culture with a heavy emphasis on local writers and artists. Around the corner on George Street and the riverbank is the grand 19th-century façade of the former **Treasury Building**, now a casino.

To the east beside the Botanical Gardens (note there are two in the city, see page 38 for the Botanical Gardens-Mount-Coot-tha) is the 1868 French Renaissance-style **Parliament House** ① *T3406 7562, www.parliament.qld.gov.au, Mon-Fri 1030-1430, free*, which was commissioned when Queensland was declared a separate colony in 1859. Visitors can join tours conducted by parliamentary attendants. Nearby is the **Old Government House** ① *2 George St, T3864 8005, www.ogh.qut.edu.au, 1000-1600, free*, built in 1862 as the official residence of the state's governors and now housing the HQ of the National Trust. It is currently undergoing interior refurbishment and will reopen to the public in 2009.

Further north, beyond the modern architecture and chic restaurants of Waterfront Place, Eagle Street Pier and the Riverside Centre, is **Customs House** ① *399 Queens St, T3365 8999, www.customshouse.com.au, Mon-Fri 0900-1700, tours Sun*. Built in 1889, it resembles a miniature version of St Paul's Cathedral in London. Directly opposite the Customs House is the city's best-known and most-photographed sight – the **Story Bridge**. It was built between 1935 and 1940 and due to the lack of bedrock has some of the deepest (42 m) foundations of any bridge in the world. Recently Brisbane has emulated Sydney's highly successful Harbour Bridge Bridge climb experience and, although far less dramatic, the Story Bridge Adventure Climb still offers great views and may appeal. The dawn or dusk trip is recommended (see page 44).

Overlooking the high-rise blocks on the southern bank of the Brisbane River is the remarkable 17-ha 'oasis in the city' that is known as the **South Bank** ① *www.visitsouthbank.com.au*. Built primarily as the showpiece for Expo 88, the 1-km stretch of parkland remains a fascinating and functional recreational space and includes riverside walks, shops, restaurants and a swimming lagoon with its very own beach. This area is also the venue for the colourful **South Bank Lifestyle Markets** ① *every Fri night, Sat and Sun*.

At the northwestern end of the park, straddling Melbourne Street, is the **Queensland Cultural Centre**, encompassing the State Library, Queensland Museum, Queensland Art Gallery, Gallery of Modern Art and Queensland Performing Arts Complex. **Queensland Art Gallery** ① *T3840 7303, www.qag.qld.gov.au, Mon-Fri 1000-1700, Sat-Sun 0900-1700, free, tours available daily*, is Brisbane's premier cultural attraction, featuring a huge and diverse collection of Aboriginal, European, Asian and contemporary Australian art. Early works include paintings by John Russell and Rupert Bunny, two of the nation's most noted expat artists, as well as more familiar international names such as Rubens, Degas, Picasso and Van Dyck. The **Gallery of Modern Art** ① *T3840 7303, www.qag.qld.gov.au, Mon-Fri 1000-1700, Sat-Sun 0900-1700, free, tours available daily*, is Australia's largest dedicated to the genre and includes the first Australian Cinémathèque, purpose-built to showcase the art of film.

Next to the art gallery is the **Queensland Museum** ① *T3840 7555, www.qm.qld.gov.au, 0930-1700, free*, which is noted for its prehistoric and natural history displays. The museum also has entertaining and educational interactive exhibits, guaranteed to keep little Einsteins amused for hours. On the opposite side of Melbourne Street is the **Queensland Performing Arts Complex**, which houses several theatres and concert venues. At the southeastern end of the South Bank you can find the **Queensland Maritime Museum** ① *T3844 5361, www.maritimemuseum.com.au, 0930-1630, $8, children $3.50*, with all the usual relics from anchors to lifebuoys. Most of the larger vessels, including the Second World War warship *The Diamantina*, sit forlornly in the adjacent dry dock. All this is best viewed from the futuristic **Goodwill Bridge**, built in celebration of the 2001 Goodwill Games.

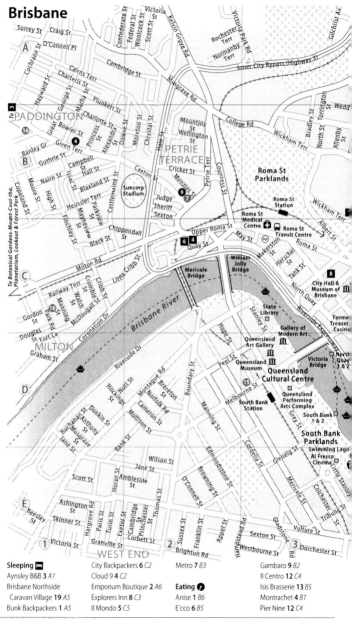

Brisbane

Sleeping
Aynsley B&B **3** *A1*
Brisbane Northside
  Caravan Village **19** *A5*
Bunk Backpackers **1** *A5*
City Backpackers **6** *C2*
Cloud 9 **4** *C2*
Emporium Boutique **2** *A6*
Explorers Inn **8** *C3*
Il Mondo **5** *C5*
Metro **7** *B3*

Eating
Anise **1** *B6*
E'cco **6** *B5*
Gambaro **9** *B2*
Il Centro **12** *C4*
Isis Brasserie **13** *B5*
Montrachet **4** *B1*
Pier Nine **12** *C4*

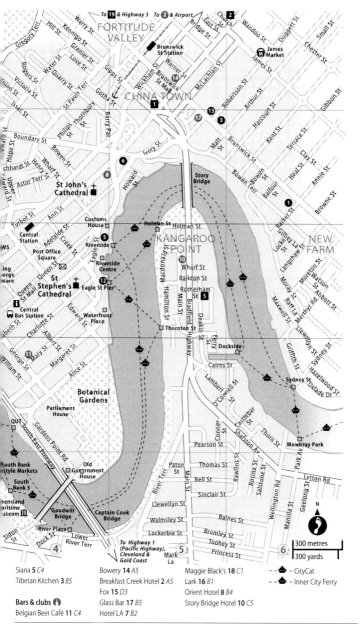

Siana 5 C4
Tibetan Kitchen 3 B5

Bars & clubs
Belgian Beer Café 11 C4

Bowery 14 A5
Breakfast Creek Hotel 2 A5
Fox 15 D3
Glass Bar 17 B5
Hotel LA 7 B2

Maggie Black's 18 C1
Lark 16 B1
Orient Hotel 8 B4
Story Bridge Hotel 10 C5

- - 🚢 - CityCat
- - 🚢 - Inner City Ferry

Brisbane suburbs

West of the city, reached via Milton Road, is the **Botanical Gardens-Mount-Coot-tha** ① *T3403 2535, 0830-1730, free, tours Mon-Sat 1100 and 1300 or pick up a free self-guided leaflet*, considered Queensland's finest subtropical gardens, featuring over 20,000 specimens of 5000 species. Within the grounds is also a **Planetarium** and **Lakeside Restaurant** as well as picnic facilities, library and gift shop (0900-1700).

Set high above the gardens is the **Mount Coot-tha Lookout**, which offers superb views across the city and out across Moreton Bay to Moreton, North Stradbroke and Bribie Islands. **Summit Restaurant** and **Kuta Café**, see page 42, provide an ideal place for lunch, dinner or just a glass of vino while soaking up the sun and the city vistas. Backing onto the lookout complex is the **Mount Coot-tha Forest Park** which consists of 1500 ha of open eucalyptus forest containing over 350 weird and wonderful native species, with a network of walking tracks. Catch bus No 471 from Ann Street or join a City Sights Tour.

Almost anywhere east of the Great Divide in Queensland, it seems you are never far away from a wildlife sanctuary and the opportunity to see (or cuddle) a koala. Brisbane is no different, hosting the **Lone Pine Koala Sanctuary** ① *Jesmond Rd, Fig Tree Pocket (southwest via Milton Rd and the western Freeway 5), T3378 1366, www.koala.net, 0830-1700, $30, children $21*, the oldest and the largest in the world. Having opened in 1927 and now housing around 130 of the famously adorable, yet utterly pea-brained tree dwellers, it offers a fine introduction, or reminder, of how unique Australia's wildlife really is. Also on display are the equally ubiquitous and marginally more bush-wise wombats, echidnas, kangaroos and the latest addition, 'Barak' the platypus. Bus No 430, from the 'koala platform' in the Myer Centre, Queen Street, will get you there, or hop aboard the Mirimar Boat Cruise on Cultural Centre Pontoon (located on the boardwalk outside the Queensland State Library) at 1120, which costs $55, children $33 (including admission) and returns at 1445, T1300 729742.

Moreton Bay and islands → *For listings, see pages 40-47.*

Brisbane's Moreton Bay and islands are easily accessible and remarkably unspoilt. Of the 300-odd islands scattered around the bay, the two largest and most popular are Moreton Island and North Stradbroke Island. Moreton, which lies 37 km northeast of the Brisbane River mouth, is almost uninhabited and famous for its 4WD opportunities, shipwrecks and pod of friendly dolphins. Further south, North Stradbroke is the largest of the islands, a laid-back place with world-class surf beaches, awesome coastal scenery and the chance to watch breaching whales and dolphins and manta rays gliding past beneath the waves. ▶▶ *For further details, see page 47.*

North Stradbroke Island

① *Stradbroke VIC, Shop 1 Kennedy Drive, Point Lookout, T3415 3044, www.stradbroke tourism.com, Mon-Fri 0830-1700, Sat-Sun 0830-1500. It stocks island maps and can assist with general information.*

Wedge-shaped North Stradbroke, or 'Straddie' as it is affectionately known, is the largest, most inhabited and most accessible of the Moreton Bay Islands. Some 30 km southeast of Brisbane, it is 36 km long and 11 km at its widest point. Separated from its southerly neighbour, South Stradbroke, by a fierce cyclone in 1896, it has become a magical tourist attraction often overlooked due to its proximity to the competing attractions of Brisbane and the Gold Coast. In many ways it is similar to Fraser Island, offering diverse and unspoilt coastal scenery and a rich biodiversity that is so typical of sand islands. The three picturesque villages of Dunwich, Amity Point and Point Lookout offer a broad range of accommodation, excellent beaches and plenty of water-based activities. Surfing is the obvious speciality.

Dunwich, a former penal colony and quarantine station, is on the west mid- section of the island and the main arrival point. The small museum ① *Welsby St, open Wed and Sat*, explores the island's rich aboriginal and early settler history. **Amity Point**, first settled in 1825, sits on the northwest corner, 17 km from Dunwich, while **Point Lookout**, the main focus for today's tourist accommodation, sights and activities, is 21 km away on the northeast corner. If you only have one or two days on the island the place to be is Point Lookout, with its golden surf beaches and dramatic headland. At the terminus of East Coast Road is the start of the **North Gorge Headlands Walk** (1 km one way). Before you set off

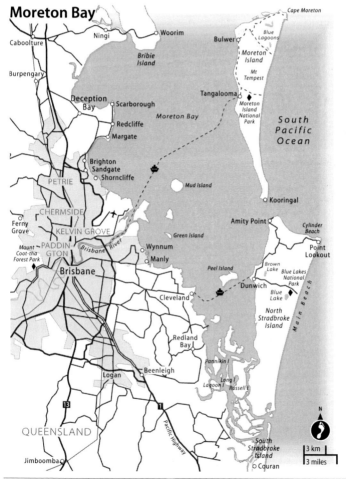

take a look at **Frenchman's Bay** below, which gives you a flavour of the dramatic scenery to come. Follow the track, through wind-lashed stands of pandanus palms, to **The Gorge**, a narrow cleft in the rock that is pounded endlessly by huge ocean breakers. Further on, **Whale Rock** provides an ideal viewpoint from which to spot migrating humpback whales between June and October. Manta rays, turtles and dolphins are also a familiar sight all year round. At the far end of the walk the vast swathe of **Main Beach** hoves into view, stretching 34 km down the entire length of the island's east coast. It offers some excellent 4WD action, fishing, surfing and a few mosquito-infested campsites. **Cylinder Beach**, back along East Coast Road, provides the best recreational spot with great surf breaks and safe swimming. If you do swim always stick to patrolled areas between the flags.

Other attractions on the island include **Blue Lakes National Park**, which is reached via Trans Island Road from Dunwich. The lake itself, a 2.5-km walk from the car park, is freshwater and fringed with melalucas and eucalypts, providing the perfect spot for a cool swim. To reach Main Beach from there requires a 4WD. **Brown Lake**, which is bigger and only 2 km outside Dunwich, is a less popular spot.

Moreton Island

Moreton Island, which lies to the north of the Stradbroke Islands, is often considered the jewel of the Moreton group by virtue of its lack of inhabitants and unspoilt beauty. It is another sand mass: almost 20,000 ha of long, empty beaches, dunes, forest, lagoons and heathlands with abundant wildlife. Other than the beauty and solitude, the greatest attractions are its opportunities for 4WD trips, fishing, camping, wreck snorkelling and diving and seeing the pod of 'wild' Tangalooma bottlenose dolphins that put in a nightly appearance at the island's **Tangalooma Wild Dolphin Resort**, see page 42. Other attractions include the Tangalooma Desert, a large sand blow near the resort, and the Blue Lagoons, a group of 15 deliberately sunken shipwrecks, which provide excellent snorkelling. If you do have the freedom of the island with a 4WD, Cape Moreton at the northeastern tip is worth a visit to see the 1857 lighthouse, which is the oldest in Queensland. Mount Tempest (285 m) dominates the heart of the island and is reputed to be the highest coastal sand dune in the world; a strenuous 5-km walk. For details, see Activities and tours page 44.

Brisbane and Moreton Bay listings

● Sleeping

Central Brisbane *p34, map p36*
Brisbane boasts more than 12,000 beds, from large 5-star hotels and modern apartment blocks to numerous backpacker and budget options plus a good selection of B&Bs, some of which present an ideal opportunity to experience a traditional Queenslander house. The only thing lacking is a selection of good motor parks within easy reach of the city centre. Although there are plenty of hostels you are still advised to book a budget bed at least 2 days in advance. There are good options on Upper Roma St, just 500 m southwest of the transit centre, and around Fortitude Valley.

$$$$ Emporium Boutique Hotel, 1000 Ann St, Fortitude Valley T3253 6999, www. emporiumhotel.com.au. Set in the heart of the Valley this hip contemporary place offers the full range of studio suites, from standard to king spa, an outstanding cocktail bar and a rooftop pool.

$$$$ Il Mondo Boutique Hotel, 25 Rotherham St, T3392 0111, www.ilmondo. com.au. Across the river on Kangaroo Point, this modern and chic hotel offers

1-3 bedroom suites and self-contained apartments, interesting aesthetics and relative peace from the centre. It is also within walking distance of all the action via a typical Brizzie ferry ride from the Holman St Wharf. In-house contemporary alfresco restaurant and a lap pool.

$$$ Explorers Inn, 63 Turbot St, T3211 3488, www.explorers.com.au. One of the better value (and certainly the best placed) of the budget hotel options. Friendly, it offers tidy (if small) doubles, twins, family rooms and singles and has a cheap but cheerful restaurant/bar. It is only 500 m from the transit centre and Queens St.

$$$ Metro Inns, 239 Wickham St, T3832 1412, www.metroinns.com.au. Sits high on the hill, like a transparent pepper pot, overlooking the CBD and offering 3-4 star standard rooms, each with a balcony to soak up the views. In-house licensed restaurant.

$$ Bunk Backpackers, corner of Ann St and Gipps St, T3257 3644, www.bunkbrisbane. com.au. This large modern establishment is well placed in the heart of the Valley. It offers doubles, twins, singles and dorms on themed floors. Modern facilities, including a pool and bar. Fast internet and travel/ jobs desk.

$$ City Backpackers, 380 Upper Roma St, 500 m southwest of the transit centre, T3211 3221, www.citybackpackers.com. Deservedly popular and well managed, it has spotless en suite doubles and dorms, modern kitchen, excellent security, roof decks, pool, internet and a great bar. It's a very sociable place that can throw a great party at the weekend.

$$ Cloud 9, 350 Upper Roma St, City, T3236 2300, www.cloud9backpackers.com.au. If you are looking for a smaller, modern establishment near the transit centre then this is the best bet. Recently opened, it offers modern facilities throughout with dorms, twins and doubles (some en suite), fast internet, free pick-ups and off-street parking. The city views from the rooftop deck add to the appeal.

Brisbane suburbs *p38, map p36*

$$$$ Brisbane Northside Caravan Village, 763 Zillmere Rd (off Gympie Rd), on the northern approach, 12 km from the CBD, T3263 4040, www.caravanvillage.com. au.This is the best motor park, offering a wide range of options from luxurycabins, en suite/standard powered and non-powered sites, pool, store, internetand an excellent camp kitchen.

$$$ Aynsley B&B, 14 Glanmire St, Paddington, T3368 2250, www.aynsley.com. au.Traditional Queenslander with good value, queen or twin en suites, parking and pool.

Moreton Bay and islands *p38*
North Stradbroke Island

There is a broad range of accommodation available on Straddie, with the vast majority being based in Point Lookout. Nevertheless, pre-booking is recommended in the summer, and on public/school holidays.

$$$$ Domain Stradbroke Resort, Home Beach, Point Lookout, T3415 0000, www. stradbrokedomain.com. Stylish modern beach shacks and villas overlooking Home Beach, with an excellent in-house café, shop, pool and gym.

$$$$ Stradbroke Island Beach Hotel and Spa Resort, East Coast Rd, Point Lookout, T3409 8188, www. stradbrokeislandbeachhotel.com.au. The former 'Straddie' has recently been fully redeveloped and now offers ultra-modern facilities all overlooking the surf beach. Great place to indulge.

$$$ Stradbroke Holiday Parks Adder Rock, East Coast Road, Point Lookout (17 km from Dunwich) T1300 551253. Located in Point Lookout it offers de luxe villas, standard cabins, powered and non-powered sites, saltwater pool, barbecue and camp kitchen.

$$ Manta Lodge YHA and Scuba Centre (above and part of the Dive Shop),1 East Coast Rd, T3409 8888, www.mantalodge. com.au. Friendly andnear the beach, with focus on dive trips. Pick-ups from Brisbane.

Moreton Island

$$$$ Tangalooma Wild Dolphin Resort, T3637 2000, www.tangalooma.com. A fine resort offering a wide range of beachside accommodation, from luxury self-contained apartments and standard rooms/units to new backpacker/budget beds, a restaurant, bistro/bar café, pools, an environmental centre, with dolphin feeding and watching, and many water sports and other activities; see page 45.

QPWS campsites, T3408 2710, www. derm.qld.gov.au. Available at The Wrecks, Ben-Ewa, Comboyuro, North Point and Blue Lagoon. The Wrecks campsite is about a 2-km walk from the resort. Each has toilets, limited supplies of water and cold showers. Fees apply.

⊘ Eating

Brisbane offers a vast choice. Outside the city centre and the Riverside (Eagle St) areas the suburbs of Fortitude Valley, New Farm (east), South Bank, the West End (south of the river) and Paddington (west) are well worth looking at. The main focuses for Brisbane's café scene are Brunswick St Mall in Fortitude Valley, South Bank parklands, West End (Boundary St) and Petrie Terrace/Paddington (Caxton and Given Terrace). Worth checking out are the stunning views from the **Summit Restaurant** at Mount Coot-tha (see page 42); or a leisurely lunch or dinner cruise on a paddle steamer (see page 44). And for something uniquely Brisbane, try the famed Moreton Bay Bug (a delicious and very weird-looking lobster).

Central Brisbane *p34, map p36*
$$ E'cco, 100 Boundary St, T3831 8344, www.eccobistro.com. Tue-Fri for lunch, Tue-Sat for dinner. Home of internationally acclaimed chef, Philip Johnson. Other than the food itself another great attraction is the unpretentious nature of the place, the bustling atmosphere and the staff.
$$ Il Centro, Eagle St Pier, T3221 6090, www.ilcentro.com.au. Sun-Fri for lunch,

Thu-Sun for dinner. Large Italian restaurant renowned for its riverside location and stunning sand crab lasagne.
$$ Pier Nine, Eagle St Pier, T3226 2100, www. piernine.com.au. Mon-Fri from 1130, Sat from 1700. Another riverside restaurant, a Brisbane institution famous for quality seafood.
$$ Siana, Riparian Plaza, 71 Eagle St, T3221 3887, www.siana.com.au. Mon-Fri lunch and dinner and from 1600 Sat. Quality mix of Thai, Chinese and Indian cuisine in stylish surroundings overlooking the river.

Brisbane suburbs *p38, map p36*
$$ Anise, 697 Brunswick St, New Farm, T3358 1558, www.anise.com.au. Tue-Sun for lunch, daily for dinner. Small and congenial wine bar/restaurant with a French- influenced menu, lengthy wine list and great foie gras.
$$ Gambaro, 33 Caxton St, Petrie Terrace, T3369 9500. Sun-Fri for lunch, Mon-Sat for dinner. An old favourite offering good seafood.
$$ Isis Brasserie, 446 Brunswick St, south towards New Farm, T3852 1155. Tue-Fri for lunch, Tue-Sun for dinner. Causing something of a stir, winning awards and maintaining a loyal following, who swear by the class and quality of both environment and cuisine consistently created by its youthful owners.
$$ Montrachet, 224 Given Terrace, Paddington, T3367 0030, www.montrachet. com.au. Mon-Fri lunch and dinner. A friendly French restaurant, home of acclaimed chef and extrovert character Thierry Galichet. Lots of French flair and ambience. Recommended.
$$ Summit, Mount Coot-tha, T3369 9922. Daily for lunch/dinner and on Sun for brunch. Further afield and well worth the trip is this Brisbane classic with its superb views across the city and Moreton Bay.
$$ Tibetan Kitchen, 454 Brunswick St, Fortitude Valley, T3358 5906. Plenty of character offering traditional Tibetan and Nepalese fare and considered by many as the best venue for samosas and curries in town. It caters well for vegetarians.

Moreton Bay and islands *p38*
North Stradbroke Island
$$ Amis, 21 Cumming Pde, Pandanus Palms Resort Point Lookout, T3409 8600. Wed-Sun. Casual fine dining with excellent views.
$$ Seashells Café, 21 Ballow St, Amity Point, T3409 7886 , T3415 3390. Daily 0800-2200. New establishment earning a good reputation. Open for breakfast, lunch or dinner with alfresco seating and bar.
$$ Stradbroke Island Beach Hotel and Spa Resort, East Coast Rd, Point Lookout, T3409 8188, www.stradbrokeislandbeach hotel.com.au. Daily for breakfast lunch and dinner from 0730. A popular spot for good value bistro meals with a large outdoor deck space overlooking Cylinder Beach.

Bars and clubs

Brisbane *p34, map p36*
Belgian Beer Café, 169 Mary St, City, T3221 0199, www.belgianbeercafebrussels.com.au. Try the traditional mussels and *frites* with a choice of 30 of the nation's finest. It also has one of the city's best beer gardens.
Bowery, 676 Ann St, Fortitude Valley T3252 0202, www.thebowery.com.au. Hailed as the best cocktail joint in the city, this New York-style bar offers class and a quiet, cosy ambience.
Breakfast Creek Hotel, 2 Kingsford Smith Drive, Breakfast Creek, T3262 5988, www. breakfastcreekhotel.com. Although a bit of a trek, this 115-year-old enterprise is something of a Brisbane institution. It retains a colonial/art deco feel, has a large Spanish beer garden and serves excellent steaks.
Fox, corner of Hope St and Melbourne St, T3844 2883. Historic place with good old-fashioned service. Also has a quality Italian restaurant attached.
Hotel LA, corner of Petrie Terrace and Caxton St, Paddington, T3368 2560. Attracts the loud and pretentious and if you can get past the over-ambitious 'fashion police' on the door, it stays open well into the wee small hours.

Lark, 1/267 Given Terrace, T3369 1299, www. thelark.com.au. Closed Mon. A colonial-style cottage converted into a quality cocktail/ wine bar, proving something of a hit for both food and drink.
Orient Hotel, corner of Queen St and Ann St, City, T3839 4625. Thu-Sat nightly until 0300. A traditional street corner Australian. It's well known for its live rock music.
Story Bridge Hotel, 200 Main St, Kangaroo Point, T3391 2266, www.storybridgehotel.com. au. In the shadow of its namesake edifice, this is a firm favourite at any time, but most famous for hosting the annual Australia Day cockroach races and the Australian Festival of Beers in Sep.

Entertainment

Brisbane *p34, map p36*
Fortitude Valley (The Valley) enjoys international acclaim (recently recognized as 'a new global hotspot' by *Billboard* magazine) and is the best place to check out the latest local rock bands, with its many pubs hosting bands from Thu-Sat. **Fortitude Valley**, the **Riverside Centre** (Eagle St, City) and **Petrie Terrace** are the main club and dance venues. For up-to-date listings and entertainment news consult the free street press publications, *Rave, Time Off* and *Scene*.

Live music
Brisbane Jazz Club, 1 Annie St, Kangaroo Point, T3391 2006. A loyal following with regulars playing on Sat-Sun, from 2030 (cover around $15).
Glass Bar, 420 Brunswick St, Fortitude Valley, T3252 0533, www.glassjazz.com.au. This is another good venue.

Festivals and events

Brisbane *p34, map p36*
An up-to-date events listing is available at www.ourbrisbane.com/whats-on/events.
New Year The year begins with a bang with celebrations and a fireworks display over the river beside the South Bank parklands.

This is repeated with even more zeal on **26 Jan**, **Australia Day**, with other hugely popular and bizarre events including the annual cockroach races; see box opposite.
Easter The **Brisbane to Gladstone Yacht Race** leaves Shorncliffe.
May Queensland Racing Festival and **Valley Jazz Festival**.
Jun Annual **Queensland Day** celebrations.
Jul Brisbane International Film Festival at the end of the month. **Mid-July** also sees the start of the 18-day **Brisbane Festival** with an international programme featuring artists from contemporary dance, opera, theatre and music from all over the globe performing alongside outstanding Australian artists.
Late Aug/Sep The 2-week **River Festival** celebrates the 'city's lifeblood' with food, fire and festivities.
Oct Fortitude Valley's Chinatown and Brunswick St become the focus for the lively **Valley Fiesta**.

O Shopping

Brisbane p34, map p36
Brisbane is *the* Queensland capital for retail therapy, with over 1500 stores and 700 shops in and around the Queens Street Mall. Two department stores, 6 shopping centres and a rash of malls and arcades all combine to provide a vast array of choice from fashion to furnishings. The city also hosts a few good markets including the **South Bank markets** on Fri night, Sat and Sun, the **Riverside and Eagle St Pier markets** on Sunday and **The Valley markets** (Brunswick St) on Sat and Sun. The new **James Market** in New Farm (2nd and 4th Sat of the month) is excellent for fresh produce and deli products and is surrounded by good cafés.

▲ Activities and tours

Brisbane p34, map p36
City Bus tours
There is a free **City Loop Bus** servicearound the CBD Mon-Fri 0700-1800 with departures every 10 mins. **CitySights,** www.citysights. com.au, also offers city tours of 1½ hrs, from $35, children $20, T131230, taking in a total of 19 stops in the inner city. Tours leave every 45 mins from Post Office Square, from 0900-1545. It's a great way to see the inner city and the views from Mount Coot-tha, with the added bonus of free bus and CityCat travel.

River cruises
Although there are a number of specialist cruise companies and a range of vessels, one of the best ways to see the sights is to utilize the hop-on/hop-off, all day Translinkservices ticket with **CityCat**, T131220, www.translink. com.au, from $4.60.
Kookaburra River Queen paddle steamers, T3221 1300, www. kookaburrariverqueens .com. A familiar sight on the river offering a range of sightseeing/ dining options: 2-hr lunch Sat/Sun, from $55; 3-hr dinner Tue, Thu-Sun 1900, from $75.
Mirimar Boat Cruises, T3221 0300, www. mirimar.com, depart daily from Cultural Centre Pontoon (located on the boardwalk outside the Queensland State Library) at 1000, from $55, children $33 (including admission, returns at 1445). Combines a cruise upriver with a visit to the Lone Pine Koala Sanctuary.

Other activities
Riverlife Adventure Centre, T3891 5766, www.riverlife.com.au. Operates from the Naval Stores at the base of Kangaroo Point Cliffs and offers abseiling and rock climbing (from $39), or kayaking (from $35). Bike and rollerblade hire (1½ hrs from $20) also available.
Story Bridge Adventure Climb, T3514 6900, www.storybridgeadventureclimb. com.au. This is emulating the success of the Sydney Bridge Climb. The secure 2½-hr climb offers dramatic views across the city from the 80-m span, with the dawn or dusk climbs adding that aesthetic edge, from $89-130.

Moreton Bay and islands *p38*
North Stradbroke Island

The VIC has all details of activities and operators and can book on your behalf. **Kingfisher Tours**, T3409 9502, www.straddie kingfishertours.com.au, offer excellent and informative 4WD tours.

Manta Lodge YHA and Scuba Centre, 1 East Coast Rd, Point Lookout, T3409 8888, www.mantalodge.com.au. Daily boat dives to try to track down manta ray, turtle and dolphin. Snorkelling, 4WD tours and sea kayaking can also be arranged. Surf and body board hire.

Straddie Adventures, T3409 8414, www. straddieadventures.com.au. An exciting range of backpacker-based tours and activities, including sand boarding, sea kayaking, surf lessons and snorkelling, full day 4WD tours.

Moreton Island

Dolphin Wild, T3880 4444, www.dolphin wild.com.au. Backpacker-oriented day cruises to Moreton Island from Redcliffe. From $115, children $65. Transfers are available from Brisbane for $25 extra.

Tangalooma Wild Dolphin Resort, T1300 652250, www.tangalooma.com, see page 42. Full day tour options (from $45), with dolphin feeding/watching from $95 (see page 40), an excellent range of island excursions and activities from sand boarding, quad biking, snorkelling and diving to scenic helicopter flights. Daily whale-watching cruises are also available Jun-Oct, from $110, children $85.

☻ Transport

Brisbane *p34, map p36*
For all public transport enquiries, T131230, www.translink.com.au.

Air

Brisbane's international and domestic airports are 16/18 km northeast of the city centre. **Jet Star**, T131538, www.jetstar. com.au; **Qantas**, T131313, www.qantas. com.au; **Tiger Airways**, T9335 3033, www. tigerairways.com.au; and **Virgin Blue**, T136789, www.virginblue.com.au, all fly regularly to all main centres and some regional destinations.

Bus

Local The Central Bus Station is downstairs in the Myer Centre, Queen St. There is a free **City Loop Bus** service around the CBD Mon-Fri 0700-1800 with departures every 10 mins. Other service fares work on a zone system from $2.30, children $1.20. For attractive day or weekly saver passes in conjunction with the CityCat, ask at a ticket office. TransLink also operates a travel card called GoCard, which stores up to $200 so you can travel seamlessly on bus, train and ferry services. You can travel on participating buses, trains and ferries using your GoCard or other valid TransLink ticket. Fares are calculated according to the number of zones travelled in a journey. All Brisbane's CityCat and CityFerry stops are within TransLink's zones 1 and 2.

Long distance All interstate and local buses stop at the multi-level Roma St Transit Centre, Roma Street, 0530-2030. Most of the major bus companies have internal offices on Level 3 (Coach Deck) and there are also lockers, internet and a visitors' information desk, T3236 2528, www.brisbanetransitcentre.com.au. Various food outlets and showers are available on Level 2. **Greyhound**, T1300 473946, www. greyhound.com.au, and **Premier Motor Services**, T133410, www.premierms.com.au, both operate north/southbound interstate and regional services.

Coachtrans, T3358 9300, www. coachtrans.com.au, runs 4 daily services to the **Gold Coast** (including the airport) and 'Unlimited Travel Passes' for city sights, airport and Gold Coast. **Crisps Coaches**, T4661 8333, www.crisps.com.au, offers south and westbound services from Brisbane to **Toowoomba/Tenterfield**. Sunshine Coast

Sunbus, T5450 7888, www.sunbus.com. au, also runs regular daily services to the **Sunshine Coast**. Brisbane Bus Lines, T3355 0034, also services the **Sunshine Coast** and **South Burnett Region**.

CityCat and ferry

Brisbane's famous, sleek blue-and-white **CityCats** glide up and down the river from Bretts Wharf (Hamilton) in the east, to the University of Queensland (St Lucia) in the west, stopping at selected wharfs on both sides of the river, daily from 0530-2230. The round trip takes about 2 hrs. Fares start at $2.30. A day ticket costs from $4.60, children $2.30, depending on zone covered. Day tickets and off-peak saver tickets also apply in conjunction with TransLink city bus services, ask at the ticket office. **CityFerry** operates an inner city and cross-river service (every 15-20 mins) at various points along the river. Fares are determined by the number of sectors crossed and start at $2.30. Pick up a copy of the *Brisbane River Experience Guide*, which highlights the main attractions and specialist tours on offer. General enquiries, T131230, www.translink. com.au.

Cycling

Brisbane is very well geared up for cyclists with over 350 km of city cycleways. Most of these have been established around the edge of the CBD along the riverbank, providing an excellent way to take in the sights and to get from A to B. VICs can supply the free and comprehensive *Brisbane Bicycle Maps* booklet. Hire from **Riverlife Adventure Centre**, T3891 5766, www. riverlife.com.au (see page 44).

Taxi

Black and White Cabs, T131008, or **Yellow Cabs**, T131924.

Train

Queensland Rail Travel Centre is located on the ground floor, Roma St Transit Centre,

T3236 2528, www.brisbanetransit centre. com.au; for general enquiries T132232, 0600-2000. **Citytrain**, T131210, www. citytrain.com.au, services greater Brisbane with networks to the Gold Coast. The main city stations are Central (top end of Edward St), Roma (Transit Centre), South Bank (South Brisbane) and Brunswick St (Fortitude Valley). Fares are based on a zone system and start at $2.30, 'one-day unlimited ticket', from $4.60. **Airtrain**, T1800 119091, www. airtrain.com.au, services the airport and Gold Coast from the city centre stations from $14.50 one-way, Gold Coast from $25.

Northbound services include the **Tilt Train**, www.tilttrain.com.au, the express service between **Brisbane** and **Rockhampton** (6½ hrs), which is recommended for those travelling to **Noosa** via Nambour or **Hervey Bay** via Maryborough (free bus connection). It departs Sun-Fri 1100 and 1700 (Rockhampton $107 and Bundaberg $67 single). **Sunlander** (**Brisbane** to **Cairns**) departs 4 times weekly from Brisbane – Sun and Thu to Cairns, First Class from $430, economy from $218. **Spirit of the Outback** travels from Brisbane to **Rockhampton** where it heads west to **Longreach**. Departs Tue 1825 and Sat 1310, from $190.

Moreton Bay and islands *p38*
North Stradbroke Island

The ferry terminal is at Toondah Harbour, Cleveland. From Brisbane take the **Citytrain** from the Roma St Transit Centre, where a **National Bus** (T3245 3333) provides pick-ups to the ferry terminal, T131230. **Stradbroke Ferries**, T3488 5300, www. stradbrokeferries.com.au, operate a car/ passenger and passenger water taxi every hour from Cleveland Mon-Fri 0600-1915, Sat-Sun 0600-1845, return from $17, children $10. **Sea Stradbroke Big Red Cat** T3488 9777, www.seastradbroke.com, runs a vehicle and passenger service from the same harbour roughly every hour, from $135 return for a car including passengers (foot passengers $11, children $6, bikes $4). The crossing for both services takes 30 mins. **North Stradbroke Flyer** (Gold Cats), T3286 1964, www.flyer.com.au, also offers a fast passenger service (end of Middle St, Cleveland), daily every half hour from 0530-1830, return from $19. Its bus meets the Cleveland train.

Once on the island, **North Stradbroke Bus Services**, T3415 2417, www.stradbrokebuses.com, meet every scheduled ferry arrival or departure and operate between Dunwich, One Mile, Amity and Point Lookout daily 0700-1900. The return fare for Dunwich to Point Lookout is about $10.

Moreton Island

Moreton Island Ferries (miCat), T3909 3333, www.moretonventure.com.au, run a vehicle and passenger service from Howard Smith Drive, Brisbane (refer to website for detailed directions) to **Tangalooma Wrecks** (1 km from the resort). Depart Mon-Sun 0830, returning at 1530 with additional sailings Fri 1830, Sun 1430 (and on public holidays), from $190 return (for a 4WD and 2 adults) and from $50 return for passengers, bikes $15. The crossing takes 30 mins.

There are no sealed roads on Moreton and independent access is by 4WD only ($44 fee for 1 month). **Moreton Island Ferries (miCat)** operates a minibus around the island as a guided day trip package only, with island activities, from $115, children $95.

For those without a 4WD vehicle the best way to reach the island is through the **Tangalooma Resort**, T1300 652250, www.tangalooma.com, which offers accommodation, day trips, tours and independent transfers, see pages 42 and 45. Its launch leaves from the terminal on the northern bank of the Brisbane River, at the end of Holt St, daily 0730 and 1000, from $45, children $25 (75 mins). Full day dolphin feeding from $95, whale watching in season (Jun-Oct) from $110. A courtesy coach operates from Roma St Transit Centre and most CBD hotels, from $10, T1300 652250.

❶ Directory

Brisbane *p34, map p36*
Banks All major bank branches with ATMs are found in the city centre, especially in the Queen St, Edward St and Eagle St malls. Foreign exchange also from **American Express**, 260 Queen St, T 1300 139060. **Travelex**, 261 Queen St, T1800 637642;Shop 149F, Queen St Mall. **Hospital** Mater Hospital (24 hr), Raymond Terrace, Woolloongabba, T3840 8111. **Roma St Medical Centre**, Transit Centre, T3236 2988. **Travellers Medical Service**, Level 1, 245 Adelaide St, T3221 3611, www.travellersmedicalservice.com.

Internet Cyber Room, Level 1, 25 Adelaide St, T3012 9331. **State Library**, South Bank, T3840 7666, 30 mins free, book a day in advance, Mon-Thu 1000-2000, Fri-Sun 1000-1700. **Pharmacy** Day and Night, 245 Albert St, T3221 8155. **Post** The central post office is at 261 Queen St, opposite Post Office Sq. Mon-Fri 0830-1730, Sat 0900-1230. Post restante post code 4000. **Useful numbers** Police, corner of Queen St and Albert St and opposite the Roma St Transit Centre, 67 Adelaide St, T3224 4444. **Emergency** T000. **RACQ**, 261 Queen St, T3872 8465.

Moreton Bay and islands *p38*
North Stradbroke Island
Banks The post offices in Dunwich, Amity and Point Lookout all act as Commonwealth Bank agents. Eftpos is available in shops and resorts. There is an ATM at the **Stradbroke Island Beach Hotel and Spa Resort**, Point Lookout. **Internet** Manta Lodge YHA and Scuba Centre, 1 East Coast Rd, Point Lookout, T3409 8888. **Post** Dunwich, Point Lookout (Megerra Pl).

Sunshine and Fraser coasts

Just an hour north of Brisbane, the spellbinding volcanic peaks known as the Glass House Mountains herald your arrival at the aptly named Sunshine Coast. For those who can drag themselves away from the coast, the hinterland promises a wealth of more unusual attractions, while north of Noosa the coastal strip gives way to the Great Sandy Region, the largest coastal sand mass in the world, with Fraser Island, the largest coastal sand island in the world.

Noosa → *For listings, see pages 58-68. See also map, page 50.*

To some the former surfing backwater of Noosa is now little more than an upmarket suburb of Brisbane. However, it does have one of the finest surf beaches in Queensland, a climate that is 'beautiful one day, perfect the next' and it is fringed with two unspoilt national parks. In the last three decades, the string of coastal communities known as 'Noosa' has metamorphosed into one of the most desirable holiday resorts and residential areas on the entire east coast with a corresponding population growth rate. Many Melbournians in particular have bought holiday properties here to escape the southern winter. But, if you can turn a blind eye to the pretentiousness of the place, it makes a worthwhile stop on your way north.

Sights
Noosa Heads is the main focus of activity with the main surf beach at **Laguna Bay** and the chic tourist shops, accommodation and restaurants along Hastings Street. To the south is **Noosa Junction**, with Sunshine Beach Road providing the main commercial shopping area. From **Noosa VIC** ① *Hastings St, Noosa Heads, T5430 5000, www.visitnoosa.com.au, 0900-1700*, get hold of the free *Noosa Guide* with a detailed road and locality maps.

To the west of Noosa Heads is the pretty 454-ha **Noosa National Park**, which offers an escape from all the sand and surf as well as some fine walks. The most popular of these is the 2.7-km **coastal track**, which starts beside the information office at the end of Park Road (T5447 3243) and takes in a number of idyllic bays and headlands, before delivering you at **Alexandria Bay**. From there you can return the way you came, explore the interior of the park, continue south to the very plush northern suburbs of **Sunshine Beach** or simply spend the day on the beach in relative isolation. Bear in mind that all the beaches that fringe the national park are unpatrolled and swimming is not recommended.

The Noosa River runs both west and south from Noosa Heads in a tangled mass of tributaries to join **Lake Weyba** (south) and **Lakes Cooroibah and Cootharaba** (west and north). **Gympie Terrace**, in Noosaville, runs along the southern bank of the river and is the focus for most river- and lake-based activities.

Sunshine Coast hinterland → For listings, see pages 58-68.

With a name like 'Sunshine Coast' it is hardly surprising that the vast majority of travellers head straight for the beach. But though the swathes of golden sand will not disappoint, if you allow some time to explore the hinterland you will find colourful markets, quaint villages, giant 'walk-in' fruits and, topping the lot, the late Steve Irwin's famous Australia Zoo. This area is best visited on a tour from Brisbane or Noosa (see page 63) or in your own vehicle. The **Noosa VIC** ⓘ *T5430 5000*, can provide information on the major attractions, along with accommodation listings and maps.

Eumundi

The historic 19th-century former timber town of Eumundi, 1 km off the Bruce Highway and 23 km west of Noosa, is pretty enough in its own right, but timing your visit to coincide with the town's famous markets is highly recommended. Every Saturday and, to a lesser extent, Wednesday morning, Eumundi becomes a creative extravaganza of over 300 arts, crafts and produce stalls, all offering excellent quality, as well as lots of atmosphere and colour. Everything, it seems, is on offer, from kites and bandannas to massages and boomerangs. The markets kick off at about 0700 and start winding up about 1500. The best time to go is early on Saturday before the day heats up and the tourist buses arrive. It can get busy and a little stressful. There are plenty of food outlets and cafés on hand for coffee and breakfast.

Blackall Range Tourist Drive

Blackall Range Tourist Drive, from **Nambour**, a busy agricultural service centre, to the Glass House Mountains, is highly recommended, offering everything from national parks with waterfalls and short rainforest walks to fine coastal views and cosy B&Bs.

Driving west from Nambour, you begin the ascent up the Blackall Range to reach the pleasant little town of **Mapleton**. As well as its own great views and attractive B&Bs, Mapleton is the gateway to **Mapleton Falls National Park**. The heady views of the 120-m falls can be accessed 17 km west on Obi Obi Road. Nearby, the 1.3-km Wompoo Circuit walk winds through rainforest and eucalypts providing excellent views of the Obi Obi Valley. Obi Obi was a noted Aboriginal warrior and *wompoo* refers to a beautiful native pigeon.

From Mapleton the road heads south along the range through **Flaxton village** and the **Kondalilla National Park**. This 327-ha park is accessed and signposted 1 km south of Flaxton and offers views of the 90-m Kondalilla Falls, from the 2.1-km Picnic Creek trail and the 2.7-km Kondalilla Falls circuit, which winds its way down through rainforest to the base of the falls. Neither of the parks offers camping facilities.

First settled by fruit growers in 1887, historic **Montville**, 5 km south of Flaxton, is the main tourist hub along the Blackall Range. With its European-style historic buildings, chic cafés, galleries and souvenir shops, it provides a pleasant stop for lunch or a stroll. Nearby, Lake Baroon also offers a pleasant spot for a picnic. Although undoubtedly very touristy, Montville has not yet been spoiled and remains a delightfully quaint contrast to the coast. From Montville the road continues south taking in the **Gerrard** and **Balmoral Lookouts**. Both offer memorable coastal views from Noosa Heads in the north to Caloundra and Bribie Island in the south.

Turning inland you then arrive at the equally pretty town of **Maleny** which, like Montville, offers many interesting arts and crafts galleries, good B&Bs and a winery. At the far end of the town turn left down the narrow Maleny–Stanley Road to access Mountain View Road (left). Heading back towards the coast you are then almost immediately offered the first stunning views of the Glass House Mountains to the south from **McCarthy's**

Lookout. A few kilometres further on is the 41-ha **Mary Cairncross Scenic Reserve**, named after the 19th-century environmentalist. Here you can admire the views, visit the environmental centre (T5499 9907), or take a stroll through the rainforest (1.7 km). From the Cairncross Reserve, the road descends towards **Landsborough**, which is the northern gateway to the Glass House Mountains.

Glass House Mountains National Park

The Glass House Mountains are indeed a wonderful sight but they do nothing for safe driving. These 13 volcanic peaks that dominate the skyline from all directions are utterly absorbing and will, if you are not careful, have you swerving off the road. Gradual weathering by wind and water over the last 20 million years created their distinctive shapes and earned them their unusual name from Captain Cook, who thought they resembled the glass furnaces in his native Yorkshire. The highest peak is **Mount Beerwah** (556 m), while everybody's favourite has to be the distinctly knobbly **Mount Coonowrin** (377 m). Although the best views are actually from Old Gympie Road – which runs north to south, just west of Landsborough, Beerwah

Noosa

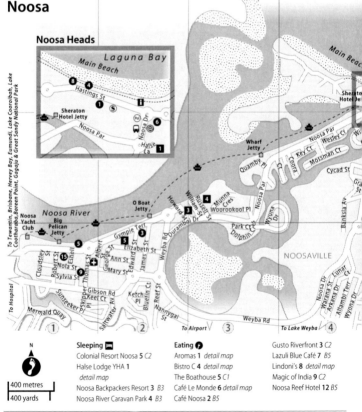

N

400 metres
400 yards

Sleeping 🛏
Colonial Resort Noosa **5** C2
Halse Lodge YHA **1**
  detail map
Noosa Backpackers Resort **3** B3
Noosa River Caravan Park **4** B3

Eating 🍴
Aromas **1** detail map
Bistro C **4** detail map
The Boathouse **5** C1
Café Le Monde **6** detail map
Café Noosa **2** B5

Gusto Riverfront **3** C2
Lazuli Blue Café **7** B5
Lindoni's **8** detail map
Magic of India **9** C2
Noosa Reef Hotel **12** B5

and Glass House Mountains Village – there is an official lookout on the southern edge of the park, 3 km west off Old Gympie Road. When it comes to bush walking and summit climbing, **Mount Ngungun** (253 m) is the most accessible (Fullertons Road off Old Gympie or Coonowrin roads) while **Mount Tibrogargan** (364 m) and Mount Beerwah also offer base viewpoints and two or three rough summit tracks. Sadly, pointy Mount Coonowrin is closed to public access due to the danger of rock falls. There is no camping allowed in the park, though several companies offer walking and climbing adventures (see Activities and tours, page 63).

Australia Zoo

ⓘ *Glass House Mountains Rd, Beerwah, T5436 2000, www.crocodilehunter.com.au, 0830-1600, $57, children $34. Free transportation is available daily from Noosa, Maroochy, Mooloolaba and Caloundra. Phone for details.*

Of all Queensland's many wildlife attractions, it is the Australia Zoo that seems to arouse people's enthusiasm the most. The reason for this is the hype and exposure of the late TV celebrity Steve Irwin (alias Crocodile Hunter), his widow Terri and daughter Bindi, to whom

the zoo is official home-base. Founded by Steve's father, the collection – thanks to his son's antics – developed faster than a crocodile could clamp its jaws around a dead chicken. The zoo houses a wide array of well-maintained displays exhibiting over 550 native and non-native species, ranging from mean-looking wedge-tailed eagles and insomniac wombats to enormous 6-m pythons and senescent Galápagos tortoises. Of course, the biggest attractions are the numerous crocodiles, or more precisely, the croc feeding, enthusiastically demonstrated daily at 1330. But what lets the place down is the sheer megalomania so apparent in the shop, with its talking Steve and Terri dolls and personal clothing lines (which even include a special kids' line after Bindi). Truly nauseating and a sad testament to modern celebrity marketing hype.

Cooloola Coast

→ *For listings, see pages 58-68.*

With access limited to 4WD only from Noosa from the south and a 76-km diversion from Gympie on the Bruce Highway from the north, the mainland – Cooloola Coast – section of the Great Sandy National Park, and its delightful, neighbouring coastal communities of Rainbow Beach and Tin Can Bay, are all too often missed by travellers in their eagerness to reach Hervey Bay and

Fraser Island. As well as the numerous and varied attractions and activities on offer within the 56,000-ha park – including huge sand blows, ancient coloured sands and weathered wrecks – Tin Can Bay offers an opportunity to feed wild dolphins. Rainbow Beach is an ideal rest stop off the beaten track, as well as providing southerly access to Fraser Island.

Ins and outs
Rainbow Beach VIC ① *8 Rainbow Beach Rd, T5486 3227, www.rainbow-beach.org, 0900-1700.* Also in Tin Can Bay ① *T5486 4855, www.tincanbay tourism.org.au.* For information on Fraser Island refer to the VIC or call T131304, www.epa.qld.gov.au. ▸▸ *See also Transport, page 67.*

Great Sandy National Park
Along with Fraser Island, Great Sandy National Park forms the largest sand mass in the world. For millennia, sediments washed out from the river courses of the NSW coast have been steadily carried north and deposited in vast quantities. Over time the virtual desert has been colonized by vegetation that now forms vast tracts of mangrove and rainforest, which in turn provide a varied habitat for a rich variety of wildlife.

The most notable feature of the park is the magnificent multi-coloured sands that extend from Rainbow Beach to Double Island Point. Over 200 m high in places and eroded into ramparts of pillars and groves, with a palette of over 40 colours, from blood red to brilliant white, they glow in the rays of the rising sun. Carbon dating of the sands has revealed some deposits to be over 40,000 years old. It is little wonder that they are steeped in Aboriginal legend. According to the Kabi tribe, who frequented the area long before the Europeans, the mighty sands were formed and coloured by the Rainbow Spirit who was killed in his efforts to save a beautiful maiden. Other features of the park include the Carlo Sand Blow, just south of Rainbow Beach, a favourite haunt for hang gliders, and the wreck of the cargo ship *Cherry Venture*, which ran aground in 1973. The views from the lighthouse on Double Island – which is actually a headland, falsely named by Captain Cook in 1770 – will also prove memorable. All the features of the park can be explored by a network of 4WD and walking trails. At the southern end of the park (accessed from Noosa), the lakes Cootharaba and Cooroibah are popular for boating and canoeing.

Rainbow Beach and Tin Can Bay
Located at the northern edge of the park, the laid-back, yet fast developing, seaside village of Rainbow Beach provides an ideal base from which to explore the park and as a stepping-stone to Fraser Island. Inskip Point, 14 km north, serves as the southerly access point to the great island paradise. Tin Can Bay, west of Rainbow Beach on the banks of the Tin Can Bay Inlet, is a popular base for fishing and boating but by far its biggest attraction is the visiting wild dolphin called 'Mystique' who appears, religiously, for a free handout, usually early each morning around the Northern Point boat ramp.

Hervey Bay → *For listings, see pages 58-68.*

The sprawling seaside town of Hervey Bay, the main gateway to Fraser Island, may lack 'kerb appeal', but more than makes up for this in the huge numbers of visitors who flood in to experience two mighty big attractions – Fraser Island and the migrating whales that use the sheltered waters of the bay as a temporary stopover. Considered by many to be the whale-watching capital of the world, Hervey Bay tries hard to stand on its own as a coastal resort and retirement destination, but – despite its low-key attractions, activities

Roach runners

Twenty years ago (or so the story goes) two Brisbanites were sitting in a bar arguing about whose suburb had the biggest, fastest cockroaches. Unable to reach a settlement, the following day they captured their very best and raced them. And with that the annual 'Cockroach Races' were born. (And who said Queenslanders are not as mad as cut snakes?) Now, every Australia Day (26 January), the Story Bridge Hotel in Kangaroo Point hosts the infamous and truly unique cocky races. Of course, the races, along with many other events and live entertainment (much of it involving the removal of girls' blouses), is merely an excuse to get utterly inebriated. Picture the scene for a second … small grandstands surround a central ring, bursting with rowdy punters, many with faces painted in national colours and wearing flags (often as the only item of clothing). The race is called and from deep within the crowd comes the sound of badly played bagpipes, heralding the arrival of the lovable little competitors. Then the sea of spectators parts and the scene is set. On the count of three, the plastic container, which covers the eager cockies in the middle of the ring, is lifted and off they run – in all directions. The crowd goes wild. The more squeamish onlookers scream as the insects run under bags, shoes and into sandwiches. As soon as the winner is declared (if, indeed, it can ever be found) it's drinks all round – and again – and again, until no one can remember who won. To say it is an experience is an understatement and it's not to missed if your visit coincides with the event. Just don't plan on doing anything the following day, except perhaps checking the contents of your shoes. Check out details at www.storybridgehotel.com.au.

and ubiquitous sweep of golden sand – it fails. The concerted attempts to keep people on the mainland for anything more than a day or a night seem futile and, as a result, it has become one of Queensland's most depressing tourist transit centres.

Ins and outs

For objective information (rare in these parts) visit the accredited **Maryborough Fraser Island VIC** ① *City Hall, Kent St, T4190 5742, www.visitmaryborough.info, and 1 km before Hervey Bay (signposted)* ① *Maryborough/Hervey Bay Rd, T4124 7626, www.visitherveybay.info, daily 0900-1700.*

Sights

Hervey Bay is one of Australia's fastest growing cities and is the main gateway to Fraser Island, the world's largest sand island. Essentially a beachfront conglomerate of north-facing suburbs, from Point Vernon in the east, through Urungan, Torquay, Scarness and Pialba in the west, it is however a popular holiday destination in its own right and in season (July-November) is arguably Australia's best venue for whale watching. Almost all major amenities are to be found along the Esplanade from the junction with Main Street in Pialba to Elizabeth Street, Urungan. The main Fraser Island ferry and whale-watching terminal is just south of Dayman Point in Urungan. The Esplanade has a footpath and cycle track, which offers a convenient way to soak up the seaside atmosphere.

   History buffs will enjoy the city's **Historical Village and Museum** ① *13 Zephyr St, Scarness, open Fri-Sun, small entry fee*. It includes over 8000 exhibits and an impressive collection of buildings including a traditional slab hut, a former church and a railway station. Blacksmith and treadle lathe demonstrations are available at weekends. In Pialba is the **Regional Gallery** ① *161 Old Maryborough Rd, Tue-Sat 1000-1600*, which showcases the work of an increasing number of local artisans and also hosts national touring exhibitions.

The 1.5-km-long **Urungan Pier** offers a pleasant breezy stroll and good fishing. Keep your eyes open for the aptly named soldier crabs on the beach at low tide.

Fraser Island → *For listings, see pages 58-68.*

Jutting out from the eastern Australian coast is the astounding 162,900-ha land mass known as Fraser Island – the biggest sand island in the world. Part of the Great Sandy National Park, which extends across to the mainland to the south, Fraser is now fully protected and was afforded World Heritage status in 1992. It is a very special place: a dynamic 800,000-year-old quirk of nature blessed with stunning beauty and a rich biodiversity. For the vast majority of visitors, the island may come as something of a surprise. Beyond a few sand blows and long, seemingly endless, stretches of beach, this is no Sahara. Blanketed in thick rainforest, pockmarked with numerous freshwater lakes and veined by numerous small streams, it surely confounds the preconceived notions of even the most experienced environmentalist. As well as its stunning beauty, sheer scale and rich wildlife, Fraser presents a great opportunity to try your hand at four-wheel driving and also plays host to one of the best resorts in the country. And despite the fact the island attracts over 300,000 visitors annually, it is still possible – only just – to find a little peace and solitude.

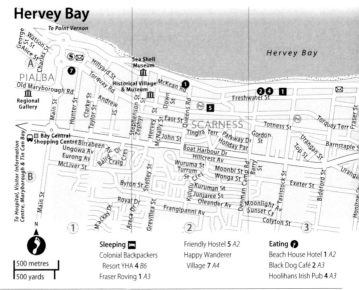

Hervey Bay

Sleeping 🛏		Eating 🍴
Colonial Backpackers	Friendly Hostel **5** *A2*	Beach House Hotel **1** *A2*
Resort YHA **4** *B6*	Happy Wanderer	Black Dog Café **2** *A3*
Fraser Roving **1** *A3*	Village **7** *A4*	Hoolihans Irish Pub **4** *A3*

Ins and outs

Getting there Vehicle and passenger ferries depart daily for Fraser Island from both Hervey Bay and Rainbow Beach. For details and the latest schedules, contact Maryborough VIC, see page 53, or see www.frasercoastholidays.info. ▶▶ *See Transport, page XXX.*

Getting around By far the best way to experience Fraser Island is to stay for at least three days and hire your own 4WD. Other than the freedom, this allows an ideal opportunity to get a feel of what an expensive 4WD is all about. Having said that, walking is hard to beat – to experience the sights, sounds and smells that would otherwise be missed. There is an eight-day walking trail and many short walk options. But with wheels or your walking boots you are advised to take detailed maps, which are available from the VIC or QPWS. Fraser is a big island.

Tourist information VICs and QPWS offices on the mainland – such as Maryborough Fraser Island VIC, see page 53 – can provide most of the necessary information.

 QPWS Great Sandy Information Centre ⓘ *240 Moorindil St, Tewantin T5449 7792, www.derm.qld.gov.au/parks/fraser.* There is also an office at **Rainbow Beach** ⓘ *Rainbow Beach Rd, T5486 3160, www.derm.qld.gov.au.*

 On the island there are QPWS ranger stations at Eurong (T4127 9128), Central Station (T4127 9191), Dundubara (T4127 9138) and Waddy Point (T4127 9190). All have variable opening times so call ahead. The resorts, especially **Kingfisher Bay**, are also valuable sources of information.

East Beach Highway (Eurong to Orchid Beach)

Fringed by pounding surf on one side and bush on the other, barrelling up and down the 92-km natural highway of East Beach is an exhilarating experience in itself. The main

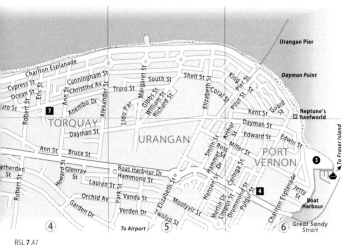

RSL **7** *A1*
Salt Café at Peppers Pier
Resort **3** *B6*

A whale of a time

Every year from August to November the waters around Hervey Bay echo to the haunting symphonies of whale song. These whales spend the warmer summer months in Antarctic waters feeding on krill before starting their annual migration north to the central and southern Great Barrier Reef where calves are born in the warm waters. Finding temporary haven in the bay's calm waters, pods of humpback whales stop to socialize and play, often breaching the surface or slapping it with fins and tail, before moving on to the far more serious business of returning to their feeding grounds in Antarctica. Other marine animals, including dolphins, turtles and occasionally dugongs, also join the fray and can be seen all year round. See below for tours.

access point for those arriving on the west coast is Eurong, where you can fuel up and head north for as far as the eye can see. Of course you will not be alone and at times the beach looks like a 4WD version of a bikers' meet on their way to a rock'n'roll gig.

There are a number of sights as you head north, the first of which is **Lake Wabby**, 4 km north of Eurong. Reached by foot – 4 km return on soft sand – Lake Wabby is one island lake that is at war with an encroaching sand blow, creating a bizarre landscape and the potential for lots of fun partaking in sand surfing and swimming. For a really stunning elevated view of the scene you can head inland for 7 km, on Cornwells Road, 2 km north of the beach car park. This in itself will test your 4WD skills. A walking track (5 km return) connects the lookout car park with the lake.

Next stop is **Eli Creek**, which offers a cool dip in crystal clear waters. Some 3 km beyond Eli Creek the rusting hulk of the *Maheno* – a trans-Tasman passenger liner that came to grief in 1935 – provides an interesting stop and a welcome landmark along the seemingly endless sandy highway. A further 2 km brings you to the unusual **Pinnacles** formation, an eroded bank of sand of varying gold and orange hues that looks like some bizarre sci-fi film set. Just south of the Pinnacles, the 43-km Northern Road circuit ventures through ancient rainforest known as **Yidney Scrub**, taking in views of the huge **Knifeblade Sand Blow**, the pretty, small **Lake Allom** and **Boomerang Lakes**, which, at 130 m above sea level, are the highest dune lakes in the world.

Back on East Beach, the colourful sandbanks continue to the **Cathedral Beach Resort** and the **Dundubara campsite**, offering the fit and adventurous walker the chance to explore the turtle-infested **Lake Bowarrady** (16 km return). From Dundubara it is another 19 km to **Indian Head**. One of the very few genuine rocks on the island, the head offers a fine vantage point from which to view the odd shark and manta ray in the azure waters below (demonstrating why swimming in the sea is ill advised around Fraser). Just beyond Indian Head, at the start of Middle Head, the track turns inland providing access to **Orchid Beach** and **Champagne Pools**. Named for their clarity and wave action, they provide perfect saltwater pools for swimming amongst brightly coloured tropical fish. Beyond the settlement of Orchid Beach and Waddy Point, travel with a 4WD becomes more difficult, with most hire companies banning further exploration north. But if you have your own vehicle, and enough experience, the northern peninsula can offer some welcome solitude and fine fishing spots all the way up to **Sandy Cape**, 31 km away.

Fraser Island

Sandy Cape

Orchid Beach
QPWS Ranger Station
Waddy Point
Airstrip
Champagne Pools
Middle Head
Wathumba
Indian Head

Hervey Bay

Worate Rd
QPWS Ranger Station
Lake Bowarrady
Dundubara
Lake Allom
Cathedral Beach

Moon Point
Bullock Rd
Boomerang Lakes
Moon Pt
Northern Rd
Happy Valley Rd
Knifeblade Sand Blow
The Pinnacles
Maheno

Yidney Scrub
Eli Creek

To Hervey Bay
Urangan

Poxans Rd
Bogimbah Rd
Happy Valley

East Beach

River Heads

Passenger
Smith Rd
South Pacific Ocean

Kingfisher Bay

Wanggoolba Creek
Lake McKenzie
QPWS Ranger Station
Lake Wabby

Mary River Heads
Central Station
Lake Birrabeen
QPWS Ranger Station
Eurong
Lake Benaroon

Dillinghams Rd
Lake Boomanjin

Toby's Gap Airstrip
Dilli Village

Hook Point
Inskip Point
To Rainbow Beach

N

5 km
5 miles

Sleeping 🛏
Eurong Beach Resort 2
Fraser Island Backpackers 1
Frasers 3
Kingfisher Bay Resort 5

QPWS Campsites ⛺

The lakes

There are over 100 freshwater lakes on Fraser, forming part of a vast and complex natural water storage system. Surprisingly for a sand island, there is 20 times more water stored naturally here than is held back by the Wivenhoe Dam, which supplies the whole of Brisbane. The most popular and visually stunning lakes are scattered around the island's southern part. By far the most beautiful and frequented is **Lake McKenzie**, which can be accessed north of Central Station or via the Cornwells and Bennet roads from East Beach. With its white silica sands and crystal clear waters, it is quite simply foolish not to visit. Make sure to go either early in the day or late, to avoid the crowds. Also take sunglasses, sunscreen and insect repellent.

Further south, **Lakes Birrabeen** and **Benaroon** offer fine swimming and are quieter than McKenzie but do not share quite the same beauty. Further south still is **Lake Boomanjin**, the largest 'perched' lake in the world, which means it ranks high on the humus podsol B Horizon with a large pH – it's very brown, in other words.

Central Station

For those arriving on the west coast, Central Station provides the first glimpse of just how wooded Fraser Island really is. Shaded by towering bunya pine and satinay and thick with umbrella-like palms, this green heart of Fraser has its own unique biodiversity. In the 50-m canopies many of the island's 240 recorded species of birds reside, from brightly coloured lorikeets and honeyeaters to tiny fairy wrens. On the ground echidna and dingoes roam and beneath it there are earthworms as long as your arm! One of the most pleasant features of Central Station are the crystal clear waters and white sandy bed of **Wanggoolba Creek**, which is the main feature on the 450-m boardwalk. Central Station also serves as the departure point for some excellent walking tracks to Lake McKenzie and the Pile Valley, where you will find yourself gazing heavenwards wondering if the trees could possibly grow any taller.

Sunshine and Fraser coasts listings

🌙 Sleeping

Noosa *p48, map p50*
Noosa is very much like a mini Gold Coast without the high-rise blocks, yet with the same massive range of 4-star resort complexes, self-contained holiday apartments and backpacker options. Here we simply skim the surface. If you have a specific idea about what you want there are various agencies who can oblige including: **Accommodation Noosa**, T1800 072078, www.accomnoosa.com.au; **Noosa Holidays**, T1800 629949, www.noosare.com. au; and **Peter Dowling**, T5447 3566, www. peterdowlingnoosa.com.au. For something a little different, try a houseboat, T5449 7611, www.luxuryafloatnoosa.com.au.

$$$$ Eumarella Shores, 251 Eumarella Rd, T5449 1738, www.eumarellashores.com. au. Next to Lake Weyba. Offers something far removed from the resorts and tourist hype. Fully self-contained colonial and log cabin-style cottages and contemporary 'eco- pavilions' sleeping 2-6 in a bush setting overlooking the lake. Minimum 2-night stay.
$$$ Colonial Resort Noosa,239-245 Gympie Terr, Noosaville, T5455 8100, www. colonialresortnoosa.com.au. In the heart of Noosaville and overlooking the river. Stylish fully self-contained rooms with decks, spa and all the usual facilities such as heated pool and secure parking.
$$ Gagaju, Boreen Point, T5474 3522, www.travoholic.com/gagaju. Characterful eco-backpackers-cum-bush-camp, located

between Lakes Cooroibah and Cootharaba, on the Noosa River. Everything is builtfrom recycled timber with dorms and shaded campsites (campfires allowed), full kitchen facilities, TV lounge room and excellent in-house half, 1 and 3-day canoe trips on the river. Pick-ups are offered from Noosa Heads.

$$ Halse Lodge YHA, 2 Halse Lane, Noosa Heads, T5447 3377, www.halselodge.com.au. At the other end of the scale is this spacious lodge, which is only a short walk from the long-distance bus stop. It is a historic 1880s Queenslander offering a good range of rooms from 6/4 dorms to doubles, twins and triple, all with shared bathrooms, bistro/bar, large quiet deck and social areas, good tour and activities desk and surf/body board hire.

$$ Noosa Backpackers Resort, 9-13 William St, Noosaville, T5549 8151, www. noosabackpackers.com. This is the main backpacker option west of Noosa Heads. It offers tidy 4-bed dorms, en suite doubles, pool, cheap meals, cable TV and internet. Free use of surfboards and kayaks.

$ Noosa River Caravan Park, 4 Russell St, Noosaville, T5449 7050. This is the best motor park/camping option in the area. Hugely popular given its riverside location and views but sadly becoming the preserve of 4WD fashionistas, which reflects the rapid influxof wealth and snobbery in the area. Powered and non-powered sites, modern amenities and barbecue. Book at least2 days in advance.

Sunshine Coast hinterland *p49*

$$$$ Eyrie Escape B&B, 316 Brandenburg Rd, Bald Knob, Mooloolah, T0414-308666, www.eyrie-escape.com.au. A 'spa witha view' at this incredible and aptlynamed place.

$$$$ Montville Mountain Inn,Main St, Montville, T5442 9499, www.montvilleinn. com.au. Central and affordable option.

Cooloola Coast *p51*

$$ Dingo Backpackers, 20 Spectrum St, Rainbow Beach, T1800 111126, www. dingosatrainbow.com. Modern, purpose-built option that offers en suite singles,

doubles, dorms, bar/restaurant, pool and internet. Despite its location it is a busy place with an excited atmosphere (at the prospect of visiting Fraser). Book ahead.

$ Rainbow Beach YHA, 18 Spectrum Av, Rainbow Beach, T5486 8885, www. frasersonrainbow.com. Just down the road from **Dingo Backpackers** is the other backpackers, which is older but comfortable, with motel-style dorms, doubles and twins, all with en suite. Facilities include internet, pool, a large well-equipped kitchen and a bar. There are also budget meals on offer and plenty of assistance with organizing a trip to Fraser or onward travel via the Cooloola beaches to Noosa.

QPWS campsites can be found at Great Sandy National Park (Cooloola). There are 20 varied sites. The main one is the Freshwater camping area, 20 km southeast of Rainbow Beach. It provides water, showers and toilets, but fires are banned. Access is by 4WD only. Booking centre, T5486 3160, Mon-Fri 1300-1500, otherwise contact the QPWS office on Rainbow Beach Rd in Rainbow Beach.

Bush camping is available just north of Rainbow Beach at Inskip Peninsula. Sealed roads provide easy access to both bay or surf side campgrounds but the only facilities are composting toilets. Phone the QPWS for more details.

Hervey Bay *p52, map p52*

The range and quality of accommodation in Hervey Bay caters for all budgets and tastes, from 5-star apartment resorts to hotels, motels, and backpacker hostels. There are also many holiday parks including four beachfront sites at Pialba, Torquay, Scarness and Burrum Heads administered by the local council. During the whale-watching season and public holidays book well ahead.

$$$$ Colonial Backpackers Resort YHA, corner of Pulgul St and Boat Harbour Drive (820), T4125 1844, www.yha.com.au. Closest to the harbour, this excellent backpackers has a fine range of options from luxury villas and 1-2 bedroom cabins, to en suite doubles and dorms, a good bistro/bar, pool, spa, internet, bike hire and tours desk.

$$$$ Happy Wanderer Village,105 Truro St, Torquay, T4125 1103, www.happywanderer.com.au. For a motor park with an excellent range of options and facilities stay here. It offers good value fully self-contained duplex villas, studio/standard units, cabins, onsite vans (shared amenities), en suite/standard powered sites and non-powered sites, pool, camp kitchen. Backpacker cabins are also available.

$$ Fraser Roving, 412 the Esplanade, T4125 3879, www.fraserroving.com.au. Enjoys a solid reputation with excellent and well-maintained facilities. Full range of rooms, spacious double en suites. Attractive package deals to Fraser Island in shocking pink 4WDs.

$$ Friendly Hostel, 182 Torquay Rd, T4124 4107, www.thefriendlyhostel.com. You are certain to get fine hospitality and some peace and quiet in this hostel. It is small and comfortable and more like a B&B, with tidy dorms (with single beds no bunks), doubles/twins and well-equipped kitchen facilities.

Fraser Island *p54, map p57*

$$$$ Eurong Beach Resort, east coast, T4127 9122, www.eurong.com. Traditional resort with a full range of options from tidy self-contained apartments, motel-style units and cabins to budget A-frame houses that can accommodate up to 8. Other budget units are also available. There is a spacious, yet fairly characterless, restaurant/bar, a pool and organized tours and activities. A well-stocked shop, café and fuel are on site. Comfortable and well situated for East Beach.

$$$$ Kingfisher Bay Resort, T4120 3333, www.kingfisherbay.com.au. This multi-award-winning resort is one of the best resorts in Australia. More an eco-village than a resort, it is highly successful in combining unique and harmonious architecture with superb facilities and a wide variety of accommodation options (fully self-contained holiday villas, lodges and luxury hotel rooms) centred on a spacious central lodge with landscaped pools and gardens. Within the main lodge are two excellent, if pricey, restaurant/bars, with a separate bistro/ pizzeria and shopping complex nearby. The resort also offers a wide range of activities and tours and hires out 4WD vehicles. There are regular daily ferry services from Urungan Boat Harbour. The resort also offers budget accommodation in its Wilderness Lodge but only through a multi-night stay option and in conjunction with its wide range of activities, tours and 4WD hire.

$$$ Fraser Island Backpackers, T1800 446655, www.fraserislandco.com.au. The traditional backpackers on the island, located midway up East Beach. Offers twins, doubles and dorms in individual en suite timber lodges. Bar and bistro, pool, internet, bottle shop and general store.

$$ Frasers at Cathedral Beach, Cathedral Beach is located 10 km north of Eli Creek, T4127 9177. This place offers tidy cabins, onsite tents and vans, all with fully equipped kitchens and non-powered sites with hot showers and a shop at Cathedral Beach.

QPWS campsites are at Central Station, Lake Boomanjin, Lake McKenzie, Lake Allom, Wathumba, Waddy Point and Dundubara. Facilities include toilets and cold showers. There are coin ($0.50/$1) operated hot showers at Central Station, Waddy Point and Dundubara.

Beach camping is permitted all along the east coast and on a few selected sites on the west coast. A nightly fee of $5 ($20 per family) applies to all campsites (Dundubara and Waddy Point must be pre-booked, all others cannot be pre-booked). QPWS fees do not apply to private resorts or campsites. And don't feed the dingoes!

⑦ Eating

Noosa *p48, map p50*

There are almost 200 restaurants in the Noosa area with around 30 along Hastings St alone. Over the years many top national

Four-wheel driving on Fraser Island

Fraser Island has virtually no sealed roads and its single-lane tracks are 4WD only. This makes it one of the best 4WD venues in Australia. Although for the layperson the tracks take some getting used to and are rough and soft in some places, access around the island is generally good, if slow. On average it takes about 30 minutes to travel 10 km on inland roads where a 35 kph speed limit is in force. Strict guidelines have been put in place for 4WD on the island and these should be adhered to at all times.

→ East Beach is, essentially, a 90-km sand highway with a speed limit of 80 kph but extreme care must be taken at all times, especially at high tide, in soft sand and crossing creeks. Avoid the temptation to let rip as this has resulted in some nasty accidents. Also apply standard road rules when meeting oncoming traffic.

→ Optimum driving conditions are two hours either side of low tide. You are also advised to release some air from your tyres in soft sand conditions.

→ All vehicles on the island require a RAM 4WD permit to be displayed on the windscreen. They can be obtained prior to arrival for $38.25 from the mainland QPWS offices, Hervey Bay City Council, 77 Tavistock Street, T4125 0222, www.derm.qld.gov.au, Hervey Bay Marina Kiosk, Boat Harbour, Urungan, T4128 9800, or River Heads Kiosk-Barge Car Park, Ariadne Street, T4125 8473. On the island permits cost a little more and can be purchased from QPWS Eurong Office. An information pack containing a detailed colour guide, camping and walking track details is supplied with the permit.

→ If you break down there are mechanical workshops at Eurong, T4127 9173, and Orchid Beach, T4127 9220. For mechanical assistance, T4127 9173. For a tow truck, T4127 9449 or T0428-353164, and be prepared to wave the contents of your bank account bye bye.

→ There are plenty of operators hiring 4WDs, but generally hire does not include fuel, ferry, food or accommodation/camping permits, nor does it include the cost of camping gear, which is an additional expense. The more professional companies will also give you a thorough briefing and maps. See Activities and tours, page 65, for companies offering tours.

→ To hire a 4WD you must at least 21, hold a current driver's licence and provide around $500 bond or credit card imprint and a permit.

chefs have set up kitchen in the region, fed by their desire to escape the big cities and the stiff competition. Many foreign chefs have also followed suit, adding a distinctly cosmopolitan range of options. Other than the expensive offerings on Hastings St in Noosa Heads, the main culinary hotspots are along Gympie Terrace and Thomas St in Noosaville. The best budget options are to be found along lower Noosa Drive and Sunshine Beach Rd in Noosa Junction.

$$$ Café Le Monde, 52 Hastings St, Noosa Heads, T5449 2366, www.cafelemonde.com. Daily 0600-late. One of the most popular socially with its large, covered, sidewalk courtyard and live entertainment 5 nights a week. It serves generous international and imaginative vegetarian dishes and is also popular for breakfast.

$$$ Lindoni's, 13 Hastings St, Noosa Heads, T5447 5111, www.lindonis.com.au. Daily 1800-2230. Of the Italian restaurants in Noosa, this place has the finest reputation, a good atmosphere and entertaining, Italian-speaking staff.

$$ Bistro C, on the Beachfront Complex,49 Hastings St, Noosa Heads, T5447 2855, www.bistroc.com.au. Daily 0730-2130. This classy restaurant offers a good traditional Australian/seafood menu and a welcome escape from the main drag overlooking the beach. Excellent for breakfast.

$$ Boathouse Restaurant, 1945 Gympie Terrace, Noosaville, T5440 5070, www. boathouserestaurant.com.au. Tue-Sun from 1000. Contemporary bistro-style cuisine including seafood, steaks and wood-fired pizzas overlooking the river. Try the much-lauded seafood platter.

$$ Gusto Riverfront, 2/257 GympieTerrace, Noosaville, T5449 7144, www.gustonoosa. com.au. Mon-Sat from 1100-late, Sun from 0800. One of the most popular restaurants in the region, offering cuisine that locals describe as 'honest and fresh' and for which they keep coming back time and again. Seafood, meat and vegetarian dishes. Book ahead.

$ Aromas, 32 Hastings St, Noosa Heads, T5474 9788. Daily 0700-late, Fri-Sat until 0100. Spacious and modern with a Mediterranean-influenced menu. Also excellent coffee, and the streetside location is a great spot to watch the world go by.

$ Café Noosa, 2/1 Sunshine Beach Rd, Noosa Heads, T5447 3949. Mon-Thu 1600-midnight, Fri-Sun 1300-midnight. Popular BYO pizza café with casual indoor or outdoor seating. Takeaway orders welcome.

$ Lazuli Blue Café, 9 Sunshine Beach Rd, towards Noosa Junction, T5448 0055. Good vegetarian dishes and value breakfasts.

$ Magic of India, across the road from Thai Breakers, Noosaville, T5449 7788. Reputed to be the best Indian takeaway in Noosa. Also open for sit-in meals Tue-Sun from 1730.

$ Noosa Reef Hotel, towards Noosa Junction, on Noosa Drive, T5430 7500. Fine views, value for money and especially good for families.

Sunshine Coast hinterland *p49*
$$ King Ludwig's German Restaurant & Bar, 401 Mountain View Rd, Maleny, T5499 9377. Wed-Sun lunch, Wed-Sat dinner. Overlooking the Glass House Mountains. Excellent food and a good atmosphere.

$$ Tree Tops Gallery, Kondalilla Falls Rd, near Flaxton, T1800 444350, www. treehouses.com.au. Also has equally excellent cabin-style accommodation.

Hervey Bay *p52, map p54*
Many of the upmarket resort complexes have restaurants offering fine dining. Cheaper eateries are to be found along the Esplanade in Torquay, Scarness and Pialba.

$$ Beach House Hotel, 344 Esplanade, Scarness, T4128 1233. Deservedly popular for both lunch and dinner, offers a good range of pub /café-style options overlooking the beach. They also have live entertainment and pool tables.

$$ Black Dog Café, corner of Esplanade and Denman Camp Rd, between Scarness and Torquay, T4124 3177. Wed-Mon 1030-1500, daily for dinner. A modern, classy restaurant with good-value Japanese dishes.

$$ Hoolihans Irish Pub, 382 Esplanade, T4194 0099. Daily from 1100. A wide range of traditional offerings with an Irish flavour. Servings are generous and it's pricey, but then there is always the quality beer!

$$ Salt Café, Shop 5, 569 Esplanade Peppers Pier Resort, Urangan, T4124 9722, www. saltcafe.com.au. Stylish contemporary café amid the Peppers complex, considered one of the best venues for fine dining.

$ RSL, 11 Torquay Rd, Pialba, T4128 1133. Daily. At the other end of town, this place can always be relied on for value for money and sedate entertainment.

Fraser Island *p54, map p57*
Resorts have restaurants/bistros and some campsites have fully equipped kitchens. See page 60. Food on the island is expensive, so if you're camping you're advised to bring all your supplies from the mainland.

🌓 Bars and clubs

Noosa p48, map p50
Reef Hotel, 19 Noosa Drive, Noosa Heads, T5430 7500. This is highly regarded and hosts 2 popular bars on two levels, with Level 1 offering a live entertainment each weekend - from resident and visiting DJs.

⛰ Activities and tours

Noosa p48, map p50
Aerial pursuits
Dimona Motor Glider Flights, based at the Sunshine Coast Airport, Maroochy, T1300 667042, www.comegliding.com.au. Trips (50 mins to 1 hr 45 mins) in something between a light aircraft and a glider, from $265-395.
Epic Horizon Paragliding, T0428-185727, www.epic-horizon.com. Tandem flights from $100.
Noosa and Maroochy Flying Services, T5450 0516, www.noosaaviation.com. Range of scenic flights from coastal trips to Fraser Island and reef safaris, $100-550.
Skydive Ramblers, T5446 1855, www. ramblers.com.au. Has a drop zone on Coolum Beach with 'photo specialist' tandems at around $350.
Sunshine Coast Skydivers, Caloundra Airport, T5491 1395, www.scskydivers.com. Large and reputable operator providing 3650- to 4250-m tandems, includingthe unusual 'night' tandem from $369(night $460).

Camel safaris
Camel Safaris, based on Noosa North Shore, T0408-710530, www.camelcompany.com. au. Safaris of 1-2 hrs along Forty Mile Beach (Great Sandy National Park/Cooloola) from $60, overnight camping $220.

Cruises and boat hire
There are numerous operators along the riverbank from whom you can hire U-Drive Boats, barbecue boats, speedboats, kayaks

and jet skis at competitive prices. There are also plenty of operators offering sedate cruises up and down the Noosa River from Noosa Heads to Tewantin and beyond.
Noosa Everglades Discovery, T5449 0393, www.noosaevergladesdiscovery.com.au. A variety of cruise options exploring the upper reaches of the Noosa River (from $99, children $70) and 4WD trips along the forty Mile Beach 'sandy highway' to see the coloured sands (from $155/$105). Informative, comfortable and entertaining. Recommended.
Noosa Ferry Cruise, T5449 8442, www. noosaferry.com. Runs regular services between all these stops, daily, from 0915-1800 (later at weekends), from $13 one way, children $6, family $45. An all-day pass costs $19.50. Sunset Cruise $19.50.
The main ferry terminals are (from west to east): Tewantin Noosa Marina (7/2 Parklyn Ct, Tewantin), Noosa Yacht Club, Big Pelican,O Boat Jetty, T Boat jetty, Noosa Wharf, Sheraton Hotel jetty.

Cycling/mountain biking
Noosa Bike Hire and Tours, T5474 3322, bikeon.com.au. Stylish outfit offering customized or scheduled guided trips according to your fitness and level of skill, as well as independent hire outlets throughout the area. Main outlet Noosa Tour Centre, Noosa Drive and Halse Lane, Noosa Heads, T5447 3845. Expect to pay around $40 per day, $20 for 2 hrs.

Horse trekking
Clip Clop Horse Treks, 249 Eumarella Rd,Lake Weyba, T0429-051544, www. clipclop treks.com.au. Wide range of exciting adventures on the waterways of the Great Sandy National Park (Cooloola), from half day (from $70), to 5-day/4-night (from around $1100). Independent hire and accommodation is also available from 2-hr treks to 4-day adventures. Prices on application.

Kayaking and canoeing
Elanda Point Canoe Company, T5485 3165, www.elanda.com.au.
Kayak Noosa , The Boathouse, 194 Gympie Terrace, Noosaville, T0448-567321, www.kayaknoosa.com. Coastal or river kayaking with the chance of encountering dolphins from $55 (2-hr sunset trips available). Independent hire from 1hr $20 to $55 per day.

Motorcycle tours
Aussie Biker Tours, 4/15 VentureDrive, Noosaville, T5474 1050, www.aussiebiker.com.au. Hire and self-guided trips.

Sightseeing tours
Fraser Island Adventure Tours, T5444 6957, www.fraserislandadventuretours.com.au. Exciting 4WD day trip to Fraser Island from Noosa, taking in the main sights of the Great Sandy National Park (Cooloola) along the way, from $145, children $110.
Noosa 4WD Eco Tours, T5449 8252, www.noosa4wdtours.com.au. Full- and half-day tours throughout the week to the Great Sandy Marine Park (Cooloola), from $95-129.
Noosa Hinterland Tours, T5448 6111, www.noosahinterlandtours.com.au. Tours throughout the week to the Hinterland taking in a winery and the Glass House Mountains, from $55, children $35; the Eumundi Markets (Wed and Sat), from $20, children $10; and the Australia Zoo on demand, from $49, children $29 (discounted zoo entry).

Spas
No doubt after a few hours on a camel or a horse your weathered cheeks and other bodily parts would greatly benefit from a spa or a massage. **Ikatan Balinese Day Spa**, 46 Grays Road, Doona, T5471 1199, www.ikatanspa.com, is a little bit out of Noosa but well worth it, or visit the **Noosa Spa** (South Pacific Resort), 167 Weyba Rd, T5447 1424, www.noosaspa.com.au.

Surfing and kitesurfing
There are more learn-to-surf operators on Main Beach than there are beach umbrellas. Generally they are all very professional and run by pros and/or experts. 2-hr session starts at about $65.
Wavesense, T0414-369076, www.wavesense.com.au, **Learn to Surf**, with world champ Merrick Davies, T0418-787577, www.learntosurf.com.au, 2 hrs from $60 and, for girls only, the **Girls Surf School**, T0418-787577, www.learntosurf.com.au.
Kitesurf, T5455 6677, www.kite-surf.com.au, and **Wind 'n' Sea**, T5455 6677, will introduce you to the world of kite surfing, from $150 for 2 hrs.
Noosa Longboards, Shop 4, 64 Hastings St, T5447 2828. Hires long/short surfboards and body boards, from $35 for 4 hrs.

Cooloola Coast *p51*
Horse trekking, diving, paragliding, canoeing and fishing all feature in the growing list of available activities and Cooloola VIC can provide detailed operator details. It is however 4WD tours that dominate, with options both north to Fraser Island and south to the Cooloola Section of the Great Sandy National Park.

4WD tours
Aussie Adventure 4WD, T5486 3599. If you want to go it alone, come here to hire 2-9 seater 4WD vehicles.

Dolphin watching
Dolphin Ferry Cruise, T0428-838836. Departs Carlo Point daily for the dolphin feeding at Tin Can Bay, from $20. For Fraser Island ferry services, see page 67.

Hervey Bay *p52, map p54*
Whale watching
The high number of visiting whales, the calm water conditions and the variety of cruises on offer has ensured Hervey Bay is the best location on the East Coast for experiencing whales up close. The choice

of cruises range from 3-hr fast catamaran trips, to morning, afternoon half-day or full-day excursions that include lunch and refreshments. There are numerous operators based at the Urungan Boat Harbour and you are advised to take a look at the various boats and compare their itineraries. With so many operators, other than cruise time, the differences really come down to minor details like the size of the group.

Blue Dolphin, T4124 9600, www.blue dolphintours.com.au. 'Whales by sail', half-day and sunset cruise option, from $70.

Mikat Whale Watch Safari, T4125 1522, www.mikat.com.au, and **Whalesong**, T4125 6222, www.whalesong.com.au, both operate cruises on large catamarans. 6-hr cruises with Mikat from $125. **Whalesong** do specialist year-round dolphin cruises, half day from $75, children $50.

Spirit of Hervey Bay, T1800 642544, www.spiritofherveybay.com. This one has the added luxury of underwater viewing rooms.

Tasman Venture II, T1800 620322, www. tasmanventure.com.au. Offers whale watching but also something different with a West Coast day tour which explorers the quiet and largely inaccessibly beaches of Fraser's west coast, with snorkelling and perhaps a bit of dolphin watching along the way, from $125.

Fraser Island *p54, map p57*

As you might expect, there are many tours on offer to Fraser from as far away as Brisbane and Noosa. To get the most from the island you really need at least 3 days, so a day tour should only be considered if you are hard pressed for time. If you want to explore the island in a short space of time try the excellent guided tour and accommodation packages on offer through the resorts, especially **Kingfisher Bay**, T1800 072555, www.kingfisherbay.com.au. Daily tours start at $169, children $99.

Air Fraser Island, T4125 3600, www.airfraser island.com.au. Recommended if you're on your own or are a couple. They will fly you out to Eurong, where you are supplied with a small, economical 4WD (with camping gear if required, fuel not included) from around $275 per day. The only drawback is that the vehicle must stay on the island and be dropped off again at Eurong. This option does avoid the expensive vehicle ferry fees and is fine if you want to fly back, but it can present problems if you wish to stay at the **Kingfisher Bay Resort** and/or get the ferry back as foot passengers from the island's west coast.

Tours from Noosa *p48, map p50*

Fraser Explorer Tours, T4194 9222, www. fraserexplorertours.com.au. Day or 2-day trips departing from either Hervey Bay or Rainbow Beach, from $165, children $99 ($309/$209).

Fraser Island Adventure Tours, T5444 6957, www.fraserislandadventuretours.com. au. Exciting 4WD day trip to Fraser Island ex Noosa, taking in the main sights of the Great Sandy National Park (Cooloola) along the way, from $145, children $110.

Fraser Island Trailblazers Tours, T5499 9505, www.trailblazertours.com.au. Good value 'down-to-sand' 3-day camping safari, via the Great Sandy National Park (Cooloola section), from $360 (2-day from $280).

Tours from Hervey Bay *p52, map p54*

Fraser Experience & Safari 4WD, 102 Boat Harbour Rd, T4124 4244, www.safari 4wdhire.com.au. For those wishing to get a group together and go independently, this is one of the most professional. They offer a range of models from $140-200 a day, camping kits from $20 per day and hire/ accommodation packages are also available. Their guided **Fraser Experience** departs Hervey Bay to Rainbow Beach then Fraser Island, 2-day tour from $285.

Fraser Explorer Tours, T4194 9222, www. fraserexplorertours.com.au. Day tour from Hervey Bay, starting at $165.

Fraser Island Company, T4125 3933,, www. fraserislandco.com.au. Offers a good range of safaris, 1 day from $145, children $85, 2 days from $269.

Nomads, T4125 3601, www. nomadshostels. com, and **Palace**, T1800 063168, are 2 backpackers offering their own vehicles, guides and budget packages (camping), from around $155. Other companies worth looking at are **Aussie Trax**, 56 Boat Harbour Drive, T4124 4433, www.fraserisland4wd. com.au, and **Fraser Magic**, 5 Kruger Court, Urangan, T4125 6612, www.fraser4wdhire. com.au.

⊖ Transport

Noosa *p48, map p50*
Air
The nearest airport is the Maroochydore (Sunshine Coast) Airport, www.sunshine coastairport.com, which is 6 km north of Maroochydore. **Jet Star**, T131538, www. jetstar.com; **Qantas**, T131313, www.qantas. com.au; **Tiger Airways**, T9335 3033, www. tigerairways.com; and **Virgin Blue**, T136789, www.virginblue.com.au, provide daily services from national centres including **Brisbane**. Local northbound bus services stop at the airport and a taxi to **Noosa Heads** will cost about $70.**Henry's**, 12 Noosa Drive, T5474 0199, www.henrys. com.au, offers express (non-stop) services between Brisbane Airport/Maroochydore Airport and Noosa Heads 7 times daily, from $25 each way.

Bus
Local Sunshine Coast Sunbus,T5450 7888, www.sunbus.com.au, has services to Noosa Heads/Tewantin north/ southbound to the Sunshine Coast west to Eumundi/Cooroy/ Nambour. A free council-run bus service every 15 mins between Tewantin and Noosa Fair is available and the information centre can provide times and routes.
Long distance The long-distance terminal is on the corner of Noosa Pde and

Noosa Drive, Noosa Heads. **Greyhound**, T1300 473946, and **Suncoast Pacific**, T131230, offer daily north/southbound services and regular services to **Tin Can Bay**. **Harvey World Travel**, Shop 2, Lanyana Way, Noosa Heads, T5447 4077, and **Palm Tree Tours**, Bay Village, Hastings St, T5474 9166, act as local booking agents.

Car
Avis, Shop 1, Ocean Breeze Resort, corner Hastings St and Noosa Drive, T5447 4933. **Budget**, 52 Mary St, Noosaville, T5474 2820. If you wish to explore the Great Sandy National Park there are several 4WD hire companies including **Thrifty**, 66 Noosa Drive, T5447 2299; and **Pelican 4WD Hire**, 66 Noosa Drive, T1800 144294.

Ferry
The **Tewantin car ferry**, T5447 1321, www. noosacarferries.com, crosses the Noosa River (end of Moorindil St) and provides access to the national park. It operates Nov-Jan Sun-Thu 0530-2230, Fri-Sat 0530-0030 and Feb-Oct Mon-Thu 0600-2230, Fri 0600-0030, Sat 0500-0030 and Sun 0500-2230, from $6.

Train
The nearest train station is at Cooroy, T132232. **Sunbus** offers services from there to Noosa Heads (No 12).

Cooloola Coast *p51*
Bus
Greyhound, T131499, and **Suncoast Pacific**, T131230, operate daily coach services to **Tin Can Bay** and **Rainbow Beach**.

Car
Rainbow Beach is 76 km east of the Bruce Highway at Gympie and the road is sealed all the way. Alternative access is by 4WD only from Tewantin, 3 km east of Noosaville, Noosa River ferry 0600-2200, from $6.

Hervey Bay *p52, map p54*
Air
Hervey Bay airport, T1800 811728, has daily scheduled flights to **Brisbane** and **Sydney** with **Jetstar**, T131538, **Qantas**, T131313, and **Virgin Blue**, T136789. The airport shuttle meets all flights, T4194 0953. Taxi T131008.

Bus
Local Wide Bay Transit, T4121 3719, www.widebaytransit.com.au, runs local hail and ride bus services between Maryborough (including the railway station) and Hervey Bay (No 5), taking in a circuit of the town along the Esplanade to Urungan and back via Boat Harbour Drive. Nos 16 and 18 also cover the main centres and Urungan Marina.

Long distance The long-distance bus terminal is in the Bay Central Shopping Centre, Boat Harbour Rd, Pialba, T4124 4000. **Greyhound**, T1300 473946, and **Premier Motor Services**, T133410, offer daily services north/ south and to **Tin Can Bay** and **Rainbow Beach**.

Car
Car hire from **Hervey Bay Rent A Car**, T4194 6626, and **Nifty Rent A Car**, 463 Esplanade, T4125 6008.

Train
The nearest train station is in Maryborough, Lennox St, T4123 9264. **Queensland Rail's** fast Tilt Train (**Brisbane** to **Rockhampton**) offers regular services north and south, T132232. Wide Bay Transit No 5 service connects with every Tilt Train for transfers to and from **Hervey Bay**, T4123 1733. **Hervey Bay Travel Centre**, Bay Central Shopping Mall, Torquay, T1800 815378, can act as booking agents.

Fraser Island *p54, map p57*
Air
There are 2 small airfields on Fraser – Toby's Gap and Orchid Beach – but most light aircraft land on East Beach at Eurong or Happy Valley.

Air Fraser Island, T4125 3600. Daily services from around $100, www.airfraserisland.com.au. It also offers packages and scenic flights, see page 65.

Boat
There are several barge options to Fraser island: **Fraser Island Barges and Ferry** have several services daily from River Heads, south of Hervey Bay, Rainbow Beach andUrangan Boat Harbour, T4194 9300, www.fraserislandferry.com.au; the **Fraser Venture Barge** also departs River Heads to Wanggoolba Creek. Both barges operate continuously between dawn and dusk departing Inskip Point daily, landing at the most southern tip of Fraser, Hook Point. Crossing time takes approximately 10 mins, from $90. The **Kingfisher Bay (Resort)**, T1800 072555, www.kingfisherbay.com.au, also operates its own passenger/4WD ferry to the resort from $85. The **Fraser Dawn Barge** operates from Urangan Boat Harbour to Moon Point– crossing time approximately 55 mins. Moon Point is directly opposite Happy Valley on Fraser Island's west coast.

ⓘ Directory

Noosa *p48, map p50*
Banks Most branches/ATMs are on Hastings St, Noosa Heads or Sunshine Beach Rd, Noosa Junction. Currency exchange at **Harvey World Travel**, Shop 2, Lanyana Way, Noosa Heads, T5447 4077.
Hospitals Noosa Hospital, 111 Goodchap St, T5455 9200; **Noosaville Medical Centre**, corner of Thomas St and Mary St, T5442 4922, Mon-Thu 0800-2000, Fri-Sun 0800-1800.
Internet Travel Bugs, Shop 3/9, Sunshine Beach Rd, Noosa Junction, T5474 8530, daily 0800-2200. **Urban Mailbox**, Ocean Breeze Resort, Shop 4, Noosa Drive, Noosa Heads, T5473 5151, daily 0900-1900 (2200 high season). **Pharmacy** Night and Day, 32 Hastings St, daily 0900-2100. **Post** 91 Noosa Drive, T5473 8591, Mon-Fri 0900-1730, Sat 0900-1230. Postcode 4567.

Hervey Bay *p52, map p54*
Banks Most branches/ATMs are
in the Central Avenue Plaza, Pialba.
Hospital Nissen St, T4120 6666.
Pharmacy Pialba Place Main St, Pialba,
T4128 1140. **Post** Post Office, 414
Esplanade, Torquay, Mon-Fri 0830-1700, Sat
0830-1200 and Central Av, Pialba, T131318.
Postcode 4655. **Useful numbers** Police,
142 Torquay Rd, T4128 5333.

Fraser Island *p54, map p57*
Food, hardware, fuel and telephones are
available at the **Eurong Beach Resort**, **Fraser
Island Retreat** (Happy Valley), **Kingfisher
Bay Resort**, **Cathedral Beach Resort** and
Orchid Beach. Additional telephones

are located at Ungowa, Central Station,
Dundubara, Waddy Point and Indian Head.
There are no banks or ATMs on the island
but most major resorts accept EFTPOS. There
are no medical services on the island. QPWS
ranger stations and resorts all have basic first
aid and can call in an air ambulance in an
emergency, T000.

For mechanical assistance on the island
contact: Eurong T4127 9173 and T0427-
279173; Orchid Beach T4127 9220. For tow
truck services contact: Eurong, T4127 9449
and T0428-353164; Yidney Rocks, T4127
9187 and T0427-279167; Orchid Beach
T4127 9220. For taxi service: Eurong, T4127
9188 and T0429-379188.

Capricorn Coast

Capricorn Coast begins north of Hervey Bay, where the great sand masses of the Fraser Coast give way to fields of sugar cane and, offshore, the start of the Great Barrier Reef. Near Bundaberg – or 'Bundy' – is Mon Repos, one of the world's most important and accessible mainland turtle rookeries. The once remote towns of 1770 and Agnes Water serve as gateway to the stunning southern reef island of Lady Musgrave, while even more beautiful Heron Island is accessed from the industrial port of Gladstone. East of Rockhampton, Queensland's 'beef capital', are the coastal resorts of Yeppoon and Emu Park, while just offshore Great Keppel Island offers many tourists their first taste of Queensland's many beautiful tropical island resorts.

Bundaberg and Southern Reef Islands → *For listings, see pages 76-82.*

Little Bundaberg sits beside the Burnett River amidst a sea of sugar cane. The city relies far more on agriculture than tourism to sustain it and as a result is usually absent from most travel agendas. Many refer to the town as 'Bundy', though this affectionate nickname is most often used to describe its famous tipple, rum, which has been faithfully distilled in Bundaberg since 1883. Not surprisingly, the wonderfully sweet-smelling distillery is the biggest tourist attraction, while others nearby include the southern reef islands of Lady Musgrave and Elliot, both of which offer excellent diving, and the fascinating seasonal action at the Mon Repos Turtle Rookery.

Ins and outs

Getting there and around Bundaberg's airport is 3 km from the city centre. All the main bus companies operate services to the city from the north and south. The **Tilt Train** is the major train service from Brisbane. The reef ferries depart from the Bundaberg Port Marina, on the lower reaches of the Burnett River, about 19 km northeast of the centre. The coastal resorts of Bargara, Burnett Heads and the Mon Repos Turtle Rookery are 15 km east. Local coach operators run regular services. ➠ *See Transport, page 80.*

Tourist information There are two VICs, with little difference between them. The accredited centre is at ① *271 Bourbong St, T4153 8888, www.bundabergregion.org, 0900-1700.*

Bundaberg

Before filling the nostrils with the sweet smell of molasses and titillating the taste buds with the dark nectar at the distillery, it is perhaps worth taking a quick, and sober, look at one or two of the historical buildings dominating the city centre. Most prominent is the 30-m clock tower of **Post Office building**, on the corner of Bourbong Street and Barolin

Street, which has been in continuous operation since 1890. A few doors down is the 1891 **Old National Australia Bank**, with its distinctive colonnades and spacious verandahs embellished with cast iron balustrades.

An equally popular retreat is the city's **Botanical Gardens Complex** ① *1 km north of the city centre, corner of Hinkler Av and Gin Gin Rd, T4152 0222, 0730-1700, $5, children $2, museums 1000-1600.* Added to the obvious botanical attractions and landscaped ponds and gardens are the **Fairymead House Sugar Museum**, which documents the history of the region's most important industry, and the **Hinkler House Memorial Museum**, T4130 4400, which celebrates the life and times of courageous local pioneer aviator, Bert Hinkler. Born in Bundaberg in 1892, Hinkler was the first person to fly solo from Australia to England, in 1928. Sadly, after going on to break numerous other records, he then died attempting to break the record for the return journey in 1933. There is also a working steam train that clatters round the gardens on Sundays.

Although a relatively small operation, the **Bundaberg Distillery** ① *Avenue St (4 km east of the city centre, head for the chimney stack), T4131 2999, www.bundabergrum.com. au, tours daily on the hour Mon-Fri 1000-500, Sat-Sun 1000- 1400, from $25, children $15,* established in 1883, provides a fascinating insight into the distilling process. The one-hour tour begins with a short video celebrating the famous Bundy brand before you are taken to view the various aspects of the manufacturing process. First stop is a huge 5-million-litre well of sweet-smelling molasses, which is gradually drawn through a maze of steel pipes, fermenters, condensers and distillers, before ending up in mighty vats within the maturing warehouses. With one vat alone being worth $5 million ($3 million of which goes to government tax) it is hardly surprising to hear the solid click of lock and key and to be mildly aware of being counted on the way out! Then, with a discernibly quickening pace, you are taken to an authentic bar to sample the various end products. Generous distillers they are too, allowing four shots, which is just enough to keep you below the legal driving limit.

Mon Repos Turtle Rookery

① *Grange Rd, off Bundaberg Port Rd, T4159 1652 or T4153 8888, www.epa.qld.gov.au. Turtle viewing Oct-May, 1900-0600 (subject to activity), information centre open daily 24 hrs Oct-May and 0600-1800 Jun-Sep, $9.60, children $5.10.*

Supporting the largest concentration of nesting marine turtles on the eastern Australian mainland and one of the largest loggerhead turtle rookeries in the world, the Coral Coast beach, known as Mon Repos (pronounced 'Mon Repo'), is a place of ecological reverence. It can be found 12 km east of Bundaberg, near the coastal resort of Bargara. During the day Mon Repos looks just like any other idyllic Queensland beach and gives absolutely no indication of its conservation value. Yet at night, between mid-October and May, it takes on a very different aura. Hauling themselves from the waves, just beyond the tideline, with a determination only nature can display, the female turtles (often quite elderly) each dig a large pit in the sand and lay over 100 eggs before deftly filling it in and disappearing beneath the waves, as if they had never been there at all. To watch this happen, all in the space of about 20 minutes, is a truly magical experience. And it doesn't end there. Towards the end of the season, from January to March, the tiny hatchlings emerge from the nest and make their way as fast as they can, like tiny clockwork toys, towards the relative safety of the water. Watching this spectacle is moving and, strangely, hilarious, despite the knowledge that only one in 1000 of the hatchlings will survive to maturity and return to the same beach to breed. Of course, like any wildlife-watching attraction, there are no guarantees that turtles will show up on any given night, so you may need a lot of patience. While you wait at the Information Centre to be escorted in groups of about 20 to watch the turtles up close, you can view static displays, or better still, join in the staff's fascinating question-and-answer sessions, where you can learn all about the turtles' remarkable natural history, and sadly, the increasing threat that humans are posing to them. Best viewing times for nesting turtles are subject to night tides between November and February. Turtle hatchlings are best viewed from 1900 to 2400, January to March.

Southern Reef Islands

Lady Musgrave Island, 83 km northeast of Bundaberg, is part of the Capricornia Cays National Park and the southernmost island of the Bunker Group. With a relatively small 14 ha of coral cay in comparison to a huge 1192-ha surrounding reef, it is generally considered one of the most beautiful and abundant in wildlife, both above and below the water. The cay itself offers safe haven to thousands of breeding seabirds and also serves as an important green turtle rookery between November and March. Then, between August and October, humpback whales are also commonly seen. With such a large expanse of reef, the island offers some excellent snorkelling and diving as well as providing a pleasant escape from the mainland.

Lady Elliot Island, about 20 km south of Lady Musgrave, is one of the southernmost coral cays on the Barrier Reef. It's larger than Musgrave and though the surrounding reef is smaller, it is very similar in terms of scenery and marine diversity. The island is also a popular diving venue with numerous wrecks lying just offshore (about $30 a dive). ▸▸ *For further details see Tours, page 79, and Transport, page 80.*

Agnes Water, 1770 and around → *For listings, see pages 76-82.*

With the dawning of the new millennium it was already obvious that both 1770 and Agnes would be changed from being fairly inaccessible, sleepy coastal neighbours into the next big thing on the southern Queensland coast. Sadly, this seems to have happened and they have fallen victim to the great East Coast property development phenomenon. As predicted, the money has moved in and the locals have moved out. Where wooded hillsides once created a soft green horizon, designer holiday homes owned by absentee landlords have appeared. Where once dunescapes created pockets of soporific seclusion, sterile and exclusive apartment resorts look set to dominate. Despite the decline, the two towns are still extremely picturesque and hemmed in by two fine national parks, Eurimbula and Deepwater. The Town of 1770 also acts as gateway to Lady Musgrave Island, an undeniable gem located 50 km offshore.

Ins and outs

Getting there and around   There are long-distance bus services from Rockhampton or Bundaberg and a train station at Miriam Vale, 55 km east. ▸▸ *See Transport, page 80.*

Tourist information   Miriam Vale VIC ⓘ *Bruce Highway, Miriam Vale, T4974 5428, www. gladstoneholidays.info, Mon-Fri 0830-1700, Sat-Sun 0900-1700*, and **Discovery Centre** ⓘ *Captain Cook Drive, Agnes Water, T4902 1533, Mon-Sat 0830-1700*, are the two main sources of local information. **QPWS** ⓘ *Captain Cook Drive, Agnes Waters, T4902 1555, www. qld.gov.au, Mon-Fri 0900-1630.*

Agnes Water and the Town of 1770

Agnes Water has a beautiful 5-km beach right on its doorstep, which offers good swimming and excellent surfing. More remote beaches offering more solitude and great walking opportunities can be accessed within the national parks. The small **museum** ① *Springs Rd, Sat-Sun 1000-1200, Wed 1300-1500, $2,* touches on Aboriginal settlement, Cook's visit and the subsequent visitations by explorers Flinders and King, as well as more recent maritime and European settlement history.

The Town (village) of 1770 nestles on the leeward side of Round Hill Head and along the bank of the Round Hill Inlet, 6 km north of Agnes, and is a popular spot for fishing and boating. It also serves as the main departure point for local national park and reef island tours and cruises, see page 79.

Deepwater and Eurimbula national parks

Deepwater National Park, 8 km south of Agnes, presents a mosaic of coastal vegetation including paperbark, banksias and heathland fringed with dunes and a sweeping beach studded with small rocky headlands. As well as fishing and walking, there are fine opportunities for birdwatching and it is often used as a nesting site by green turtles between January and April. The roads within the park are unsealed so 4WD is recommended.

To the northwest of Agnes is Eurimbula National Park. Indented by the Round Hill Inlet and Eurimbula Creek, it is an area covered in thick mangrove and freshwater paperbark swamps. It is less accessible than Deepwater and best explored by boat. Other than the interesting flora and fauna, highlights include the panoramic views of the park and coastline from the Ganoonga Noonga Lookout, which can be reached by vehicle 3 km from the park entrance, 10 km west of Agnes Water. Again a 4WD is recommended, especially in the wet season.

Rockhampton and around → *For listings, see pages 76-82.*

Straddling both the Tropic of Capricorn and picturesque Fitzroy River, Rockhampton – or 'Rocky' as it is affectionately known – is the dubbed the 'beef capital' of Australia. First settled by Scots pioneer Charles Archer in 1855 (yet strangely bestowed the anglicized suffix 'Hampton', meaning 'a place near water'), the city enjoyed a brief gold rush in the late 1850s before the more sustainable bovine alternative finally sealed its economic fate. Although most visitors stay only very briefly, on their way to sample the coastal delights of Yeppoon and Great Keppel Island, Rocky has a truly diverse range of tourist attractions, from the historical and cultural to the ecological and even subterranean. Then, of course, there is the town's legendary gastronomic delight, in the form of a steak the size of a small European country.

Ins and outs

Tourist information Capricorn Region VIC ① *Gladstone Rd, Rockhampton, T4927 2055, www.capricorntourism.com.au, daily 0900-1700,* is in the Capricorn Spire, which marks the point of the Tropic of Capricorn (23.5° south), and caters for city and region. **Rockhampton VIC** ① *208 Quay St, T4922 5625, www.rockhamptoninfo.com, Mon-Fri 0830-1630, Sat-Sun 0900-1600,* is housed in the grandiose 1902 Customs House. ►► *See Transport, page 80.*

City centre

With its mineral and agricultural heritage, there are numerous historical buildings dominating the city centre. These include the 1902 **Customs House**, which now houses the VIC, the 1895 **Post Office**, on the corner of East Street and Denham Street, the 1890 **Criterion Hotel**, on

Quay Street, and the 1887 **Supreme Court**, on East Lane, which has been in continuous use now for over a century. As well as its numerous historical buildings, Rockhampton also boasts six bull statues, in celebration of its status as the beef capital of Australia.

Train enthusiasts will enjoy the **Archer Park Steam Tram Museum** ① *Denison St, T4922 2774, www.steamtram.rockhampton.qld.gov.au, Sun-Fri 1000-1600, $7.30, children $4.20, tram operates Sun 1000-1300*. The town also has a number of art galleries. Best of the lot is the **Rockhampton Art Gallery** ① *62 Victoria Pde, T4927 7129, Tue-Fri 1000-1600, Sat-Sun 1100-1600, free*, which displays a long-established collection of mainly 1940-1970s Australian works as well as some more recent contemporary acquisitions.

The small but tidy **Rockhampton Zoo** ① *T4922 1654, 0800-1700, free*, on Spencer Street, has many natives on hand including koala and tame kangaroos and a charming pair of chimps called Cassie and Ockie (as in Dokie). Almost next door are the spacious **Botanical Gardens** ① *0600-1800*, first established in 1869. Amongst its leafy avenues of

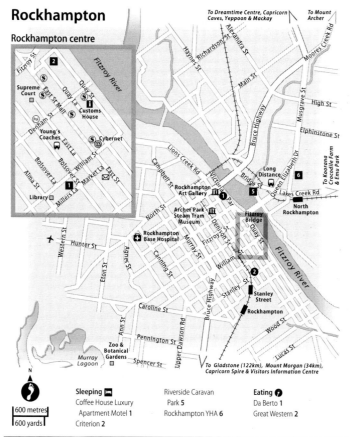

Rockhampton

Rockhampton centre

Sleeping ▬
Coffee House Luxury
  Apartment Motel **1**
Criterion **2**

Riverside Caravan
  Park **5**
Rockhampton YHA **6**

Eating ❶
Da Berto **1**
Great Western **2**

600 metres
600 yards

palms and cycads are a fernery, a Japanese garden and the peaceful garden tearooms. **Murray Lagoon** is also a fine place to stroll around.

Around the city

Though not quite on a par with the Tjapukai Aboriginal park near Cairns (see page 115), the **Dreamtime Centre** ⓘ *6 km north of the Rockhampton city along the Bruce Highway, T4936 1655, www.dreamtimecentre.com.au, Mon-Fri 1000-1530, $13.50, children $6.50, guided tours start daily at 1030,* is an entertaining introduction to Aboriginal and Torres Strait heritage using a wide range of displays and hands-on activities. Set in 12 ha of parkland just off the Bruce Highway, 6 km north of the city centre, a guided or self-guided tour allows you to witness some masterful didgeridoo playing, before exploring the various displays outside in the Torres Strait Islander Village. These include traditional gunyahs (shelters) and the giant Dugong Complex, with artefacts and building materials. There is also a native plant garden where you can learn about their use as food and medicine. For many the highlight of their visit is the opportunity to throw a boomerang so it actually comes back.

Established over 20 years ago, **Koorana Crocodile Farm** ⓘ *Coowonga Rd, Emu Park, 33 km east of the city, T4934 4749, www.koorana.com.au, 1000-1500, $22, children $11, tours at 1030-1200 and 1300-1430, no public transport,* was the first private croc farm in Queensland and is home to some mighty large characters. Tours are available and there is an interesting video presentation that will avail you of many facts, the most memorable being that crocodile dung was once used for contraception (though quite how, thankfully, remains an enigma). **Mount Morgan**, 38 km southwest of the city, has a steam railway and a small but well-presented museum ⓘ *1000-1600, $5, children $1,* celebrating its highly productive gold and copper mining heritage. There is also a bat-infested cave nearby where dinosaur footprints were discovered in 1954. **Mount Archer**, which looms large at 604 m above Rocky's northeastern suburbs, has a fine summit walk and lookout. Access is from the end of Moores Creek Road, north of the Bruce Highway. Vehicular access to the summit is from Frenchville Road, off Norman, which is off Moores Creek Road.

Capricorn Caves

ⓘ *Olsen's Caves Rd, T4934 2883, www.capricorncaves.com.au, 0900-1600, standard tours $22, children $11; 3-hr caving from $60 (1300); 2-hr geological fossil tour from $35. Accommodation packages also available.*

This limestone cave system, 23 km north of Rockhampton, is well worth a visit. Privately owned and open to the public for over a century, the caves offer a memorable combination of subterranean sights and sounds and are home to an array of unusual wildlife. An entertaining guided tour takes you through numerous collapsed caverns, beautifully lit caves and narrow tunnels, to eventually reach a natural amphitheatre where stunning acoustics are demonstrated with classical music and then, utter silence. The venue is so special it is often used for weddings and Christmas carol concerts. During December and January, exiting visitors can witness a brilliant natural light spectacle created by the rays of the sun.

The cave system has been home to tens of thousands of bats and the odd harmless python for millennia, and although very few are seen, it adds that essential Indiana Jones edge. The more adventurous can go on an exhilarating two- to four-hour caving tour and come face to face with the bats and pythons while squeezing through the infamous 'Fat Man's Misery'. Also on offer is a new specialized cave geo tour revealing an ancient geological landscape and the marine fossils encrusted on the cave walls, evidence of the coral reef that existed 390 million years ago.

Yeppoon and around → *For listings, see pages 76-82.*

Blessed by a cooling breeze and a string of pretty beaches, the small seaside settlements of Yeppoon, Rosslyn Bay and Emu Park are the main focus of the Capricorn Coast and the region's principal coastal holiday resorts. Yeppoon – the largest – offers a wealth of affordable accommodation and safe swimming, while 7 km south, Rosslyn Bay provides the gateway to Great Keppel Island. One of the highlights of the area is the vast coastal wilderness of the **Byfield National Park** – a sanctuary for a rich variety of water birds and venue for some fine 4WD adventures.

Although most non-natives stop only briefly on their way to Great Keppel Island, the surrounding coastline offers plenty to see and do. There are beaches and headlands dotted all along the 16-km stretch of road between Yeppoon and Emu Park. South of Yeppoon the small national parks of **Double Head**, above Rosslyn Harbour, and **Bluff Point**, at the southern end of Kemp Beach, provide short walks and viewpoints across to Great Keppel Island. South of the Bluff, **Mulambin Beach** stretches south to **Pinnacle Point** and the entrance to **Causeway Lake**, a popular spot for fishing and boating. From there the road skirts **Shoal Bay** and **Kinka Beach**, considered by many as the best in the region, before arriving in Emu Park.

West of Yeppoon, just off the main highway, is the knobbly volcanic peak known as **Mount Jim Crow** (221 m). Who Mr Crow was exactly remains a mystery, but the peak was steeped in Aboriginal legend well before his arrival and can be climbed, with a bit of scrambling, from the old quarry.

To the north of Yeppoon, the seemingly boundless **Byfield Coastal Area** is one of the largest undeveloped regions on the east coast of Australia and, although the vast majority of it is taken up by the inaccessible Shoalwater Bay Military Training Area, the biodiversity of **Byfield National Park**, on its southern fringe, offers plenty of opportunity for camping, walking, boating, fishing, birdwatching and 4WDs. The heart of the park is reached via the Byfield Road and Byfield State Forest, but you'll need a 4WD, especially if you want to reach Nine Mile Beach. This is perhaps what makes the park so special. If such luxuries are beyond your budget then you can still get a feel for the place from the 'wetlands' west of the Rydges Capricorn Resort, or the Sandy Point Section of the park, to the north. Although the road is unsealed it is easily negotiable by 2WD and offers numerous access points to Farnborough Beach where you can have a stretch of pristine sand almost entirely to yourself. **Rydges Capricorn Resort** itself is also well worth a look, see page 78.

Great Keppel Island → *For listings, see pages 76-82.*

Great Keppel Island (1400 ha) is the largest of 18 islands in the Keppel group, which sits within easy reach of Rosslyn Bay. For many, Great Keppel provides the first real taste of Queensland's idyllic tropical islands. Although not quite on a par with Magnetic Island, it has a wealth of beautiful sandy beaches, walks and activities, with a good range of places to stay.

Despite having 17 beaches to choose from, few visitors venture beyond the main hub of activity at **Fisherman's Beach**, which fronts the main resort and provides ferry access. You are far better to be more adventurous and seek out the quieter spots. A 20-minute walk south is **Long Beach**, which in turn provides access to **Monkey Beach**, 35 minutes away, across the headland to the west. North of the resort, beyond the spit, is **Putney Beach**, which offers pleasant views across to Middle Island. There are numerous walks around the island, with the most popular being the 45-minute trek to **Mount Wyndham**, the highest point on the island. Longer excursions of around 1½ hours will take you to the realms of solitude and the island's northeastern beaches, including **Svendsen's**, **Sandhill** and **Wreck Beach**, or further still to the unremarkable light beacon on the island's southeast coast. Walking maps and descriptions are readily available from the ferries and resorts. With so many walks and beaches you will probably have very little time for anything else, but do check out the tame and beautiful rainbow lorikeets that frequent the resort's **Keppel Café**.

While Great Keppel Island is the main focus of activity, some of the other, smaller islands in the group offer more solitude, good snorkelling and camping. **Middle Island**, lying north of Great Keppel, is home to an underwater observatory that sits above a sunken Taiwanese wreck teeming with monster cod and other bizarre sea creatures. There is a QPWS campsite, but you will need to take your own water and gas stove. Other QPWS campsites are located at **Considine Beach**, **North Keppel Island**, and **Humpy Island**, renowned for its good snorkelling. Both sites have seasonal water supplies and toilets. For more details and permits contact the QPWS office ① Yeppoon Courthouse, Normanby Street, Yeppoon, T4939 5385, Mon-Fri 0900-1630. All the islands have a complete fire ban. **Pumpkin Island** (6 ha), just to the south of North Keppel, is privately owned but offers some accommodation.

Capricorn Coast listings

⊜ Sleeping

Bundaberg and Southern Reef Islands *p69*

Beyond the usual rash of motels, Bundaberg has little choice. The town is short on quality backpackers with most catering for workers seeking cheap long stays. If you have your own transport you are advised to head for the seaside resort of Bargara (12 km east) where you will find a number of pleasant low-key resorts and beachside motor parks.

$$$$ Kacy's Bargara Beach Hotel and Motel, corner of Bauer St and the Esplanade, Bargara, T4130 1100, www.bargaramotel. com.au. A range of apartment and standard rooms and a in-house restaurant.

$$$ Big 4 Cane Village Holiday Park, Twyford St (2 km south of Bundaberg, off Takalvan St), T4155 1022, www.cane-village-holiday-park.qld.big4.com.au. The best motor park in town, it has en suite/standard cabins, powered and non-powered sites and a camp kitchen.

$$$ Villa L'sha, 6 Albatross Court, Moore Park Beach, Bundaberg, T4154 8220, www. villa-l-sha.com. Contemporary villa B&B, set in a tropical garden and near the beach. Queen en suite, kitchenette and pool. Excellent value.

$$ Bargara Beach Caravan Park, the Esplanade, Bargara, T4159 2228, www. bargarabeach.com.au. Spacious option near the amenities in Bargara, has good facilities and a camp kitchen.

$$ Bargara Gardens Motel and Villas, 13 See St, Bargara, T4159 2295, www. bargarabeachvillas.com.au. A good budget motel option with self-contained villas in a quiet tropical garden setting and near the beach.

$ Feeding Grounds Backpackers , 4 Hinkler Av, North Bundaberg, T4152 3659, www. footprintsadventures.com.au. Tempting to say with a name like that it has to be good; however, despite the name this is a reputable, quality establishment and the recent adjunct to a well-established tour company specializing in entertaining tours to the turtle rookery.

QPWS campsite, T4971 6500 (Gladstone), on Lady Musgrave Island. No water, and fires banned. Bookings essential and needs to be arranged well in advance.

Agnes Water, 1770 and around *p71*

There is a good range of accommodation but both towns are getting increasingly busy, especially around Christmas and public holidays, so book ahead.

$$$$ Beachshacks, 578 Captain Cook Drive, 1770, T4974 9463, www.1770beach shacks. com. Characterful, spacious, modern, fully self-contained bungalows complete with thatched roofs and decks overlooking the beach and next door to the local store and bottleshop.

$$$$ Captain Cook Holiday Village, 300 m further inland on Captain Cook Drive, 1770, T4974 9219, www.1770holidayvillage. Set in the bush and offers a good range of options from self-contained en suite cabins to campsites and a good bistro/bar. Fires are permitted and there is access to Agnes Water main beach.

$$ Beachside Backpackers 1770, 12 Captain Cook Drive, Agnes Water, T4974 7200, www.1770beachsidebackpacker.com. au. This is the newer of the 2 backpackers in Agnes and offers self-catering and luxury apartments as well as the usual hostel-style dorms all with modern facilities including internet café, pool and yoga classes. The **Freckles Bar and Grill** is a popular feature of the complex and offers cheap backpacker meals.

$$ Cool Bananas 2 Springs Rd, Agnes Water, T4974 7660, www.coolbananas. net.au. Of the 2 backpackers in Agnes, this has the most activity. It is a fine place, and very popular, with modern, purpose-built facilities, fast internet, off-street parking and a wealth of organized activities, including surf lessons from $17 and even flying lessons (yes, as in plane) from $50. Excellent staff. Free pick-ups from Bundaberg on Mon, Wed and Fri.

$ 1770 Camping Grounds, in 1770, T4974 9286. This is the most popular camping ground. It sits beachside on Captain Cook Drive and has powered and non-powered sites, a small camp kitchen and a shop. Fires are permitted.

QPWS campsites, at Wreck Rock, Deepwater National Park, 11 km south of Agnes, with toilets, rainwater supply and a cold shower, self-registration (fires are banned) and Bustard Beach, Eurimbula National Park, with bore water and toilets, self-registration; fires are banned. For more information on both parks contact the QPWS in Agnes Water, T4902 1555.

Rockhampton *p72, map p73*

There are plenty of good places in the centre of the city, and numerous motels and motor parks scattered around the outskirts and along the Bruce Highway.

$$$$ Coffee House Luxury Apartment Motel, corner of Williams St and Bolsover St, T4927 5722, www.coffeehouse.com.au. A tidy, modern establishment with well-appointed, fully self-contained apartments, executive and standard rooms. A fine café and internet.

$$$ Capricorn Caves Eco-Lodge and Caravan Park, Capricorn Caves, 23 km north of the city, T4934 2883, www.capricorncaves. com.au. Handy for visiting the caves.

$$$ Rockhampton YHA, located across the river on MacFarlane St, T4927 5288, www.rockhamptonbackpackers.com.au. Rather plain but well maintained and good facilities, it has standard doubles, some with en suite and dorms, new en suite cabins, a well-equipped kitchen, internet and tours desk. Onward trips to the coast and Great Keppel a speciality.

$$ Criterion, Quay St, T4922 1225, www. thecriterion.com.au. Try this for a traditional, historical edge, overlooking the river, old fashioned and characterful rooms at good rates.

$ Riverside Caravan Park, next to the river just across the Fitzroy Bridge, 2 Reaney St, T4922 3779. Basic, 3-star park. Convenient to the city centre, but only has powered and non-powered sites with limited facilities.

Yeppoon and around p75
$$$$ Rydges Capricorn Resort,
Farnborough Rd, T4925 2525, www.
capricornresort.com.au. This hugely popular
resort is set in the perfect beachside spot on
the fringe of the Byfield National Park. The
focus of its popularity is not surprisingly its
superb pool, golf courses and huge range of
activities. It offers slightly ageing apartments,
suites and rooms with all the usual facilities,
including 2 restaurants, a bistro and café.
Although designed for extended package
holidays it often offers attractive short-stay
deals, especially on weekdays and in the low
season. Bookings essential.
**$$$ Big 4 Capricorn Palms Holiday
Village**, Wildin Way, Mulambin Beach (1 km
south of Rosslyn Bay), T4933 6144, www.
capricorn- palms-holiday-village.qld.big4.
com.au. This is the best motor park in the
area with everything from deluxe villas to
non-powered sites, a good camp kitchen
and pool.
$$$ Ferns Hideaway Resort, located near
Byfield, 50 km north of Yeppoon, T4935
1235, www.fernshideaway.com.au. Set deep
in the rainforest, in near perfect isolation
beside a creek, this colonial-style resort
lodge offers log cabins with open fires and
spa, basic budget rooms, campsites and a
licensed bar and restaurant.
$$ Sunlover Lodge, 3 Camellia St, T4939
6727, www.sunloverlodge.com.au. Further
afield in Kinka Beach is this excellent lodge,
with a fine range of quiet, modern, fully self-
contained cabins and villas, some with spa
and all within a short stroll of the beach.

Great Keppel Island p75
The island is well known for offering a broad
range of accommodation from luxury to
budget. Before making a decision on island
accommodation budget travellers should
look into the numerous packages available,
including those from Rockhampton/
Yeppoon backpackers. This will save
considerably on independent travelling
costs.

$$$ Great Keppel Island Holiday Village
('Geoff and Dianna's Place'), T4939 8655,
www.gkiholidayvillage.com.au. A laid-back
place with everything from a self-contained
house to cabins, doubles, twins, dorms and
custom-built tents. Fully equipped kitchen,
free snorkel gear and organized kayak trips.
$$$ Self-contained cabins, Pumpkin
Island, T4939 4413, www.pumpkinisland.
com.au. Each of the 5 cabins sleep 5-6 (from
$350), camping area with fresh water, toilet,
shower and barbecue (from $25).

🍴 Eating

**Bundaberg and Southern Reef
Islands** p69
$$ Bargara Beach Hotel and Motel, corner
of Bauer St and the Esplanade, Bargara,
T4130 1100. Good bistro restaurant with
Australian/Chinese, wood-fired pizza.
$$ Viva Italia, corner Bourbong and
Bingera streets, T4151-1117. Licensed Italian
restaurant offering value pastas and pizzas.
$$-$ Grand Hotel, corner of Targo St and
Bourbong St, T4151 2441. Modern, licensed
restaurant offering traditional pub grub,
value breakfasts and good coffee.
$ Ann's Kiosk, the Botanical Garden,
Bundaberg, T4153 1477. Daily 1000-1600.
Ideal for a light lunch in quiet surroundings.

Agnes Water, 1770 and around p71
$$-$ Agnes Water Tavern, 1 Tavern Rd,
Agnes Water, T4974 9469. Daily for lunch
and dinner. A popular haunt with long-term
locals (now becoming an endangered
species). Offers good value meals and has a
pleasant garden bar.
$$-$ Deck, Captain Cook Holiday Village,
1770 (see page 77). Tue-Sat for lunch
and dinner. Good value, local seafood, great
views and a nice atmosphere.

Rockhampton p72, map p73
Unless you're a strict vegetarian, then you
hardly need a menu in Rocky. Big around
here (literally) are the steaks.

$$ Criterion, see page 77, and the **Great Western**, 39 Stanley St, T4922 1862, are the best bets for steaks. Both are open daily from about 1100-late.
$$-$ Da Berto, 62 Victoria Pde, T4922 3060. Open daily for lunch and dinner. Quality contemporary Italian option overlooking the river. Mon night specials.

Yeppoon and around *p75*
$ Causeway Lake Kiosk, beside the Causeway Bridge (between Rosslyn Bay and Kinka Beach). Daily until about 2000. The best fish and chips in the area.
$ Keppel Bay Sailing Club, above the beach on Anzac Parade, T4939 9500. Daily for lunch and dinner. Good value and a great view.
$ Shorething Café, 1/6 Normanby St, Yeppoon, T4939 1993. Good breakfasts, coffee and internet.

Great Keppel Island *p75*
Other than the resort eateries (see Sleeping, page 78) there is **Keppel Island Pizza**, on the waterfront, T4939 4699, Tue-Sun 1230-1400, 1800-2100.
   The resorts have limited groceries and they are pricey so you are advised to take your own food supplies.

▲ Activities and tours

Bundaberg and Southern Reef Islands *p69*
Day trips (by air) from Bundaberg to Lady Elliot Island cost from $299, children $162, T5536 3644, www.ladyelliot.com.au.
Bundaberg Dive Academy, Shop 3A, Targo St, T4152 4064, www.bundabergdiveacademy.com. This place offers a fine range of land- and water-based accommodation and diving course packages that are good value for money compared with the high-profile operators further north.
Footprints Adventures, T4152 3659, www.footprintsadventures.com.au. For local tours look no further than the dedicated team

here. Turtle rookery night trips (Jan to late Apr) from $50.
Lady Musgrave Barrier Reef Cruises, departs Town of 1770 (transfers from Bundaberg), T1800 072110, www.lmcruises.com.au. Day trips daily (0800-1745), from $160, children $80. Certified diving is available, from $40, introductory dives from $75. Whale-watching trips operate between Aug-Oct. Camping transfers from $320.

Agnes Water, 1770 and around *p71*
1770 Environmental Tours, 1770 Marina, T4974 9422, www.1770larctours.com.au. An exciting and unique eco/history tour/cruise on board an amphibious vehicle (LARC), along the coast north of 1770 to Bustard Head and Pancake Creek. There are 2 tours on offer: **Paradise Tour** (Mon, Wed and Sat 0900-1600) explores the beaches, Aboriginal middens and the stunning views from the Bustard Head Light Station and neighbouring cemetery, with a spot of sand boarding en route, from $148, children $88. **Afternoon Cruise** (on demand, 1630) is a 1-hr exploration of Round Hill Creek and Eurimbula National Park, from $35, children $16. Book ahead.
1770 Great Barrier Reef Cruises, based at the Marina, T4974 9077, www.1770reefcruises.com. Day trips and camping transfers to Lady Musgrave Island (51 km east of 1770), from $160, children $80 (plus $5 reef tax). The cruise, dubbed the 'See More Sea Less' allows a whole 6 hrs on the reef, including a stop on a floating pontoon that acts as an ideal base for snorkelling, diving and coral viewing. Departs daily at 0800. Lunch included and bookings essential. A shuttle bus is available from Bundaberg. Camping transfers to the island cost $320. For more information on Lady Musgrave Island, see page 71.

Rockhampton *p72, map p73*
Farm stays
There are several renowned farm/station stays in the region, where you can go

horse riding, on 4WD adventures, help to rehabilitate abandoned or injured kangaroos and even learn how to milk a cow. These include **Myella Farmstay**, 125 km southwest of the city, T4998 1290, www.myella.com..

Sightseeing tours
Mt Etna Little Bent-Wing Bat Tours, T4936 0511. Guided tours to see tens of thousands of cave dwelling bats in the 'bat cleft' located in the Mt Etna Caves National Park. Dec-Jan only, 1730 on Mon, Wed, Fri and Sat, from $9, children $5. Own transport required.
Mount Morgan Guided Tours, T4938 1823. Trips of 2 hrs taking in the town, mine and some Jurassic caves, from $27, children $12.

Yeppoon and around *p75*
Rydges Capricorn Resort , Farnborough Rd, T1800 075902, www.capricornresort.com. au. Offers horse treks (from $80), eco-tours (from $45) and canoe trips (from $55).

Great Keppel Island *p75*
All the main places to stay offer their own range of activities and tours but day trippers can access a huge variety of water-based activities and equipment from the beach hut directly opposite the ferry drop-off point. The island also has fine snorkelling and diving.
Freedom Flyer Cruises, T4933 6244, www. keppelbaymarina.com.au. Range of cruise packages beyond their basic transfers to Great Keppel. Transfers from $47, children $27. Coral cruise in a glass-bottom boat with fish feeding, boom netting and snorkelling, from $23, children $15. All day from $135. Coach transfers from Rockhampton are available. Book ahead.
Great Keppel Island Holiday Village, T4939 8655. Excellent sea kayaking and snorkelling trips from $55.
Keppel Reef Scuba Adventures, Putney Beach, T4939 5022, www.keppeldive.com. Dive shop just beyond the Spit. Qualified dive from about $85 including gear, introductory dive from $100, depart 0830 daily. Also offer island and beach drop-offs.

⊖ Transport

Bundaberg and Southern Reef Islands *p69*
Air
Bundaberg airport is 3 km south of the city centre via the Isis Highway. **Qantas**, T131313, flies daily to **Brisbane**, **Rockhampton**, **Mackay** and **Townsville**.
For **Lady Elliot Island**, SeAir, T5536 3644, www.ladyelliot.com.au, offers flight transfers from **Bundaberg** and **Hervey Bay** from $254, children $136. See also Activities and tours above (and for Lady Musgrave Island).

Bus
Local services run by **Duffy's Coaches**, 28 Barolin St, T4151 4226, www.duffysbuses. com.au around the city, the Coral Coast, Rum Distillery, Bargara, Burnett Heads, Bundaberg Port Marina, several times daily. The long-distance bus terminal is at 66 Targo St, between Woondooma St and Crofton St. **Greyhound**, T1300 473946, and **Premier Motor Services**, T133410, offer interstate services north and south.

Train
The station is in the heart of the city on the corner Bourbong St and McLean St. The **Tilt Train** is the preferred service between **Brisbane** and **Rockhampton** but other north/southbound services pass through daily, T132235. **Stewart and Sons Travel**, 66 Targo St, T4152 9700, acts as booking agents for air, bus and train operators.

Agnes Water, 1770 and around *p71*
Bus
Greyhound, T1300 473946, offers part-transfers to Agnes (from the Bruce Highway) stopping at the Fingerboard Junction Service Station (about 30 km south of Agnes and 20 km east of Miriam Vale). There is a transfer bus from there. **Bananas Backpackers** offer their own pick-ups from Bundaberg.

Car/4WD
The twin towns are best accessed from the Bruce Highway at Miriam Vale (55 km), or from the south via Bundaberg (120 km).

Train
The nearest station is in Miriam Vale, T132232.

Rockhampton p72, map p73
Air
Rockhampton Airport is 4 km west of the city centre. **Jet Star**, T131538; **Qantas**, T131313; **Tiger Airways**, T03-9335 3033; and **Virgin Blue**, T136789, have regular schedules to main centres north, south and west. A taxi to town costs about $20.

Bus
Capricorn Sunbus, T4936 2133, www.sunbus.com.au, is the local suburban bus company. **Young's Coaches**, 274 George St, T4922 3813, www.youngsbusservice.com.au, runs regular daily services to the train station, **Yeppoon** (No 20); **Rosslyn Bay** (cruise boats); **Emu Park** and **Mount Morgan** (No 22). The main local terminal is on Bolsover St. The long-distance bus terminal, T4927 2844, is located at the Mobil service centre, George St. **Greyhound**, T1300 473946, and **Premier Motor Services**, T133410, offer north/southbound services.

Train
The station is 1 km south of the city centre at the end of Murray St (off Bruce Highway). **Tilt Train** is the preferred daily service to **Brisbane**. Other slower services north/southbound are the budget **Sunlander** and luxury **Queenslander**. **Spirit of the Outback** heads west to **Longreach** Tue and Sat. There is a travel centre at the station, T132232.

Yeppoon and around p75
Bus
Young's Coaches, 274 George St, T4922 3813, have regular daily services to Yeppoon (Route 20), **Rosslyn Bay** (cruise boats) and **Emu Park**.

Great Keppel Island p75
Air
Great Keppel has its own airfield but services vary. For details, contact the VIC.

Bus
Young's Coaches, T4922 3813, run regular daily services from **Rockhampton** to **Rosslyn Bay** (No 20).

Ferry
Both the major ferry companies are based at Rosslyn Bay Harbour, 7 km south of Yeppoon. **Freedom Fast Cats**, T4933 6244, www.keppelbaymarina.com.au, are based at the new Keppel Bay Marina. They have a travel centre, shop, café and internet. Yacht charters are also available. The basic return fare to Great Keppel (30 mins) is $47, children $27. Ferries depart daily at 0900, 1130 and 1530. See also Activities and tours, page 79. To reach the other islands, Rosslyn Bay ferry companies offer cruises daily to Middle Island. Other than Middle Island, all water transport must be arranged privately through the **Keppel Bay Marina**, T4933 6244.

❶ Directory

Bundaberg and Southern Reef Islands p69
Banks All the major branches have ATMs and can be found on Bourbong St. **Hospitals** After Hours Medical Clinic, Mater Hospital, 313 Bourbong St, T4153 9539. Mon-Fri 1800-2300, Sat 1200-2300, Sun 0800-2300. Bundaberg Base Hospital, Bourbong St, T4150 1222. **Internet** Cosy Corner, Barolin St (opposite the post office), T4153 5999, Mon-Fri 0700-1930, Sat 0700-1700, Sun 1100-1700. **Pharmacy** Amcal, 128 Bourbong St, T4151 5533. **Post** 157b Bourbong St, T131318. Mon-Fri 0900-1700, Sat 0830-1200. Postcode 4670. **Useful numbers** Police, 254 Bourbong St, T4153 9111.

Agnes Water, 1770 and around *p71*
Banks There is a **Westpac Bank** and
ATM facilities in the Agnes Water's
Shopping Complex. **Internet** Bananas
Backpackers,2 Springs Rd.

Rockhampton *p72, map p73*
Banks All the main branches with ATMs
are centred in and around the CBD on
East St. **Commonwealth Bank** offers
currency exchange services. **Hospital**
Rockhampton Base Hospital, Canning
St, T4920 6211. **Internet** Cybernet, 12
William St, T4927 3633. Mon-Fri 1000-1730,
or the **Library**, corner of William St and Alma
St, T4936 8265, Mon, Tue, Fri 0915-1730,
Wed 1300-2000, Thu 0915-2000, Sat 0915-
1630. Book in advance. **Post** 150 East St,
Mon-Fri 0830-1730. Postcode 4700. **Useful
numbers** Police, corner of Denham St and
Bolsover St, T4932 3500.

Contents

Central & Far North Queensland

Central Coast

This is the home straight on the long trek north to Cairns and there's still an awful lot to pack in. The town of Mackay is the base from which to explore the reef island groups of Brampton, Newry and Carlisle. Inland, the lush slopes of Eungella National Park are home to wonderful waterfalls and unusual wildlife. Back on the coast the rush is on to reach the fast developing resort of Airlie Beach, gateway to the sublime Whitsunday Islands. Further north, Magnetic Island lives up to its name, attracting tourists with its beautiful beaches, while inland the historic gold-mining town of Charters Towers offers many their first taste of Queensland 'outback'. North again is Mission Beach, like a mainland version of Magnetic Island, while, offshore, as always, are the tropical reef islands.

Mackay and around → *For listings, see pages 97-110.*

Driving towards Mackay at night in early summer is a surreal experience. For miles around, sugar cane fields are awash with the orange glow of flames. Although the sugar cane industry is in crisis, and the burning of harvested cane fields in preparation for the next crop a less frequent sight, when it does happen it looks like the world is on fire. After Scots pioneer John Mackay recognized the region's agricultural potential in 1862 it grew to become the largest sugar-producing area in Australia and still hosts the biggest bulk processing facilities in the world. Although not tourist-oriented, Mackay provides a welcome stop halfway between Brisbane and Cairns and is also the gateway to several Barrier Reef and Whitsunday Islands and a fine base from which to explore the superb Eungella and Cape Hillsborough national parks.

Ins and outs
Mackay VIC ① *320 Nebo Rd (Bruce Highway), T4944 5888 www.mackay region.com, Mon-Fri 0830-1700, Sat-Sun 0900-1600*, housed in a former sugar mill, offers booking services for local and island accommodation and tours. There is a smaller VIC in the Town Hall ① *63 Sydney Rd, T4951 4803*. **QPWS** office ① *DPI Building, 30 Tennyson St, T4944 7800, www.epa.qld.gov.au, Mon-Fri 0830-1700*, offers information and permits for island and national park camping. ►► *See Transport, page 106.*

Mackay
Although most of Mackay's attractions are to be found beyond the city limits, the centre, with its palm-lined main street and pleasant river views, is worth a look. The heart of the city boasts some notable historical buildings, including the impressive façades of the **Commonwealth Bank** (1880) ① *63 Victoria St*, the former **Queensland National Bank**

(1922) ⓘ *corner of Victoria St and Wood St*, the **Town Hall** (1912) ⓘ *63 Sydney St,* which houses the VIC and a small historical display, and the old **Customs House** (1902) ⓘ *corner of Sydney St and River St*. The VIC stocks a free *Heritage Walk* leaflet.

The **Artspace Mackay** ⓘ *Gordon St, Civic Centre Precinct, T4961 9722, www. artspacemackay.com.au, Tue-Sun 1000-1700, free*, is a recent and welcome architectural addition to the city, housing an art gallery and museum showcasing the social and natural history of the region. The sugar industry features heavily but this is interspersed neatly with many contemporary displays including the school trophies of the city's most famous daughter, Olympic gold medal runner Cathy Freeman.

The beaches north of Mackay are well known for their tropical beauty and fine swimming and are a great place to recharge the travel batteries. The best spots are at **Black's Beach**, **Dolphin Heads** (Eimeo Beach) and **Bucasia Beach** and are best accessed from the Mackay–Bucasia Road off the Bruce Highway.

Aside from the lure of the beach, there is an opportunity to visit to one of the local sugar mills. The **Polstone Sugar Cane Farm** ⓘ *Masottis Rd, Homebush, T4959 7298, offers tours Mon, Wed and Fri at 1330, Jun-Nov, from $16, children $7.*

Brampton and Carlisle islands

The islands of Brampton (464 ha) and Carlisle (518 ha) are part of the **Cumberland Islands National Park**, which lies 32 km northeast of Mackay. Both are practically joined by a sandbank that can be walked at low tide and have a rich variety of island habitats, rising to a height of 389 m on Carlisle's Skiddaw Peak and 219 m on Brampton's namesake peak. The waters surrounding both islands are part of the Mackay/Capricorn Section of the Great Barrier Reef Marine Park, offering some excellent dive sites. There are 11 km of walking tracks on Brampton giving access to Brampton Peak as well as several secluded bays and coastal habitats. In contrast walking on Carlisle Island is rough, with no well-formed paths.

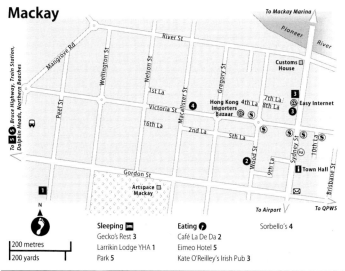

Mackay

200 metres
200 yards

Sleeping 🛏
Gecko's Rest **3**
Larrikin Lodge YHA **1**
Park **5**

Eating 🍴
Café La De Da **2**
Eimeo Hotel **5**
Kate O'Reilley's Irish Pub **3**

Sorbello's **4**

State phone codes and time difference

There are no area phone codes. Use a state code if calling outside the state you are in. These are: 02 for ACT/NSW (08 for Broken Hill), 03 for VIC and 07 for QLD.

Note that NSW operates daylight saving, which means that clocks go forward one hour from October to March.

Instead you are better to explore the beaches or take to the water with a snorkel and mask, especially in the channel between the two islands. Day trips aren't available and the minimum stay is one night.

Newry Islands

The Newry group, also part of the Great Barrier Reef Marine Park, consists of six national park islands 50 km northeast of Mackay. Like the Cumberlands, they are hilly, diverse in coastal habitat types and rich in wildlife, including sea eagles, ospreys, echidna and bandicoots. Green sea turtles also nest between November and January on the largest of the group – Rabbit Island. There are 2 km of walking tracks on Newry Island leading through rainforest and open forest to elevated viewpoints.

Cape Hillsborough National Park

Although positively petite compared to most of Queensland's other mainland national parks, Hillsborough is no less impressive, boasting some superb coastal habitats, views and beaches. It is also particularly famed for its tame, beach-loving wildlife such as kangaroos, the aptly named pretty-faced wallabies and the distinctly more ugly scrub turkeys. There are four diverse walking tracks ranging from 1.2 km to 2.6 km in length, including the Juipera Plant Trail, which highlights the food plants once utilized by the Juipera Aboriginal people.

Eungella National Park and Pioneer Valley

The 80-km inland excursion from Mackay via the Pioneer Valley to Eungella (pronounced 'young-galah') offers an excellent diversion from the coast and access to what the Aboriginal people once called 'the land of the clouds'. Whether shrouded in mist or gently baking under the midday sun, Eungella and its exquisite national park possess a magic as special as the wildlife that lives there and the Aboriginals who once did.

Immediately west of Mackay, the Mackay–Eungella Road branches off the Peak Downs Highway and follows the southern bank of the Pioneer River to the small sugar cane town of **Marian**. In **Mirani**, 10 km further west of Marian, you can find out why the two were so called, and if they were indeed sisters, at the small museum on Victoria Street. Just beyond Mirani is the **Illawong Fauna Sanctuary** ① *T4959 1777, www.illawong-sanctuary.com, 0930-1730, $15, children $6*. It's a fairly low-key affair but worth stopping to take a walk through enclosures full of emus, wallabies and roos. The sanctuary also has accommodation, a café and its own tour company, **Gum Tree Tours**.

A further 29 km past Mirani, beyond the small hamlet of Gargett and 1 km east of Finch Hatton Township, is the turn-off to the **Finch Hatton George section** of the Eungella National Park. In the dry season the 10-km road is suitable for 2WD, but in the wet, when several creek crossings are subject to flooding, the final 6-km gravel road often requires 4WD. At the gorge there is a private bush camp (see page 98), picnic site and access to the memorable **Wheel of Fire Falls** (5 km return) and **Araluen Falls walks** (3 km return).

Back on the main highway, the road head towards the hills before climbing up dramatically 800 m to the small, pretty township of **Eungella**. At the crest of the hill, past a few worrying gaps in the roadside barriers, is the historic **Eungella Chalet**, with its spacious lawns, swimming pool and views to blow your wig off; see page 98. As well as being an ideal spot for lunch, it is also a popular launch pad for hang-gliders.

From the chalet the road veers 6 km south, following the crest of the hill, before arriving at Broken River. Here you will find a picnic area, QPWS campsite and the **Eungella National Park Ranger Station** ① *T131304, 0800-0900, 1130-1230 and 1530-1630*. They will give you all the necessary detail on the numerous excellent short walks in the vicinity. There is also a platypus viewing platform nearby but bear in mind they can only be seen around daybreak. The park is also home to a host of other unique species including the Eungella honeyeater, the brown thornbill and the infinitely wonderful Eungella gastric brooding frog. The latter, as its name suggests, has the unenviable habit of incubating its eggs in its stomach before spitting the young out of its mouth.

Airlie Beach → For listings, see pages 97-110.

From a sleepy coastal settlement, Airlie Beach and its neighbouring communities of Cannonvale and Shute Harbour (known collectively as Whitsunday) have developed into the

Airlie Beach

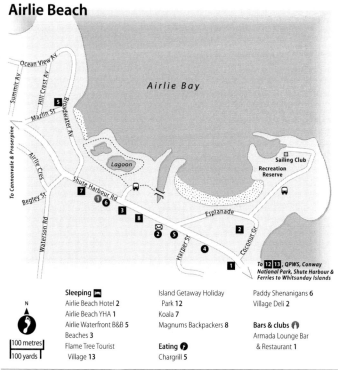

Sleeping 🛏
Airlie Beach Hotel 2
Airlie Beach YHA 1
Airlie Waterfront B&B 5
Beaches 3
Flame Tree Tourist
  Village 13

Island Getaway Holiday
  Park 12
Koala 7
Magnums Backpackers 8

Eating 🍴
Chargrill 5

Paddy Shenanigans 6
Village Deli 2

Bars & clubs 🍸
Armada Lounge Bar
  & Restaurant 1

Scenic flights from Airlie Beach

There are several options for scenic flights from Airlie Beach. Most of the operators are based at the airfield between Airlie and Shute Harbour. Helicopter flights are also offered from the waterfront in Airlie; a 10-minute scenic flight around the bay costs from $95. In general, a flight of 5-20 minutes over the town and inner islands (South Mole, Long and Daydream islands) will cost around $130. A scenic trip to Whitehaven with no stopover will cost around $290, while a 40-minute Whitehaven Beach flight with 2-hour stopover will cost from $399. Extended trips to the outer reef with stopovers will cost up to $530. **HeliReef Whitsunday**, T4946 8249, www.avta.com.au, has a range of flight-seeing options by helicopter, fixed-wing and floatplane. **Air Whitsunday**, T4946 9111, www.airwhitsunday.com.au, and **Island Air**, T4946 9120, www.avta.com.au, both have a fleet of fixed-wing land and seaplanes and offer both tours and island transfers, from $130.

main gateway to the Whitsunday Islands. With over 74 islands, many idyllic resorts and a long list of beaches, including Whitehaven, which is often hailed as among the world's best, it comes as no surprise that little Airlie has seen more dollars spent in the name of tourism in recent years than almost anywhere else in the state. With all the offerings of the Whitsunday Islands lying in wait offshore, most people use Airlie simply as an overnight stop but the town itself can be a great place to party or just relax and watch the tourist world go by.

Ins and outs
Getting there and around The nearest airports are at Proserpine and Hamilton Island. Long-distance bus services run from Cairns and Sydney, stopping at all major centres and cities along the way. Both north and south services run three times weekly. The train station is at Proserpine. The main centre is small and easily explored on foot. See page 104 for tours to the Whitsundays and below for tourist information details. ▸▸ *See Transport, page 107.*

Sights
Right in the heart of town, and the focus for many, is the new and glorious **lagoon** development. In the absence of a proper beach (and the accompanying threat of marine stingers between October and May) it has to be said that the local authorities have created a fine (and safe) substitute. In anticipation of going out to the islands you can secure some good views of them in the **Conway National Park** between Airlie and Shute Harbour. There is a self-guided 6.5-km circuit walk through mangrove forest on the way to a lookout on the summit of Mount Rooper offering a slightly obscured view of Hamilton, Dent, Long and Henning Islands.

Whitsunday Islands National Park → *For listings, see pages 97-110.*

With over 70 sublime, sun-soaked islands, the Whitsundays are not only the largest offshore island chain on the east coast of Australia but the biggest tourist draw between Brisbane and Cairns. It is hardly surprising. Many of the islands are home to idyllic resorts, from the luxurious Hayman and Hamilton to the quieter, more affordable, South Molle, as well as a plethora of beautiful, pristine beaches. Here, for once, the term paradise is not merely tourist board hyperbole.

Whitsunday Islands

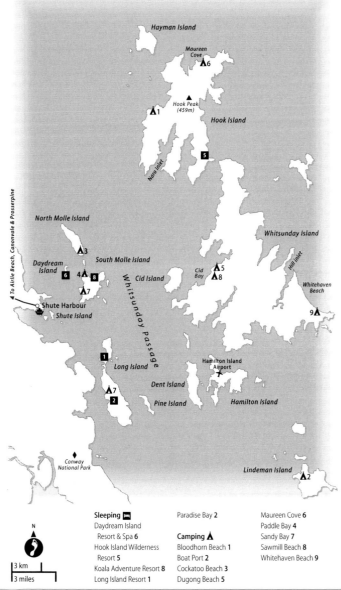

Hayman Island

Maureen Cove
▲ 6

Hook Peak
(459m)

Hook Island

▲ 1

5

Nora Inlet

North Molle Island

Whitsunday Island

▲ 3

South Molle Island

Daydream
Island

6   4 ▲ 8

Cid Island

Cid
Bay

▲ 5
▲ 8

Hill Inlet

Whitehaven
Beach

▲ 7

To Airlie Beach, Cannonvale & Prosserpine

Shute Harbour
Shute Island

Whitsunday passage

9 ▲

1

Long Island

Hamilton Island
Airport

▲ 7

Dent Island

2

Pine Island

Hamilton Island

Conway
National Park

Lindeman Island

▲ 2

N

3 km
3 miles

Sleeping 🛏
Daydream Island
Resort & Spa **6**
Hook Island Wilderness
Resort **5**
Koala Adventure Resort **8**
Long Island Resort **1**

Paradise Bay **2**

Camping ▲
Bloodhorn Beach **1**
Boat Port **2**
Cockatoo Beach **3**
Dugong Beach **5**

Maureen Cove **6**
Paddle Bay **4**
Sandy Bay **7**
Sawmill Beach **8**
Whitehaven Beach **9**

Ins and outs

Tourist information Whitsunday VIC ① *Bruce Highway, 192 Main St, Proserpine, T4945 3711, www.whitsundaytourism.com, Mon-Fri 0900-1700, Sat-Sun 1000-1600*, is the main accredited VIC for the islands. **QPWS office** ① *corner of Shute Harbour Rd and Mandalay St, Airlie Beach, T4946 7022, www.epa.qld.gov.au, Mon-Fri 0900-1700, Sat 0900-1300*, is very helpful. Operators are always changing in the region so you are advised to visit the VIC first to get all the very latest information, especially surrounding water transport logistics. The VIC can supply all camping information and issue permits. Note, to obtain a permit you must have proof of return transportation. **Island Camping Connections**, T4946 5255, offers independent transportation by water taxis and hires out camping gear. Shute Harbour scheduled ferry services stop on most major island resorts. ►► *See Transport, page 107.*

South Molle Island

South Molle (405 ha) is one of three little Molles (South, Mid and North) sitting about 8 km from Shute Harbour. Being in such close proximity to the mainland, and therefore relatively cheap to reach, South Molle is popular with day trippers. With its varied habitats and hilly topography, the island offers some excellent walking and sublime views. The best of these is undoubtedly the 6-km **Spion Kop walk** that climbs through forest and over open grassland to some superb viewpoints across the outer islands. The resort on the island is both pleasant and casual (see Sleeping, page 99).

Long Island

Aptly named Long Island is the closest island to the mainland and runs parallel with the uninhabited coastal fringes of the Conway National Park. A national park in its own right, much of its 800 ha of dense rainforest is inaccessible, save for a loose network of tracks that connect a number of pretty beaches near the major resorts at the northern end.

Daydream Island

One of the smallest of the Whitsunday Islands – with a name almost as nauseating as the staff's shirts – Daydream is one of the closest islands to the mainland (just 5 km away) and the most accessible. As such its congenial, if compact, modern resort has become a popular holiday venue. On offer for guests are a host of activities including sail boarding, jet-skiing, parasailing, reef fishing, diving, snorkelling, tennis and even croquet. Don't expect too many walking tracks, other than the very short variety to the bar. Walking on little Daydream is like circling a small buffet table trying to decide what to choose. It is best just to sit back by the pool, shade your eyes from the staff's shirts and, well … daydream.

Whitsunday Island

At over 100 sq km, Whitsunday Island is the biggest in the group, boasting perhaps their biggest attraction – the 6-km white silica sands of **Whitehaven Beach**. Aerial views of this magnificent beach and the adjoining Hill Inlet repeatedly turn up in the pages of glossy magazines and on postcards as the epitome of the term 'tropical paradise'. Though best seen from the air, the beach is easily accessed by numerous day trips and island cruises, though in many ways this is its downfall. Thankfully uninhabited and without a resort, Whitsunday's only available accommodation comes in the form of eight QPWS campsites scattered around its numerous bays and inlets.

Hook Island

Hook is the second largest island in the group and the loftiest, with Hook Peak (459 m) being the highest point of all the islands. Like the others it is densely forested, its coastline punctuated with picturesque bays and inlets. The most northerly of these, **Maureen Cove**, has a fringing reef that offers excellent snorkelling. Lovely Nara Inlet, on the island's south coast, has caves that support evidence of early Ngalandji Aboriginal occupation. It is also a popular anchorage for visiting yachties.

Lindeman Island

Lindeman Island, 20 sq km, is one of the most southerly of the Whitsunday group and the most visited of a cluster that make up the **Lindeman Island National Park**. It offers all the usual natural features of beautiful inlets and bays and has over 20 km of walking tracks that take you through rainforest and grassland to spectacular views from the island's highest peak, Mount Oldfield (7 km return, 212 m). The island has seven beaches, with Gap Beach providing the best snorkelling.

Townsville → For listings, see pages 97-110.

Considered the capital of Queensland's north coast and the second largest city in the state, Townsville attracts a considerable number of both domestic and international visitors drawn by its enviable tropical climate and the huge range of activities on offer, not to mention the considerable attraction of Magnetic Island lying offshore. If you are short of time Townsville presents a fine opportunity to venture briefly outback with the grand old gold-mining town of Charters Towers less than a two-hour drive west.

Ins and outs

Tourist information The **VIC** ① T4778 3555, 0900-1700, is several kilometres south of town on the Bruce Highway. There is an information booth in the Flinders Mall ① T4721 3660, Mon-Fri 0900-1700, Sat-Sun 0900-1300, and next to the Museum of Queensland ① 70-102 Flinders St East, T4721 1116, www.townsvilleholidays.info, Mon-Sun 0900-1700. **QPWS** ① Marlow St, T4796 7777. ⇥ See Transport, page 108.

Sights

SS Yongala is a passenger ship that sank with all 121 crew – and a racehorse called Moonshine – during a cyclone in 1911. Located about 17 km off Cape Bowling Green, it is often touted as one of Australia's best dives, offering diverse habitats and a huge range of species, including enormous manta rays, colourful coral gardens and even the odd human bone. Since the wreck sits at a depth of 29 m and is subject to strong currents, the dive presents a challenge and requires an above average level of competency. See Activities and tours, page 105 for details.

The long-established **Reef HQ Aquarium** ① 2-68 Flinders St East, T4750 0800, www.reefhq.org.au, 0930-1700, $25, children $19, is not on a par with Sydney Aquarium's remarkable Reef Exhibit, but it still provides an excellent introduction to the reef. The centrepiece is a huge 750,000-litre 'Predator Exhibit', complete with genuine wave action, a part replica of the famous (local) Yongala wreck, an 'interactive island' and myriad colourful corals, fish and the obligatory sharks. Feeding takes place on most days at 1500, but equally interesting is the 'Danger Trail', a guided presentation (daily at 1300) that introduces some of the most deadly and dangerous creatures on the reef, such as the nasty box jellyfish. The star of the show, however, is the stonefish, which has to be the ugliest fish on the planet.

Next door to Reef HQ, the newly renovated **Museum of Tropical Queensland** ① *Flinders St East, T4726 0600, www.mtq.qld.gov.au, 0930-1700, $14, children $8*, provides an impressive insight into the region's maritime history, with the story of *HMS Pandora*, the British 17th-century tall ship that is closely linked with that of the better known *HMS Bounty*. It was the *Pandora* that was dispatched by the British Admiralty in 1790 to bring the Bounty mutineers to justice, but her own voyage to the South Pacific proved no less notorious. After capturing 14 of the mutineers on the island of Tahiti and going in search of those who remained on the *Bounty*, the *Pandora* ran aground on the Barrier Reef, with the loss of 31 crew. The wreck was rediscovered near Cape York in 1977, resulting in a frenzy of archaeological interest, and the many exhibits and artefacts are on show in the museum today. There is an interactive science centre to keep the less nautically inclined suitably engaged. The café has fine views across the river.

Fringing the shoreline east of the city centre is **The Strand**, which, along with the Museum of Queensland, is the new showpiece of the city and part of its recent multi-million dollar facelift. Said by some to be the most attractive public waterfront development in Australia, it provides an ideal spot to soak up the rays, take a stroll or break

Townsville

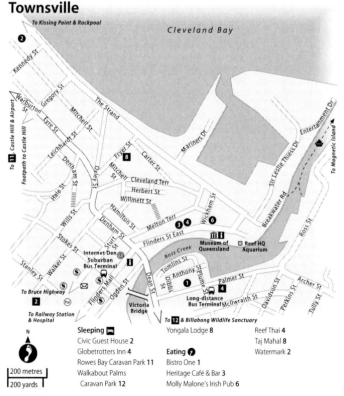

Sleeping
Civic Guest House **2**
Globetrotters Inn **4**
Rowes Bay Caravan Park **11**
Walkabout Palms
Caravan Park **12**
Yongala Lodge **8**

Eating
Bistro One **1**
Heritage Café & Bar **3**
Molly Malone's Irish Pub **6**
Reef Thai **4**
Taj Mahal **8**
Watermark **2**

a leg on rollerblades. It is also designed to serve as protection against cyclones, but you won't find any signs advertising the fact. One of the most attractive features of the Strand is the collection of 50-year old Bunyan fig trees that look like columns of melted wax. At its westerly terminus – **Kissing Point** – there is a man-made rockpool, which provides safe swimming year round and complete protection from the infamous 'marine stingers'. There is also a popular fish and chip shop and seafood restaurant next to the pool, but unless you want an enforced hunger strike while you wait in line, it is best avoided.

As well as the enigmatic sugar shaker building, Townsville's skyline is dominated by **Castle Hill**, which glows orange in the rays of the rising sun. If you cannot drag yourself out of bed to see for yourself, then you can always make the climb to the summit by car or on foot and take in the memorable views, day or night. Access by car is at the end of Burk Street, off Warburton Street. The Goat Track to the summit is off Stanton Street, at the end of Gregory Street, also off Warburton.

Billabong Wildlife Sanctuary ① *17 km south of the city, next to the Bruce Highway, T4778 8344, www.billabongsanctuary.com.au, 0800-1700, $30, children $19,* is one of the best in Queensland. Fringing an authentic billabong (water hole or stagnant pool), it houses an extensive collection of natives, from the leggy cassowary to the sleepy wombat. There are many tame roos and emus lazing on paths around the park, as well as more dangerous individuals such as crocs and poisonous snakes. Various shows and talks throughout the day give you an opportunity to learn about the animals and, if you wish, to handle the more docile serpents and baby crocs. Don't miss the smelly fruit bat colony next to the lake.

Magnetic Island → *For listings, see pages 97-110.*

Magnetic Island is Townsville's biggest tourist attraction and the most easily accessible tropical island bolthole on the reef. Lying only 8 km offshore and baking in over 320 days of sunshine a year, 'Maggie' has always been a popular holiday spot, but its discreet permanent population also adds charm and an authenticity lacking in most of the resort-style islands. In fact, it is considered by many in the region as the most desirable suburb in Townsville. With its amenities concentrated in the eastern and northeastern fringes of the island, Maggie boasts a much larger area of wild and fairly inaccessible terrain giving an overall impression of wilderness and escape. With over half the island given over to national park, encompassing over 40 km of walking tracks, 20 picture-postcard bays and beaches, as well as a wealth of activities and some great budget accommodation, not to mention a resident population of koalas, the island certainly does earn its name in the number of visitors it attracts, though the real derivation is from Captain Cook (who else?) whose compass had a small fit as he passed by in 1770.

Ins and outs

Getting there and around There are regular ferry services from Townsville to Nelly Bay. The best way to explore the island is to hire a 4WD or moke. The four main villages spread along its eastern coastline are served by public transport. Tours are also available. ▸▸ *See Transport, page 108.*

Tourist information VIC ① *Shop 1, Nelly Bay, T4758 1862, 0800-1630,* is a short walk from the ferry. It offers transportation, accommodation and activity bookings. Also refer to the **QPWS office** ① *22 Hurst St, Picnic Bay, on the island, T4778 5378, www.derm.qld.gov.au/ parks/magnetic-island/index.html.*

Sights

With over 20 beaches to choose from there are plenty of places to set up camp and just relax. Although there is excellent swimming and some good snorkelling spots – most notably the left side of Arthur Bay – care must be taken during the stinger season from October to May, when you are advised to swim only in the netted areas at Picnic Bay and Horseshoe Bay. The most popular beaches are **Rocky Bay**, between Picnic Bay and Nelly Bay, and **Alma Bay**, just north of Arcadia, though the most secluded and most beautiful are **Arthur Bay**, **Florence Bay**, **Radical Bay** and **Balding Bay**, at the northeast corner of the island. All four are accessed via the unsealed Radical Bay Track, 8 km north of Picnic Bay (but note that all vehicle hire companies place restrictions on unsealed roads, so you may have to walk). Beyond these bays is **Horseshoe Bay**, the biggest on the island and a popular spot for swimming and water sports.

There are many excellent walking tracks on the island with the two most notable being the **Horseshoe Bay to Arthur Bay track** (3 km, two hours one way) and in the same vicinity, the **Forts Walk** (2 km, 1½ hours return). The Horseshoe Bay to Arthur Bay track can be tackled in either direction and takes in all the secluded bays and some low-lying bush. Many allow themselves extended stops at one of the beaches since it can be very difficult to drag yourself away. The Forts Walk starts at the Radical Bay turn-off and follows the ridge past some old gun emplacements to the old observation tower lookout. This track is also one of the best places to observe koalas. Late afternoon (when they are awake and feeding) is the best time to see them. Another short walk to **Hawking's Point lookout** above Picnic Bay is also worthwhile. It starts at the end of Picnic Street (600 m, 30 minutes). To visit the more remote areas on the south and west coast requires your own 4WD, a boat or a very long trek. The unsealed track west starts from Yule Street, Picnic Bay, beside the golf course. Sadly, the island's highest peak Mount Cook (497 m) is inaccessible. Magnetic Island is a superb and relatively cheap venue to learn to dive. There are also some excellent dive sites around the island, including the wreck of the *Yongala*.

Hinchinbrook Island National Park → *For listings, see pages 97-110.*

From the moment you first see it, Hinchinbrook Island casts its irresistible spell. Even from afar, the green rugged peaks possess a dramatic air of wilderness. Heading north from Townsville, the Bruce Highway passes Ingham before crossing the Herbert River. It then climbs to reach the breathtaking lookout across to Hinchinbrook, its mountainous outline and velvety green cloak of rainforest seemingly almost connected to the mainland by the huge expanse of impenetrable mangrove swamps and smaller islands.

Ins and outs

The beachside town of **Cardwell** is the jumping-off point for Hinchinbrook. It is fast developing into a tourist resort and provides a welcome stop on the route north. The lengthy main drag, Victoria Street, hosts most amenities, accommodation and numerous operators offering fishing, cruising, flightseeing or wildlife-watching activities, as well as the **QPWS Rainforest and Reef Centre** ⓘ *by the jetty, T4066 8601, www.great greenwaytourism.com and www.epa.qld.gov.au, Mon-Fri 0830-1630, Sat-Sun 0900-1500,* which provides local tourist information and details of seasonal eco-cruises and issues permits for Hinchinbrook Island National Park.

Around the island

At almost 40,000 ha, Hinchinbrook is the largest island national park in the world and, having changed little since white settlement in Australia, remains one of the most unspoilt. Crowned by the 1142 m peak of Mount Bowen, it is a wonderland of sheer cliffs, forested slopes and pristine beaches inhabited with some of the state's weirdest and most dangerous wildlife. And unlike many of its peers along the Queensland coast, Hinchinbrook presents more of a challenge than a relaxing excursion. Most who choose to visit the island do so for a day, but you can stay longer at one of two designated campsites or in the lap of luxury at its one and only (expensive) resort, **Hinchinbrook Island Wilderness Lodge & Resort**, see page 101. For true explorers, though, there is only one mission – the famed **Thorsborne Trail**. This 32-km, 4-day (minimum) bushwalk, also known as the East Coast Trail, is one of the best in the country and takes in a wide range of habitats along the east coast, from Ramsay Bay in the north to George Point in the south. Given its obvious popularity, only 40 intrepid souls are allowed on the track at any one time and you must book, sometimes up to a year in advance. The best time to do it is from April to September, which avoids the very wet and the very dry, but the topography of Hinchinbrook can create inclement weather at any time. The track is not graded and in some areas is rough and hard to traverse and insect repellent is an absolute must. The QPWS centre, see Ins and outs above, provides detailed information on the track and issues the relevant camping permits. Its excellent broadsheet *Thorsborne Trail* is a fine start.

Mission Beach and Dunk Island → *For listings, see pages 97-110.*

Taking its name from a former Aboriginal mission established in the early 1900s, Mission Beach is the loose term given to an idyllic 14-km stretch of the Queensland coast from Bingil Bay in the north to the mouth of the Hull River to the south. The area is not only noted as the main tourist centre between Townsville and Cairns, but for the importance of its rainforest biodiversity, being home to many unique plants and animals. These include the umbrella-like licuala palm and the rare cassowary. There is plenty to see and do here, but it is as much a place to relax from the rigours of the road, as it is to explore its many natural delights. The superb offshore resort of Dunk Island is no exception.

Ins and outs
Tourist information Mission Beach VIC ⓘ *El-Arish-Mission Beach Rd, Porter Promenade, T4068 7099, www.missionbeachtourism.com, 0900-1700,* is a powerhouse of information, fuelled with the great enthusiasm of both the management and volunteers. The area is hard to navigate, so be sure to secure the free *Street and Business Directory*. ►► *See also Transport, page 109.*

Mission Beach
Wet Tropics Environmental Centre ⓘ *next door to the VIC, 1000-1700,* offers a fine introduction to the rainforest ecology and habitats of the region. If you plan on doing any rainforest walks, this is the place to get directions and all the relevant details. The centre also acts as a nursery for rainforest plants, collected, by all accounts, from cassowary droppings! Also of note are the records kept of the great bird's all-too-frequent disagreements with local automobiles. Before leaving this area, take a look at the large tree just to the south of the VIC and Environmental Centre. It is the seasonal home to a large colony of metallic starlings and in spring (August) becomes a hive of activity when the birds return to their own extensive and exclusive piece of real estate, in the form of countless, beautifully woven nests.

The main tracts of accessible rainforest are to be found in the **Tam O'Shanter State Forest** that dominates the region and contains one of the largest tracts of coastal lowland rainforest in northern Queensland. There are a number of excellent walks on offer, but take plenty of insect repellent. The best and the most moderate of these is the **Licuala Walk**, accessed and signposted off the Tully-Mission Beach Road. It's a 1.2-km stroll under the canopy of the rare and beautiful licuala palms. On a hot day the torn lily pad-like leaves offer a cool and quiet sanctuary. There is also a special 350-m section designed for kids, where they can 'follow the cassowary footprints' to find a surprise at the end of the walk. If you are fit enough for a longer walk, the 7-km (two hours) **Licuala-Lacey Creek Track** also starts at the car park. This track cuts through the heart of the Tam O'Shanter Forest and links Licuala with Lacey Creek, taking in the upper Hull River, a giant fig and lots of mosquitoes on the way. At Lacey Creek there is another short rainforest walk (1.1 km, taking 45 minutes), accessed and signposted off the El-Arish-Mission Beach Road. Just north of Mission Beach and Clump Point is the 4-km (2 hours) **Bicton Hill Track**. It is a stiff, yet pleasant climb to the summit though views are rather disappointing once you get there. Yet another option is the historic, 8-km (4 hours' return) **Kennedy Track** (named after local explorer Edmund Kennedy), which heads from South Mission Beach to the mouth of the Hull River.

Other than the rainforest and Dunk Island, the big attractions in these parts are the beaches. There are over 65 to choose from, blending together into one 14-km long stretch of glorious, soft sand backed by coconut palms. While sunbathing here might be heavenly enough, you may also be tempted into the water to swim and to snorkel. But if your visit is between October to May, play it safe and stick within the netted areas off Mission and South Mission beaches, in order to avoid 'stingers'.

Dunk Island

Once named (far more suitably) Coonanglebah by the Aboriginals, meaning 'The Island of Peace and Plenty', this island was renamed Dunk by Captain James Cook in 1770 after Lord Dunk, First Lord of the Admiralty. But whatever its official label, this 730-ha national and marine park, lying less than 5 km off Mission Beach, certainly offers plenty and is one of the most beautiful island parks and resorts north of the Whitsundays. What is perhaps most attractive for the visitor is the fact that it is so easily accessible.

Whether staying at the resort or as day visitors, the vast majority come to relax big style, but if you can drag yourself away from the beautiful stretch of palm-fringed beach either side of the wharf in **Brammo Bay**, you can experience the island's rich wildlife or sample some of the many activities on offer. The island has 13 km of walking tracks and the reception in the main resort building can provide free maps and information. There are plenty of options, from the short 15-minute stroll to see **Banfield's Grave** at the eastern end of the resort complex, to a complete Island Circuit (9.2 km, three hours) that takes in the remote **Bruce Arthur's Artists Colony/Gallery** ⓘ *Mon-Thu 1000-1300, $4.* The energetic may also like to attempt the stiff climb (5.6 km, three hours' return) to the summit of Mount Kootaloo (271 m), the island's highest peak.

The resort itself offers a day visitor's package that includes lunch and access to the bar, some sports facilities and the attractive **Butterfly Pool** (from $40), tickets available at **Watersports**, next to the wharf. If you really want to push the pampering boat out, book a session at the heavenly **Spa of Peace and Plenty** where you can choose from a wide range of alluring treatments, with such evocative names as the Floral Rain or Taste of Tahiti. Also book at **Watersports**.

Queensland Outback

The former gold-mining settlement of Charters Towers, 132 km west of Townsville, offers a great outback experience and is only two hours away, via the sealed Flinders Highway. This was the second largest city in Queensland at the turn of the 20th century – a place known as 'The World', where people's wildest dreams of wealth could come true. In its heyday, its gold mines yielded over six million ounces ($25 million) of the precious metal. Nowadays it's better known for its beef production than its mineral resources, but is a fascinating example of a quintessential outback town.

With the help of the National Trust, Charters Towers has made some sterling efforts in the restoration of its heritage buildings and mining relics. The **Ghosts of Gold Heritage Trail** begins at the **VIC** ① *74 Mosman St, T4761 5533, www.charterstowers.qld.gov.au, 0900-1700*, which is housed in the former band hall building between the former Stock Exchange and City Hall. It covers a number of venues throughout the city and helps to bring to life the colourful stories, legends, incredible feats and the characters of the gold rush.

The trail includes the old **Stock Exchange Building** ① *0900-1500*, built originally as a shopping arcade in 1888 and converted into a stock exchange in 1890 before being fully restored in 1970. Next door is the magnificent former 1892 Australian Bank of Commerce building. The unusually named Ay Ot Lookout, on the corner of Hodgkinson Street and the High Street, was built in 1896 and reflects the architectural excellence of the era. Guided tours of the interior are conducted throughout the week, 0800-1500.

On the outskirts of the city, east via Gill Street and Millchester Road, are the remains of the **Venus Battery Mill** ① *0930-1630, guided tours on the hour, $12, child $6*, the largest surviving battery relic in Australia. Interactive displays tell the story of how the battery was used to extract the precious metal, and as you wander around its eight huge stampers and former cyanide ponds it certainly stirs the imagination back to the days when it was in full production. Just south of the city on the Flinders Highway are the Dalrymple Sale Yards, one of the largest stock sale yards in the state with countless head of beef cattle transported in by monstrous road trains – a true reminder that you are now in real outback country.

Nearby, Towers Hill has superb views across the city, especially at sunrise or sunset. At an open-air amphitheatre in the evening the film *Ghosts After Dark* is screened. Access is from the south end of Mosman Street, off Black Jack Road. Film tickets from the VIC. The VIC can also book an excellent city tour.

Central Coast listings

● Sleeping

Mackay and around *p84, map p85*
$$$$ Broken River Mountain Retreat, Broken River (for Eungella National Park), Eungella Dam Rd, T4958 4000, www. brokenrivermr.com.au. A range of studio, 1- and 2-bedroom self-contained cabins, restaurant (open to the public) and an exciting range of in-house activities from night spotting to canoeing.

$$$ Bucasia Beachfront Caravan Park, 2 Esplanade, Bucasia Beach, T4954 6375. Some 10 km north of the city, this is one of several good motor parks in the area. It has 3 stars and has self-contained villas, cabins, powered and non-powered sites and memorable views across to the Whitsunday Islands.
$$$ Cape Hillsborough Nature Resort, Casuarina Bay in Cape Hillsborough National Park, T4959 0152, www.capehillsborough resort.com.au. Beachfront cabins, motel

units or powered and non-powered sites. Fires permitted. There is a small store, pool, restaurant and bar lounge with internet.

$$$ Eungella Holiday Park, North St (take the first right beyond the chalet), Eungella, T0437479205, www.eungella- holidaypark. com.au. Self-contained cabin, powered and non-powered sites.

$$$ Historic Eungella Chalet Mountain Resort, Chelmer St, Eungella, T4958 4509, www.eungellachalet.com.au. As well as the magnificent views it has a wide range of options, from self-contained cabins with open fires to motel rooms and backpacker (weekday only) beds, an à la carte restaurant, public bar and pool.

$$$ The Park, Bruce Highway Mackay, T4952 1211, www.toptouristparks.com.au. In the south, 6 km to the city centre and handy for the main highway, this 3-star motor park offers villas, cabins, powered and non-powered sites, and a good camp kitchen in a garden setting.

$$ Gecko's Rest 34 Sydney St, T4944 1230, www.geckosrest.com.au. Centrally located, purpose-built hostel with a/c singles, dorms, singles, doubles and twins. Free shuttle.

$$ Larrikin Lodge YHA, 32 Peel St (200 m south of the bus terminal), T4951 3728,www.larrikinlodge.com.au. Backpackers will find a warm welcome here, the city's budget mainstay for some time now. It offers standard dorms, doubles and one family room with all the usual facilities in a traditional 'Queenslander'. Internet and entertaining in-house tours to Eungella National Park. A 3-night 'tour' package with 1 night in Mackay and 2 at the Eungella Chalet costs a very reasonable $180.

$$ Platypus Bush Camp, Finch Hatton Gorge Rd (for Eungella National Park), T4958 3204, www.bushcamp.net. Created by a friendly and laid-back bushman called Wazza, it gets mixed reviews and features a characterful collection of basic open-air huts and campsites, set amongst the bush and beside the river. The huts range from single, through doubles to the notably more distant

Honeymoon Hut, with its exclusive platypus-spotting opportunities. Other camp features include an open-air communal kitchen and sauna (all constructed from local cedar wood) and a fine swimming hole. Campfires are authorized. A bit pricey, but certainly different.

QPWS campsites At Broken River (for Eungella National Park), with toilets, drinking water, showers and gas barbecues, permits available at the Ranger Station (T4958 4552) which has a small food kiosk attached. Also at Newry Island and Outer Newry Island. The latter has a hut (maximum of 10 at any one time). Rabbit Island has a QPWS campsite with toilets and a seasonal water tank. Also available at Smalley's Beach at the western end of Cape Hillsborough National Park, T4944 7800, limited fresh water. There's a basic site at Carlisle Island, all supplies must be imported, seasonal water tank but a back-up supply should be taken anyway. Basic bush campsites are also on Goldsmith, Scawfell, Cockermouth, Keswick and St Bee's Islands. Permits and fees apply to all sites. Book ahead with the QPWS, 30 Tennyson St, Mackay, T4944 7800, www.epa.qld.gov.au.

Airlie Beach *p87, map p87*

Despite having numerous smart resorts, apartments and backpackers aplenty, Airlie can hardly keep pace with its own popularity and you are advised to book ahead. Many backpackers offer accommodation and activity combo deals, often booked from afar, but though these can be attractive in price, they can severely limit your choice.

$$$$ Airlie Waterfront B&B, corner of Broadwater Av and Mazlin St, T4946 7631, www.airliewaterfrontbnb.com.au. This is one of the best B&Bs in the region and certainly the best located for all amenities.

$$$$ Airlie Beach Hotel, corner of Esplanade and Coconut Grove, T4946 1999, www.airliebeachhotels.com.au. No-nonsense centrally located hotel with recently renovated standard rooms, motel-style units and self-contained suites. Cable TV, internet, 2 restaurants, bar and off-street parking.

$$$ Flame Tree Tourist Village, 2955 Shute Harbour Rd, T4946 9388, www. flametreevillage.com.au. Further east near the airfield, low-key in a quiet bush setting, with a camp kitchen and within easy reach of the ferry terminal.

$$$ Island Getaway Holiday Park, a short walk east of the town centre (corner of Shute Harbour Rd and Jubilee Pocket Rd), T4946 6228. This 4-star motor park is a popular option offering value units, cabins, camp-o-tels and powered and non-powered sites. Good camp kitchen and some very tame possums.

$$ Airlie Beach YHA, 394 Shute Harbour Rd, T4946 6312. YHA members will get the usual discounts at this friendly motel-style option.

$$ Bush Village Backpackers Resort, 2 St Martins Rd, Cannonvale, T4946 6177, www. bushvillage.com.au. For a little bit of peace and quiet this is an excellent option. It is friendly with tidy and spacious self-catering cabins with a/c, en suite doubles, dorms, pool and a regular shuttle into town.

$$ Koala, Shute Harbour Rd, T4946 6446, www.koalaadventures.com, and

$$ Magnums Backpackers, 366 Shute Harbour Rd, T4946 6266, www.magnums. com.au, are the main players when it comes to the major party-oriented backpackers located right in the heart of the town. In many ways they are the heart of the town! At the end of the day (or night) they are all pretty similar and certainly fiercely competitive, always trying to outdo each other on the small details. But in essence they all have the full range of dorms, singles and doubles, boast lively bars, nightclubs, a pool, good value eateries and internet. They can also advise on activities and trips (though this advice will not be completely objective).

Whitsunday Islands *p88, map p89*

$$$$ Daydream Island Resort and Spa, T4948 8426, www.daydreamisland. com. Daydream is the closest island to the mainland and one of the smallest, making it a popular base. This 4-star luxury resort is modern, offering attractive multi-night package deals and good facilities including a luxury spa, open-air cinema and organized activities.

$$$$ Long Island Resort and Barefoot Lodge, Long Island, T4946 9400, www. longislandresort.com.au. Offering its guests the perfect arrival point in Happy Bay, both atmosphere and amenities are casual but stylish. There are 2 options: the standard resort and the budget Barefoot Lodge that has access to resort facilities.

$$$$ Paradise Bay, Long Island, T4946 9777, www.paradisebay.com.au. In almost perfect isolation on the island's western side, this is an architect's dream realized. It strives very successfully to create a relaxing eco-friendly retreat with a focus on the place rather than the amenities. Although basic and expensive, visitors very rarely leave disappointed. The accommodation is in comfortable en suite beachfront units. The hosts are very professional and friendly and there is a moody yet enchanting pet kangaroo. The lodge has its own yacht which is part of an optional, and comprehensive, daily activities schedule. 3-night packages available.

$$$ Hook Island Wilderness Resort, Hook Island, T4946 9470, www.hookislandresort. com. Located towards the southeastern end of the island, this is a low-key resort popular with budget travellers. It offers en suite and standard cabins and dorms along with numerous activities, an underwater observatory, café-bar, pool and spa.

$$$ Koala Adventure Island Resort, South Molle Island, T1800 466444, www. southmolleisland.com.au. A pretty relaxed place aimed at the younger set, offering a full range of accommodation from beach bungalows to dorms, all with the usual mod cons and allowing day trippers access to the pool, bar/bistro and some activities. It is also noted for its evening entertainment.

QPWS campsites Whitsunday Island
There are 8 QPWS campsites here. The most
popular is Whitehaven Beach, southern
end. It can accommodate up to 60 and
has toilets, but no water supply. The only
campsites with water are Sawmill Beach and
Dugong Beach, both of which fringe Cid
Bay on the island's western side. They are
connected by a 1-km walking track.

Hook Island There are 5 QPWS campsites
here, with Maureen Cove and Bloodhorn
Beach (Stonehaven Bay) being the most
popular. None has a water supply.

Lindeman Island The only campsite here
is at Boat Port, with toilets but no water.

Long Island This has a campsite on the
western side of the island at Sandy Bay. It is
a fine, secluded spot backed by rainforest,
through which there is a track allowing you
to explore and reach viewpoints overlooking
the other islands. There are toilets but no
water supply.

South Molle 2 campsites, at Sandy Bay and
Paddle Bay with toilets but no water supply.
There are 2 other sites on small offshore
islands and at Cockatoo Beach on North
Molle, but if the resort cannot offer you a
lift in one of its vessels, independent access
must be arranged. Cockatoo Beach site has
seasonal water supplies.

Townsville *p91, map p92*
$$$ Rowes Bay Caravan Park, west of the
Strand on Heatley's Parade, T4771 3576,
www.rowesbaycp.com.au. Close to town
and beach, offering villas, cabins, powered
and non-powered sites and camp kitchen.
$$$ Walkabout Palms Caravan Park, 6
University Rd, Wulguru, T4778 2480, www.
walkaboutpalms.com.au. This 4-star park
has good facilities and is connected to the
24-hr petrol station. Although not central to
the city (7 km away) it's in a good position
for the transitory visitor right on the main
north-south highway.
$$ Civic Guest House, 262 Walker St,
T4771 5381, www.backpackersinn.com.au. A
little less conveniently situated, but the pick

of the bunch. It has a wide range of rooms
(some with en suite and a/c), good general
facilities, a spa and interesting in-house trips.
$$ Globetrotters Inn, 121 Flinders St East,
T4771 5000. Choice of modern 4-share
rooms or your own en suite motel-style
room with TV and fridge. Pool and internet
café. Dive/stay packages a speciality.
$$ Yongala Lodge, off the Strand on Fryer
St, T4772 4633, www.historicyongala.com.
au. Named after the famous local shipwreck,
offers a range of contemporary motel
units from single to 2-bedroom, a pleasant
Mediterranean/international restaurant and
is a pebble's throw from the waterfront.

Magnetic Island *p93*
Picnic Bay, the main arrival point,
offers many amenities but most of the
accommodation is evenly spread down the
east coast. There is plenty of choice, from
luxury poolside apartments to a hammock,
and most are virtually self contained. For
full listings contact the VIC. Book ahead for
budget accommodation and during school
and public holidays.
$$$$ Magnetic Island Tropical Resort,
56 Yates St, Nelly Bay, T4778 5955, www.
magnetic islandresort.com. An excellent
choice, offering modern, A-frame self-
contained chalets with good facilities.
Restaurant/bar, pool and spa, amidst a bush
setting. Recommended.
$$$ Marshall's B&B, 3-5 Endeavour Rd,
Arcadia, T4778 5112. This eco-friendly
option, next door to Magnetic North
Apartments, offers basic, but good value
singles and doubles in a traditional
Queenslander house and is surrounded
by spacious gardens with the odd friendly
wallaby for company. Fans. Free night
standby special (ie buy 2, get 3) Oct-Jun.
$$ Base Backpackers, 1 Nelly Bay Rd, Nelly
Bay, T4778 5777, www.stayatbase.com.
South of Nelly Bay on the beach, this newly
branded backpackers is regaining popularity
after renovation. It has an interesting range
of accommodation options, from dorms to

ocean-view *bures* (traditional South Pacific thatched huts). Modern facilities, café, dive shop and home to the notorious full moon parties.

$$ Bungalow Bay Koala Village (YHA), 40 Horseshoe Bay Rd, Horseshoe Bay, T4778 5577, www.bungalowbay.com.au. Set in spacious grounds, offering everything from a/c chalets (some en suite) and en suite multi-share to camp and powered sites with camp kitchen. Regular, mass lorikeet feeding. Lively place with popular late night bar and bistro, pool, spa and internet but a little further away from the beach.

$$ Magnums, 7 Marine Pde, Arcadia, T4778 5177, www.magnums.com.au. A busy, sprawling place with 30 a/c motel-style units (including dorms) close to all local amenities. Pool, spa, restaurant/bar and bistro. Internet.

Hinchinbrook Island National Park *p94*

There are as yet limited accommodation options in Cardwell. Hinchinbrook VIC can help with finding accommodation.

$$$$ Hinchinbrook Island Wilderness Lodge and Resort, Hinchinbrook Island, T4066 8270 www.hinchinbrookresort.com. au. This exclusive place offers an excellent, though somewhat expensive, sanctuary, with an eco-friendly setting and all mod cons. Don't expect a party atmosphere or a place overrun with activities as this is a resort that is proudly in tune with the wilderness and environment that surround it. A perfect place at which to indulge, relax and pamper yourself.

$$$ Kookaburra Holiday Park and Hinchinbrook Hostel (YHA), 175 Bruce Highway (north of the jetty), Cardwell, T4066 8648, www.kookaburraholidaypark.com.au. YHA affiliated, this has everything from self-catering villas to campsites as well as dorms, doubles and twins in the hostel section. Good facilities, including a pool, tours and activities bookings, internet and free bike hire for guests.

Camping Facilities on Hinchinbrook Island are at Scraggy Point (The Haven), on the island's northwest coast, and Maucushla Bay, near the resort. Toilets and gas fireplaces.
Bush camping sites on Hinchinbrook Island have been established along the Thorsborne Trail with Zoe Bay offering toilets and water. Open fires are not allowed and you will require a gas stove and water containers. Camping permits for all sites must be obtained from the QPWS Rainforest and Reef Centre, see page 94 for contact details, or email to hinchinbrookcamp@env.qld.gov.au.

Mission Beach and Dunk Island *p95*

Although there is a smattering of resorts in the area, the many excellent and characterful B&Bs and self-contained accommodation are recommended.

$$$$ Sejala, 1 Pacific St, Mission Beach, T4088 6699, www.sejala.com.au. 5-star luxury in the form of a stunning beachfront villa with private pool or a choice of 3 arty (and cheaper) self-contained beach huts with shared plunge pool.

$$$$ Beachcomber Coconut Caravan Village, Kennedy Esplanade, Mission Beach South, T4068 8129, www.beachcomber coconut.com.au. There are several motor parks in the area including this very tidy beachside option. Recommended.

$$$$ Dunk Island Resort, Brammo Bay, Dunk Island, T4068 8199, www.dunk-island. com. This 4-star resort offers a delightful range of units and suites, excellent amenities and a wealth of activities and sports on offer. Book well ahead. Children welcome.

$$$$ Hideaway Holiday Village, 60 Porters Prom, Mission Beach village, T4068 7104, www.missionbeachhideaway.com.au. This motor park is a little sterile but has good facilities and is very handy for the beach and village amenities. Pool, camp kitchen and internet.

$$$ Absolute Backpackers, 28 Wongaling Beach Rd, Wongaling Beach, T4068 8317, www.absolutebackpackers.com.au. Newly renovated, popular place with a social atmosphere, offering 10-, 8- and 4-bed dorms and separate doubles with fans or a/c and a well-equipped kitchen. It is also close to the happening bar in the **Mission Beach Resort** and the main shopping complex.

$$$ Beach Shack, 86 Porter Promenade, 1 km north of Mission Beach village, T4068 7783, www.missionbeachshack.com. This complex is a colourful 2-storey house opposite the beach and within walking distance to the village centre. It offers tidy dorms and doubles, 2 kitchens, spas and a relaxed, friendly atmosphere.

$$$ Dragonheart B&B Resort, Bingil Bay, T4068 7813, www.dragonheartbnb. com. A friendly welcome and separate accommodation in Balinese-style cottages (with en suite) set in the rainforest. It also has a pool. A good choice and good value.

$$$ Licuala Lodge, 11 Mission Circle, Mission Beach, T4068 8194, www.licuala lodge.com.au. Excellent award-winning pole house B&B with doubles, singles, and a memorable 'jungle pool' and spa. Dinner available on request.

$$$ Sanctuary Retreat, 72 Holt Rd, Bingil Bay, T4088 6064, www.sanctuaryatmission .com. An interesting eco-retreat; wildlife enthusiasts will love it. The minimalist and secluded forest huts are in a setting designed to nurture and attract the local wildlife rather than scare it away. Restaurant, internet and pick-ups. Good value.

$$$ Scotty's Beach House Hostel, 167 Reid Rd, Wongaling Beach, T4068 8676, www. scottysbeachhouse.com.au. Closer to the beach than **Mission Beach Backpackers Lodge**, this is a well-established and popular place, offering a range of unit-style dorms and doubles surrounding a fine pool, a very relaxed atmosphere, restaurant and reputedly the best bar in town.

$$$ Treehouse YHA, Frizelle Road (off Bingil Bay Road), Bingil Bay, T4068 7137, www.treehousehostel.com.au. Always popular, this pole house has doubles, twins and dorms a pool and all the usual amenities. Its only drawback is its distance from the beach but shuttle buses regularly ply the route.

QPWS camping ground, Dunk Island, is discreetly located next to the resort. Permits can be purchased from **Watersports** on the island. Barbecues and showers.

Queensland Outback

Charters Towers is the stepping stone to popular outback stations, with comfortable accommodation and the quintessential outback experience. Charters Towers VIC has details.

$$$-$$ Aussie Outback Oasis Big4 Holiday Park, 76 Dr George Ellis Drive, T4787 8722, www.aussieoutbackoasis.com. au. One of several motor parks with good facilities in the town that offers the full range of accommodation options.

$$$-$$ Bluff Downs, T4770 4084, www. bluffdowns.com.au. A historic 40,000-ha working cattle station, set on the spectacular deepwater lagoons of the Basalt River, 80 km north of the city. A range of activities, from mustering to fossil hunting, and a/c backpackers' quarters, homestead rooms and a cottage.

⊘ Eating

Mackay and around *p84, map p85*
$$ Sorbello's , 166B Victoria St, T4957 8300. Daily 1200-2000. The best Italian restaurant in town.

$$-$ Café La De Da, 70 Wood St, T4944 0203. New establishment; good quality and value.

$ Eimeo Hotel, Mango Av, Dolphin Heads, 12 km away, T4954 6106. Daily 1200-2000. Cheap counter meals with spectacular views over Eimeo Beach and the Whitsunday Islands.

$ Hideaway Café, just beyond the chalet, Eungella, T4958 4533. Daily 0800-1700. Well worth a stop. The delightful Suzanna has created her own piece of paradise, with spacious gardens, home-made pottery and a wishing well. Take a tour of the imaginative and international menu while supping a coffee and soaking up the views across the valley.

$ Kate O'Reilley's Irish Pub, 38 Sydney St, T4953 3522. The best for pub grub.

Airlie Beach *p87, map p87*

$$-$ Beaches Backpackers and **Magnums** (see page 101), have popular bar/bistros offering a wide variety of good-value dishes (including the obligatory roo burgers) and a lively atmosphere. The 2-for-1 pizzas in the **Magnums** complex are also a bargain. Both are open for lunch and dinner.

$$-$ Chargrill, 382 Shute Harbour Rd, T4946 6320. Popular for seafood and meat dishes and has live entertainment most nights until 0300.

$$-$ Paddy Shenanigans, 352 Shute Harbour Rd, T4946 5055. This Irish pub also offers good value bar meals and is a fine place to remain for a night out.

$ Village Deli, 366 Shute Harbour Rd, T4946 5745. Tucked away at the back of the shopping complex, opposite the post office, good coffee, healthy snacks, fruit smoothies and breakfast in peaceful surroundings.

Townsville *p91, map p92*

There are reputable, upmarket restaurants in most major hotels and motels. Palmers St has taken over from Flinders St East as the preferred venue of the local gourmand, offering a wide range of international, mid-range options.

$$ Bistro One, 30-34 Palmer St, T4771 6333. Popular, especially for seafood.

$$ Molly Malone's Irish Pub, corner of Wickham St and Flinders St East, T4771 3428. For pub grub, tidy surroundings and congenial atmosphere.

$$ Reef Thai , 455 Flinders St, T4721 6701. Daily 0530-late. Takeaway service. Locally recommended, with a seafood edge.

$$ Taj Mahal, 2/235 Flinders St East, T4772 3422. Good Indian cuisine.

$$ The Watermark, 72-74 The Strand, T4724 4281. Modern Australian cuisine amid chic and contemporary surrounds and great ocean views.

$ Heritage Café and Bar, 137 Flinders St East, T4771 2799. Nice atmosphere, varied and good value blackboard of dishes.

Magnetic Island *p93*

The restaurants and cafés on Maggie tend to be casual affairs and close early. Most of the major resorts and backpackers have cafés, bistros, or à la carte restaurants all open to the public. Self-caterers will find grocery stores in all the main centres mostly open daily until about 1900.

$$-$ Man Friday, 37 Warboys St, Nelly Bay, T4778 5658. Wed-Mon from 1800. Mexican, traditional Australian and international dishes with vegetarian options.

$ Noodies, on the waterfront, Horseshoe Bay, T4778 5786. Another place offering fine seafood and overlooking the beach.

$ Sandbar Restaurant, 11 Cook Rd, Arcadia, T4778 5477. Good atmosphere and seafood.

Mission Beach *p95*

Most eateries are concentrated in and around the Village Green Shopping Complex on Porter Promenade in Mission Beach village, but between here and Wongaling Beach you won't be short of choice.

$$$ Mission Beach Restaurant and Bar, corner of Banfield Rd and Wongaling Beach Rd, Wongaling Beach, T4068 8433. Daily for dinner except Wed. For fine dining with an international menu try this classy joint. Cleverly designed in typical, though modern, Queenslander style, on poles and open plan, it is stylish with food to match. Recommended.

$$ Greek Tavern, corner of Webb St and Banfield Parade, T4068 8177. As the name suggests, predominantly Mediterranean oriented cuisine, but also some Asian and Australian options. Great views over Wongaling Beach and good for a quiet romantic dinner.

$ Café Gecko, Shop 6, The Hub, Porter Promenade, T4068 7390. Daily 0900-1700. Seems to change management regularly but maintains quality when it comes to a caffeine fix.

$ Scotty's Beachhouse Bar and Grill, 167 Reid Rd, off Cassowary Drive, Wongaling. This place has a lively atmosphere and offers budget bistro meals.

🎵 Bars and clubs

Airlie Beach *p87, map p87*
Beaches Backpackers and **Magnums** (see page 101) have streetside bars that are popular and the best place to meet others for the obligatory wild night out.
M@ss, at **Magnums**, is a nightclub that rips it up well into the wee hours (sometimes quite literally, with wet T-shirt competitions and foam parties).

Magnetic Island *p93, map pXXX*
The major backpackers provide most of the island's entertainment and have late bars.
Magnums, Arcadia (see page 101).
Live bands most nights and full-on pool competitions.
Picnic Bay Hotel has pool competitions every Tue.

⛰ Activities and tours

Mackay and around *p84, map p85*
Jungle Johno Tours, T4951 3728, www.larrikinlodge.com.au/ jungle-tours. A popular option, offering entertaining eco-tours and camping trips to Eungella National Park and the Finch Hatton Gorge. Platypus spotting is a speciality. A 3-night 'tour' package with 1 night in Mackay YHA and 2 nights at the Eungella Chalet costs a very reasonable $180.
Mackay Reeforest Tours, T4959 8360, www.reeforest.com. Wider range of day tours to Hillsborough and Eungella National Parks and in season the Farleigh Sugar Mill Tour, from $145, children $95.

Airlie Beach *p87, map p87*
With numerous dive shops, umpteen cruise operators, over 74 islands and almost as many vessels, the choice of water-based activities and trips is mind blowing. The 2 most popular trips are Whitehaven Beach and Fantasea's floating Reefworld pontoon, which offers the chance to dive, snorkel or view the reef from a semi-submersible or underwater observatory. Note that both

options are also the most commercial and most crowded. The main ferry companies also offer island transfers and island day tripper specials with South Molle being a popular and good value choice.

Cruises
All offer a wide array of day cruises to the islands, the outer reef, or both. A day cruise will cost from $95-200.
Fantasea (Blue Ferries) Cruises, T4967 5455, www.fantasea.com.au. The major player with fast catamarans.
Whitehaven Express, T4946 1585, www.whitehavenxpress.com.au. Well-established operator offering day trips to Whitehaven from $150.

Diving
The outer reef offers the clearest water and most varied marine life. There are numerous options with all local dive shops and most of the larger cruise companies offering day or multi-day trips and courses.
Dive Australia, Sugarloaf Rd, T4946 1067, www.scubacentre.com.au. A range of 3-day liveaboard Open Water Courses from $649.
Reefjet, Shop 2, Abel Point Marina, T4946 5366, www.reefjet.com.au. Excellent day cruise to the Bait Reef (outer reef) and Whitehaven Beach with dive and snorkelling options from $140.

Fishing
MV Moruya, T4948 1029, www.fishingwhitsunday.com.au. Entertaining half, full and multi-day trips from Shute Harbour, from $150.

Kayaking
Salty Dog Sea Kayaking, T4946 1388, www.saltydog.com.au. Half day guided trips from $70, full day from $125, overnight (from $360) or 6-day (from $1490), island camping adventures and independent kayak hire from $50 per day. The trips guarantee plenty of beautiful scenery as well as a spot of island bushwalking and snorkelling.

Ocean rafting
Ocean Rafting, T4946 6848, www.ocean rafting.com.au. Runs a 6½-hr fast cruise around the islands and Whitehaven Beach on board their rigid inflatable. Includes snorkelling, guided rainforest and Aboriginal cave walk from $108, children $69.

Sailing
Again the choices are mind-boggling. A whole host of vessels from small dinghies to world-class racing yachts are available for day, night or multi-day adventures. Depending on the vessel type, as well as accommodation and food, a day cruise will cost about $150 while a 2-day/2-night will cost from $350-550; a 3-day/2-night trip around $450-700 and a 3-day/3-night from $550-1000.

Townsville *p91, map p92*
Diving
There are several companies in Townsville or on Magnetic Island (which is often the preferred location) offering a wide variety of trips for certified divers wishing to experience the *Yongala*. It's best to shop around.
Adrenalin Dive, 9 Wickham St, T4724 0600, www.adrenalinedive.com.au. Range of courses/trips to the *Yongala* wreck, from $220.

Sightseeing tours
Kookaburra Tours, T0448 794798, www. kookaburratours.com.au. Range of tours including entertaining full day trips to the Wallam Falls (Australia's tallest) on Tue and Charters Towers on Wed from $125.

Magnetic Island *p93*
Cruises/sailing
Jazza's Sailing Tours, 90 Horseshoe Bay Rd, T4778 5530, www.jazza.com.au. Good value, 6-hr cruise aboard the 12-m *Jazza* from $100, children $50 (includes lunch).
Tropic Sail, T4772 4773, www.tropicsail. com.au. Hire of yachts from $440 per night and day sailing trips from Townsville.

Diving
Pleasure Divers, 10 Marine Pde, T4778 5788, www.pleasuredivers.com.au. Reputable 2-4 day course/trips (including *Yongala* wreck) from $220.

Flights
Red Baron Sea Planes, Horseshoe Bay, T4758 1556, www.redbaronseaplanes.com. A unique opportunity to fly in a Grumman Sea Cat (used in the film *The Phantom*) and the only one of its type in the world, from $350.

Golf
Magnetic Island Country Club, Picnic Bay, T4778 5188, www.magvac.com. Small 9-hole golf course, visitors welcome, $14 ($20 for 18 holes).

Horse trekking
Bluey's Ranch, 38 Gifford St, Horseshoe Bay, T4778 5109, www.horseshoebayranch. com.au. Horse treks from 2 hrs to half day, from $100.

Sightseeing tours
Magnetic Island Bus Service, Nelly Bay, T4778 5130. 3-hr guided tours from Nelly Bay, 0900 and 1300, from $35, children $18, family $88.
Tropicana Guided Adventure Company, Harbour Terminal, T4758 1800, www. tropicanatours.com.au. Multifarious award-winning 4WD trips with entertaining and multi-talented guides. Full day (8 hrs) '7-days-in-1' trip recommended from $198, children $99.

Water sports
Magnetic Island Sea Kayaks, Horseshoe Bay, T4778 5424, www.seakayak.com.au. Half-day sea kayaking adventures from $85, which also includes a beach breakfast.

Hinchinbrook Island National Park
p94

Hinchinbrook Ferries Eco-Tours, Cardwell, T4066 8585, www.hinchinbrookferries.com. au. Full day national park discovery trips from $125.

Mission Beach and Dunk Island *p95*
Many of the Mission Beach operators incorporate Dunk Island in their kayak and jet ski tours. Snorkelling on Dunk is poor compared to the reef.

Skydiving
Jump The Beach, T4031 5466, www. jumpthebeach.com. Great value tandem jumps on to Mission Beach or Dunk Island: 2750 m and 3350 m from $210, 4250 m from $295.
Paul's Parachuting, based in Cairns, T1800 005 006, www.paulsparachuting.com.au. Tandems with landings on Mission Beach at similar prices.

Water sports
Calypso Dive and Snorkel, 20 Wongaling Beach Rd, T4068 8432, www.calypsodive. com. Purpose-built dive centre in Mission Beach; as well as a full range of courses it offers wreck dives and a blast around Dunk Island on jet skis from $230.
Coral Sea Kayaking, T4068 9154, www. coral seakayaking.com. Full day sea kayaking voyages to Dunk Island with plenty of time to explore and a fine lunch from $128 (half-day coastal exploration, $77).
Dunk Jet Sports, T4068 8432, www.dunkjet sports.com. 2-hr circumnavigation of Dunk Island on jet ski, from $230, or full day including lunch with plenty of time to relax and explore Dunk itself. From $330. Departs South Mission Beach 0830.
Watersports, next to the wharf on Dunk Island. Offers independent day visitors a host of equipment and water-based activities from a mask and snorkel hire to windsurfing, waterskiing and parasailing.

⊜ Transport

Mackay and around *p84, map p85*
There is no public transport to Eungella, though it is possible to make arrangements with local tour operators (see page 104).

Air
Mackay Airport, T4957 0255, is 2 km south of the city centre, along Sydney St and is served by **Jet Star**, T131538; **Qantas**, T131313; **Tiger Airways**, T9335 3033, www.tigerairways .com; and **Virgin Blue**, T136789. All have daily services throughout Queensland and New South Wales. **Air Whitsunday**, T4946 9111, www.airwhitsunday.com. au, has shuttle services to **Proserpine** and **Hamilton Island**. Taxis meet all flights and cost about $20 into town.
For **Brampton and Carlisle islands**, local companies also fly to and from Hamilton Island and daily to and from Mackay. A launch service for resort guests is available Thu-Mon at 1130 from Mackay Marina, T4951 4499. Campers can take a scheduled launch and walk to the QPWS campsite or arrange to be ferried directly to the island through the resort. **Qantas** flies to Brampton from Australian state capitals. For more information contact the QPWS office, Mackay.

Boat
For the Newry Islands access is by private boat from the boat ramp at Victor Creek, 4km west of Seaforth. For details contact **QPWS**, T1300 130372, www.derm.qld.gov. au/ parks/newry-islands/index.html.

Bus
Local Mackay Transit, Casey Av, T4957 3330, www.mackaytransit.com.au, is a hail 'n' ride bus service to Northern Beaches (Mon-Fri, No 7) and Mirani (No 11). Day Rover tickets are available.
Long distance Greyhound, T1300 473946, stops at the terminal on Milton St, between Victoria and Gordon St, T4951 3088.

Taxi
Mackay Taxis (24 hrs), T131008.

Train
The station is 5 km southwest of the city centre on Connor's Rd, between Archibald St and Boundary Rd off the Bruce Highway. **Queensland Rail**, T132332. Taxis meet most trains and cost $20 in to the centre. Regular buses leave from Nebo Rd (Bruce Highway).

Airlie Beach *p87, map p87*
Air
The nearest airports are in Proserpine, 36 km west, and Hamilton Island in the Whitsunday Islands. Both are served by **Qantas**, T131313, and **Island Air Taxis**, T4946 8249, www.avta.com. au, who provide local island transfers from **Mackay**, **Proserpine** or **Shute Harbour**. **Whitsunday Transit** buses meet flights in Proserpine.

Bus
Local Whitsunday Transit, T4946 1800, www.whitsundaytransit.com.au, offers daily buses from **Proserpine Airport** to **Shute Harbour** (through Airlie) from $8.50 (Explorer Pass). Buses between **Cannonvale** and **Shute Harbour** operate daily between 0600-1845, from $5 one way. Day pass, $8.50.
Long distance Buses stop beside the lagoon in the heart of town or next to the Sailing Club in the Recreation reserve. Either way most accommodation is within walking distance or you will be met by private shuttle. **Greyhound**, T1300 473946, runs regular daily services.

Taxi
Whitsunday Taxis, T131008.

Train
The nearest station is in Proserpine, 36 km west of Airlie, with 8 trains weekly including the **Brisbane-Cairns Tilt Train**. For bookings, call **Queensland Rail**, T132232. The station is served by **Whitsunday Transit**, T4946 1800, linking Proserpine with Airlie Beach and Shute Harbour, which meets all arrivals.

Whitsunday Islands *p88, map p89*
Air
Proserpine Airport, 36 km west of Airlie Beach, on the mainland, and Hamilton Island Airport, provide air access. Both are serviced by **Qantas**, T131313. **Lindeman** is the only other island with an airfield.
Island Air Taxis, T4946 9102, www.avta. com.au, provides local island transfers by fixed-wing or helicopter from **Mackay**, **Proserpine** or **Shute Harbour**. **Air Whitsunday**, T4946 9111, www.airwhit sunday.com.au, also offers fixed-wing and seaplane services. All local fixed-wing, helicopter and seaplane companies also offer scenic flights (see box, page 88).

Boat
Shute Harbour, east of Airlie Beach, is the main departure point for ferry services to the Whitsunday islands. Ask at the VIC for the latest transfer services and day packages.
Cruise Whitsundays, Abel Point Marina, Airlie Beach, T4946 4662, www.cruise whitsundays.com, offers an island resort transfer service to Hamilton, Daydream Island Resort and Spa, Long Island, and the Koala Adventure Resort on South Molle. Cruise Whitsundays also operates a connecting service from Whitsunday Coast Airport (Proserpine) through to Daydream and Long Islands. The average transfer cost is around $45. They also offer day packages, day trips to Whitehaven Beach (from $165) and their own Reef Pontoon at Knuckle Reef (from $199).
Fantasea , T4967 5455, www.fantasea.com. au, offers daily services and day packages to **Hamilton** (6 daily, from $45 return). They too offer a range of day tripper and adventure cruises that include their 'Reefworld' pontoon out on the reef; the island resorts (with use of resort facilities

and lunch) are also on offer from $225. Their main office is at the ferry terminal, with another office at Shop 11, Shute Harbour Rd, Airlie Beach, T4967 5455. Ferry schedules are available at the VICs. **Whitehaven Express**, T4946 6922, www.whitehavenxpress.com. au, has a daily trip to Whitehaven Beach from Abel Point Marina (Cannonvale) at 0900, from $150, children $75. **Island Camping Connections**, T4946 5255, based at the ferry terminal, runs island transfers for campers by water taxi, from $45-150. Book ahead.

Bus
Whitsunday Transit, T4946 1800, www. whit sundaytransit.com.au, has regular daily services from **Proserpine** to **Shute Harbour** (through Airlie Beach).

Townsville *p91, map p92*
Air
Townsville is serviced from all major cities by **Qantas**, **Jet Star**, and **Virgin Blue**. The airport, T4727 3211, is about 5 km west of the city in the suburb of Garbutt.

Bus
Local Townsville's Sunbus, T4725 8482, www.sunbus.com.au, runs regular daily suburban services. Fares are from $2.50, day pass from $10.
Long distance Premier Motor Services, T133410, and **Greyhound**, T1300 473946. Westbound destinations include **Charters Towers**. Most coaches stop at the Sunferries Terminal, Breakwater, Sir Leslie Thiess Drive, T4772 5100. Daily 0600-1930.

Car
Main companies at the airport. **Network**, 25 Yeatman St, T4725 3210.

Train
The station, Blackwood St, just south of the Flinders Mall, next to the river, has a travel centre, T4772 8546 (confirmations and timetable), T132232 (bookings), www.

traveltrain.qr.com.au. The **Sunlander**and **Tilt Train** operate regular services between **Brisbane** and **Cairns**; the **Spirit of the Tropics** operates a twice-weekly service from **Brisbane** to **Townsville** and the **Inlander** runs twice-weekly services to **Mount Isa**.

Magnetic Island *p93*
The island speed limit is a strict 60 kph. Fuel is available around the island.

Bus
Interstate buses stop in the centre of **Cardwell** off the Bruce Highway on Brasenose St.
Magnetic Island Bus Service, T4778 5130, runs up and down the east coast, between Picnic Bay to Horseshoe Bay every hour or so from 0600-2340. Tickets are sold on the bus from $2.50. 1-day ($15) and 2-day ($18) unlimited passes are generally the preferred option. They also offer 3-hr guided tours from Picnic Bay at 0900 and 1300 from $40, children $20.

Cycle and scooter hire
Magnetic Island Photos, Picnic Bay Mall, T4778 5411, rents bikes. **Road Runner Scooter Hire**, 64 Kelly St, T4778 5222, scooters. Bikes can also be hired from some hostels.

Ferry
Passenger ferries arrive at the Nelly Bay wharf. Vehicular ferries arrive at Geoffrey Bay, Arcadia. **Fantasea Ferries**, Ross St, Townsville South, T4796 9300, www. magneticislandferry.com.au, have regular sailings to Nelly Bay, Mon-Fri 0520-1805, Sat-Sun 0710-1805, from $164 (vehicle with up to 6 passengers) return. Passenger only $26. **Sunferries Magnetic Island**, T4726 0800, www.sunferries.com.au, offers regular daily sailings from the Bayswater Terminal to Nelly Bay 0535-1840 and from $29 return, children $15.

Moke and 4WD

One of the highlights of Maggie is exploring the island by mini-moke or toy-like 4WDs. **Moke Magnetic**, based at 112 Sooning St, Nelly Bay, T4778 5377, www.moke magnetic. com, hires mokes and vehicles seating up to 8 from about $75 per day, with 60 km of fuel for free. Deposit $200. **Tropical Topless Car Rentals**, 138 Sooning St, T4758 1111, has a fleet of colourful (and topless) 4WD, comfortable, good value and economical, from about $75 per day, flat rate, unlimited kilometres. Credit card deposit.

Hinchinbrook Island *p94*

Hinchinbrook Island Ferries, Cardwell, T4066 8270, www.hinchinbrookferries. com.au, is the main operator in Cardwell and provides the northerly access to the island (including the resort, $85). It also offers day cruises from $125, children $65. Irregular schedule Nov-May. **Hinchinbrook Wilderness Safaris** (Bill Pearce) T4777 8307, www.hinchinbrook wildernesssafaris.com. au, provide southerly access from Lucinda (from $46 one-way, $57 return), east of Ingham, and a range of day tours and cruises. Most people doing the Thorsborne Trail attempt it from north to south using **Hinchinbrook Island Ferries** for the northerly drop-off and **Hinchinbrook Wilderness Safaris** for southerly pick-up. Sailings vary according to season.

Mission Beach and Dunk Island *p109*
Air

Dunk has its own airport and regular flights are available via **Cairns** from major Australian cities. **Qantas Link** from Cairns several times daily with onward connection with **Hinterland Aviation**, T4035 9323,www. hinterlandaviation.com.au.

Boat

Quickcat, T4068 7289, www.quickcatcruises. com.au leaves Clump Point for Dunk daily at 0830, 1000 and 1400, from $56 return. Quickcat also visit the outer reef and Beaver Cay which is a beautiful spot offering much better snorkelling than Dunk Island, from $138. Quickcat offers coach pick-ups from **Cairns**. Prices vary, so do shop around. **Dunk Island Express**, T4068 8310, departs from the beach opposite their office on Banfield Parade, Wongaling Beach, 5 times daily, from $30, children $15 return. **Quick Cat Cruises** and **Dunk Island Express** offer local courtesy pick-ups.

Bus

Mission Beach Bus and Coach, T4068 7400, run the daily **Bingil Bay** to **South Mission Beach** service, single fare $3, day ticket $12, children $6. **Greyhound**, **Premier Motor Services** and **Coral Coaches** have regular daily services from north and south stopping outside the post office on Porter Promenade in Mission Beach. **Mission Beach Connections**, T4059 2709, offers daily shuttles from **Cairns** (departing 0730 arriving at 0925 and departing Mission Beach 0730 arriving **Cairns** 0945) from $47 single. It links up with the **Tilt Train** in Tully.

Queensland Outback

Daily Greyhound bus service to/from Townsville, 1 hr 40 mins, from $44. The Inlander train service operates twice-weekly services from Townsville to Mount Isa, Sun and Thu from $27. The station is on the corner of Gill St and Enterprise Rd, Charters Towers, T132232, www.traveltrain.com.au.

ⓘ Directory

Mackay and around *p84, map p85*
Banks Branches at Victoria St and Sydney St. **Hospital** Mackay Base Hospital, Bridge Rd, T4968 6000. **Internet** Easy Internet, 22 Sydney St, T4953 3331, Mon-Fri 0830-1730, Sat 0800-1300. **Hong Kong Importers Bazaar**, 128 Victoria St, T4953 3188, Mon-Fri 0845-1715, Sat-Sun 0900-1400. **Pharmacy** Night and Day, 65 Sydney St (next door to the post office). 0800-2100. **Post** 69 Sydney St. Open

Mon-Fri 0800-1700. Postcode 4740. **Useful numbers** Police, Sydney St, T4968 3444.

Airlie Beach *p87, map p87*
Banks Most (with ATMs) on Shute Harbour Rd in Airlie and Cannonvale. Currency exchange at **Magnums**. **Medical services** Whitsunday Diving Medical Centre, 257 Shute Harbour Rd, T4946 6241. **Pharmacy** Night and Day, 366 Shute Harbour Rd, Airlie, T4946 7000. **Post** Shop 6A/366-370 Shute Harbour Rd. Mon-Fri 0900-1700. **Useful numbers** Police, 8 Altmann Av, Cannonvale, T4946 6445.

Townsville *p91, map p92*
Banks Most in and around the Flinders Mall. Currency exchange at **Westpac Bank**, 337 Flinders Mall. **Hospital** Townsville Hospital, 100 Agnes Smith Drive, T4796 1111. **Internet** Internet Den, 265 Flinders Mall, T4721 4500, Mon-Fri 0900-2100, Sat-Sun 1000-2000. **Post** Sturt St, T4760 2020, Mon-Fri 0830-1730. **Useful numbers** Police, corner of Sturt and Stanley streets, T4759 7777.

Magnetic Island *p93*
Banks The post office, Nelly Bay, acts as Commonwealth Bank agents. There are ATMs at **Picnic Bay Hotel, Magnums Resort** and **Horseshoe Bay Store**. **Internet** VIC, Nelly Bay, free with bookings and in Picnic Bay at most backpackers. **Medical services** Sooning St, Nelly Bay, T4778 5614. **Pharmacy** Magnetic Island Pharmacy, Shopping Centre, 55 Sooning St Nelly Bay, T4778 5375, Mon-Fri 0900-1730, Sat 0900-1300. **Post** 98 Sooning St, Nelly Bay. Mon-Fri 0830-1700, Sat 0900-1100. Postcode 4819. **Useful numbers** Police, T4778 5270.

Mission Beach and Dunk Island *p95*
Bank/Post Post office, Porter Promenade, Mission Beach, is Commonwealth Bank Agent. ATMs in the **Mission Beach Supermarket** and at **Comfort Resort Mission Beach**. **Internet** Piccalo Paradiso, Shop 3/ 41 David St, Mission Beach, and **Mission Beach Information Station**, shop 4, **Mission Beach Resort Shops**, Wongaling Beach. **Medical services** Medical Centre, Cassowary Drive, Mission Beach, T4068 8174. **Useful numbers** Police, corner of Cassowary Drive and Web Rd, Mission Beach, T4068 8422.

Far North Queensland

Far North Queensland offers more to see and do than any other region in Australia. The bustling tourist centre of Cairns is the gateway to the Great Barrier Reef and Wet Tropics Rainforest that, between them, offer a seemingly endless choice of activities, from world-class diving to wilderness outback tours. West of Cairns the lush, green plateau of the Atherton Tablelands is a cool retreat from the coast, while to the north, Cape Tribulation and Port Douglas are popular excursions. Few venture beyond Port Douglas but those adventurous souls who try will experience the very best that 4WD has to offer, and be exposed to some of Australia's true wilderness.

Cairns → *For listings, see pages 126-138.*

Wedged between rolling hills to the west, the ocean to the east and thick mangrove swamps to the north and south, Cairns is the second most important tourist destination in Australia, only after Sydney. With the phenomenal Great Barrier Reef on its doorstep, Cairns was always destined to become a major tourist hotspot, but the attractions don't end there. With the ancient rainforest of Daintree National Park just to the north, this is one of the very few places on earth where two such environmentally rich and diverse World Heritage listed national parks meet.

Ins and outs
Getting there Many hotels and hostels provide shuttle services to and from the airport, on the northern outskirts of the town, www.cairnsairport.com.au. **Coral Reef Coaches** ⓘ *T4098 2800, www.coralreefcoaches.com.au*, offers regular services to and from the city and throughout the region, from $15. **Cairns City Airporter (Australia Coach)** ⓘ *T4087 2900*, runs services to the city and to/from Port Douglas, Cape Tribulation and Mission Beach. A taxi costs about $20, T131008. The interstate coach terminal is next to the Reef Fleet Terminal on Spence Street. Cairns Railway Station is located beside Cairns Central Shopping Complex. Coach and rail services from all major towns nearby, Brisbane and beyond. ➼ *See Transport, page 136.*

Getting around The centre of Cairns is compact and easily negotiable on foot. The waterfront with its new lagoon complex serves as the social focus of the city during the day along with the many hostels, hotels, shops and restaurants along the Esplanade and in the CBD. South of the CBD, the new Lagoon and Trinity Pier complex gives way to Trinity Inlet and Trinity Wharf, where the reef ferry and interstate coach terminals are based. Local bus operators serve the outskirts of the city. Bike hire is readily available. Buy maps from **Absells Map Shop**, Main Street Arcade off Lake Street (85), T4041 2699.

Cairns

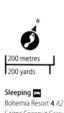

200 metres
200 yards

Sleeping

Bohemia Resort **4** *A2*
Cairns Coconut Caravan
Resort **32** *E1*
Cairns Holiday Park **6** *A1*
Cairns Rainbow Inn **9** *C2*
Caravella Hostels **10** *D4, E4*
Dreamtime Travellers
Rest **13** *F1*
Fig Tree Lodge & Willie
McBride's **14** *A2*
Geckos **16** *F1*
Gilligan's Backpackers
Resort **27** *F3*
Hides **18** *F3*
Kookas B&B **29** *A2*
Njoy **20** *D2*
Nomads Beach House **5** *A2*
Travellers Oasis **26** *F1*

Eating

Adelphi's Greek Taverna **8** *E3*
Barnacle Bill's **1** *F4*
Café China **3** *G3*
Dundee's **5** *G3*
Fish D'Vine **19** *G3*
Fusion Organics **2** *E3*
Gaura Nitai's Vegetarian **6** *G3*
International Food Court **7** *F4*
Mudslide Café **4** *E3*
Red Ochre Restaurant **13** *F3*

Bars & clubs

Cairns Rhino Bar
& Bistro **10** *F4*
Courthouse Hotel **11** *F4*
PJ O'Briens **12** *F3*
Trybox **13** *G3*
Tropos **10** *F3*
Woolshed **18** *F3*

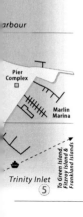

arbour

Pier
Complex

Marlin
Marina

Trinity Inlet
(5)

To Green Island,
Fitzroy Island &
Frankland Islands

Tourist information The number of independent commission-based information centres and operators in Cairns is famously out of control. For objective information and advice on accommodation and especially activities, visit the accredited **Tourism Tropical North Queensland** ① *Gateway Discovery Centre, 51 the Esplanade, T4051 3588, www.tropicalaustralia.com.au, 0830-1730.* The **QPWS office** ① *5B Sheridan St, T4046 6602, www.epa.qld.gov.au, Mon-Fri 0830-1630,* has detailed information on national parks and the Barrier Reef Islands, including camping permits and bookings. Also useful are www.wettropics.gov.au and www.greatbarrierreef.org.

Sights

The majority of tourist activities in Cairns are focused on the Great Barrier Reef. The choice is vast and includes diving and snorkelling, cruising, sailing, kayaking and flightseeing. On land the choices are no less exciting with everything from bungee jumping to ballooning. See page 132 for details. The city itself also has many colourful attractions.

The **Lagoon Complex**, which overlooks the mudflats of Trinity Bay, is the city's biggest attraction and its new social hub. Cleverly designed and with shades of the popular Brisbane and Airlie Beach urban lagoons, it is now the place to see and be seen. A café and changing rooms are onsite.

Cairns Regional Art Gallery ① *corner of Abbott St and Shields St, T4046 4800, www.cairnsregionalgallery.com.au, Mon-Sat 1000-1700, Sun 1300-1700, $5, free for children,* is housed in the former 1936 Public Curators Offices. Since 1995 the gallery has been an excellent showcase for mainly local and regional art as well as national visiting and loan exhibitions. The **KickArts Centre of Contemporary Arts** ① *96 Abbott St, T4050 9494, www.kickarts.org.au, Tue-Sat 1000-1700, café and bar from 1100-late, free,* intriguingly guarded on the outside by five man-sized jelly babies, is home to three resident arts companies and is never short of artistic programmes. Visiting international exhibitions also feature. Also worth a visit is the **Tanks Art Centre** ① *46 Collins Av, T4032 6600, www.tanksartscentre.com, Mon-Fri 1000-1600*, on the northern outskirts of the city. Three former diesel storage tanks are now used as a dynamic exhibition and performance space for the local arts community.

The **Rainforest Dome** ① *T4031 7250, www.cairnsdome.com.au, 0800-1800, $22, children $11*, housed in the glass rooftop dome of the **Reef Hotel Casino**, is a strange mix of hotel, casino and small zoo, but once you are inside the dome itself it soon proves a very enjoyable experience and a far better bet than $20 on the card tables downstairs. There are over 100 creatures, from the ubiquitous koalas to 'Goliath' the salty croc. For some divine inspiration head for **St Monica's Cathedral** ① *183 Abbott St, entry by donation*, to see the unique stained glass windows known as the 'Creation Design'. The huge and spectacularly colourful display even includes the Great Barrier Reef, complete with tropical fish. Leaflets are on hand to guide you through the design.

If you know very little about the reef and its myriad fascinating and colourful inhabitants, and especially if you are going snorkelling or are a first-time reef diver, you would greatly benefit from an appointment with **Reef Teach** ① *2nd floor, Mainstreet Arcade, between Lake St and Grafton St, T4031 7794, www.reefteach.com.au, Tue-Sat show at 1830, $15*. Created by the rather over-animated Irish marine biologist and diver Paddy Cowell and his equally enthusiastic staff, it offers an entertaining two-hour lecture on the basics of the reef's natural history, conservation and fish/coral identification.

Skyrail Rainforest Cableway and Kuranda Scenic Railway

Skyrail ① *T4038 1555, www.skyrail.com.au, daily 0815-1715, $42 one way ($61 return), children $21 ($31), price excludes Cairns transfers*. **Kuranda Scenic Railway** ① *T4036 9333, www.ksr.com.au, departs Cairns 0830 and 0930 (except Sat), departs Kuranda 1400 and 1530, $45 single ($68 return), children $23*.

The award-winning Skyrail Rainforest Cableway, 15 minutes north of Cairns on the Captain Cook Highway, is highly recommended in both fine or wet weather and is perhaps best combined with a day tour package to Kuranda via the Kuranda Scenic Railway (see below). The once highly controversial Skyrail Gondola project was completed in 1995 and at 7.5 km is the longest cable-gondola ride in the world. It gives visitors the unique opportunity to glide quietly above the pristine rainforest canopy and through the heart of the World Heritage listed **Barron Gorge National Park**.

From the outset the mere prospect of such an intrusion into the ancient forest caused international uproar. Botanists and conservationists the world over were immediately up in arms and high-profile local demonstrations took place. But for once, all the fears and protestations proved groundless and now Skyrail has proved a highly impressive project that encompasses environmental sensitivity and education, with a generous dash of fun thrown in for good measure.

The journey includes two stops: one to take in the views and guided rainforest boardwalk from Red Peak Station (545 m) and another at Barron Falls Station where you can look around the entertaining Rainforest Interpretative Centre before strolling down to the lookouts across the **Barron River Gorge** and **Barron Falls**. The interpretative centre offers a range of displays and some clever computer software depicting the sights and sounds of the forest both day and night, while the short walkway to the falls lookout passes some rather unremarkable remains of the 1930s Barron Falls hydroelectric scheme construction camp. A word of warning here: prepare to be disappointed. Ignore the postcards or promotional images you see of thunderous, Niagara-like falls. They only look like that after persistent heavy rain and/or during the wet season. Sadly, for much of the year – from April to December – the falls are little more than a trickle. From the Barron Falls Station you then cross high above the Barron River before reaching civilization again at the pretty Kuranda Terminal. When crossing the rainforest you may be lucky enough to see the unmistakable Ulysses butterfly, which has now become a fitting mascot symbolic of the North Queensland rainforest.

The Kuranda Scenic Railway wriggles its way down the Barron Gorge to Cairns and provides an ideal way to reach the pretty village of Kuranda (see page 119). To add to the whole experience, you are transported in a historic locomotive, stopping at viewpoints along the way (which provides respite from the rambling commentary). Skyrail can be combined with the Kuranda Scenic Railway for around $88, children $44. Tickets available on the web, from travel agents, tour desks, hotels, motels, caravan parks and at the VIC.

Tjapukai

ⓘ T4042 9900, www.tjapukai.com.au, 0900-1700, day rates $35, children $17.50; night rates $99, children $50.

Tjapukai, pronounced 'Jaboguy', is an award-winning, multimillion dollar Aboriginal Cultural Park lauded as one of the best of its kind in Australia. It is the culmination of many years of quality performance by the local Tjapukai tribe. The 11-ha site, located next to the Skyrail terminal in Smithfield, offers an entertaining and educational insight into Aboriginal mythology, customs and history and, in particular, that of the Tjapukai. The complex is split into various dynamic theatres that explore dance, language, storytelling and history and there is also a mock-up camp where you can learn about traditional tools, food and hunting techniques. For many, the highlight is the opportunity to learn how to throw a boomerang or to play a didgeridoo properly without asphyxiating. To make the most of the experience give yourself at least half a day. Tjapukai also offers a new 'Tjapukai by Night experience', which begins at 1930 with an interactive, traditional and dramatic *corroboree* ritual, which is followed by an impressive buffet of regional foods and an entertaining stage show. Transfers are readily available for an extra charge and there's a shop and quality restaurant.

Other excursions

North of the airport the thick mangrove swamps give way to the more alluring northern beaches and the expensive oceanside resorts of **Trinity Beach** and **Palm Cove**. Both make an attractive base to stay outside the city or a fine venue in which to swing a golf club or to catch some rays. The VIC has listings. Other than Trinity Beach and Palm Cove the most northerly of the beaches, **Ellis Beach** is recommended. The northern beaches are also home to the **Cairns Tropical Zoo** ⓘ *Clifton Beach, 22 km, T4055 3669, www.cairnstropical zoo.com, 0830-1730, $32, children $16*, which houses crocs, snakes, wombats and a range of species unique to tropical North Queensland. It is very touchy-feely and there are various shows on offer with everybody's favourite – the 'Cuddle a Koala Photo Session' – taking place daily at 0930 and 1430, $16 extra.

Some 40 km north of Cairns, on the road to Port Douglas, is **Hartley's Crocodile Adventures** ⓘ *T4055 3576, www.crocodileadventures.com, 0830-1700, $32, children $16*, one of the best wildlife attractions in the region. Long-term resident and near octogenarian croc 'Charlie', was, until his death in September 2000, the star exhibit. Despite his demise, the park has been greatly enhanced by a recent relocation and impressive renovations, and still hosts plenty of heavyweights (fed daily at 1100 and 1500). There are plenty of other animals in evidence, including the ubiquitous koala, wallabies and cassowaries. There's also a restaurant and shop. Just north of Hartley's Creek is the Rex Lookout from where you can get your first glimpse of Port Douglas and the forested peaks of the Daintree National Park and Cape Tribulation in the distance.

Northern Great Barrier Reef islands → *For listings, see pages 126-138.*

Cairns is the principal access point to the some of the top attractions of the Great Barrier Reef. The GBR is sometimes referred to as the largest single living entity on earth and is certainly the largest coral reef on the planet, stretching 2000 km from Cape York to the Tropic of Capricorn and up to 250 km at its widest point. Diving is the great attraction here, but if that's not your thing, then you should at least take a day cruise to one of the islands to sample the good life and go snorkelling. If you seek solitude there are a number of islands that can be visited independently and where camping is permitted, but you must arrange all transportation. Bookings and permits are essential. For information contact the QPWS Office in Cairns. For Lizard Island, see page 125.

Green Island
Once you arrive in Cairns it won't take long before you see postcards of Green Island, a small outcrop of lush vegetation, fringed with white sand and surrounded by azure and green reefs. The island, named after Charles Green, the chief observer and astronomer on board Captain Cook's ship, *Endeavour*, is a textbook cay – formed by dead coral – and will fulfil most people's fantasy of a tropical island. Only 45 minutes (27 km) away by boat, and part of the inner reef, it is the closest island to Cairns and, at 15 ha, one of the smallest islands on the reef. It is home to an exclusive resort but is designed more the day tripper in mind, with concrete pathways leading to food outlets, bars, dive and souvenir shops, a pool and some well-trodden beaches.

Despite its size, you can still grab a snorkel and mask and find a quiet spot on the bleached white sand. The best place to snorkel is by the pier itself, where the fish love to congregate around the pylons. Here you may see what appears to be a large shark. It is, in fact, a shark ray or 'bucket mouth', a charming and friendly bottom feeder and totally harmless. Another fine set of dentures can be seen at **Marineland Melanesia** ⓘ *T4051 4032, 0930-1600, $15, children $7.50,* in the heart of the island, with its small collection of aquariums and marine artefacts, all presided over by Cassius, a crocodile with plenty of attitude. If you are unable to go diving or snorkelling, you can still experience the vast array of colourful fish and corals from a glass-bottom boat or a small underwater observatory ($6) both located by the pier. Although nothing remarkable, the latter was reputedly the first underwater observatory in the world.

There are a number of tour options for Green Island, giving you the opportunity to combine, diving and/or snorkelling to the outer islands with a few hours exploring the island. Or you may just want to pay the ferry fare and use the island's facilities, go snorkelling or laze on the beach. You can walk right round the island (1.5 km) in 20 minutes.

Fitzroy Island
Fitzroy, part of the inner reef, just 6 km off the mainland and 25 km south of Cairns, is a large 339-ha continental island surrounded by coral reef. It is mountainous and offers more of an escape than the others, with pleasant walking tracks through dense eucalyptus

and tropical rainforests rich in wildlife. One of the most popular walks is a 4-km circuit to the island's highest point, 269 m, with its memorable views and modern lighthouse. A scattering of quiet beaches provide good snorkelling and diving. The best beach is **Nudey Beach** which is not, as the name suggests, a base for naturists. It can be reached in about 20 minutes from the island's resort. Fitzroy was used by the Gunghandji Aboriginal people as a fishing base for thousands of years and in the 1800s by itinerants harvesting bêche-de-mer, or sea cucumbers. It is named after Augustus Fitzroy, Duke of Grafton, who was the British prime minister when the *Endeavour* left England.

Frankland Islands

A further 20 km south of Fitzroy Island is the Frankland Group, a small cluster of continental islands of which 77 ha are designated a national park. The islands are covered in rainforest and fringed with white sand beaches and coral reef. They offer a wonderfully quiet retreat in comparison to the larger, busier islands. There are QPWS camping areas on Russell and High Islands. Permits and bookings can be obtained through the QPWS in Cairns.

Atherton Tablelands → *For listings, see pages 126-138.*

The Atherton Tablelands extend inland in a rough semi-circle from the Cairns coast to the small mining settlements of Mount Molloy in the north, Chillagoe in the west and Mount Garnet in the south: in total an area about the size of Ireland. At an average height of over 800 m, and subsequently the wettest region in Queensland, the Atherton Tablelands are most extraordinary: here, you'll find lush fields and plump cattle, tropical forests busting with birdsong, huge brimming lakes, high – and at times thunderous – waterfalls and even kangaroos that live in trees (see page 122). The further west you go the drier it gets until, at the edge of the Great Divide Range, the vast emptiness of the outback takes over. Given their inherent beauty, the Tablelands, especially the small and pretty settlements like Yungaburra, are the favourite retreat of Queensland's coastal dwellers, as well as tourists in search of peace and quiet, greenery and, above all, cooler temperatures.

Ins and outs

Getting there and around If you are short of time the best way to see the region is as part of a tour from Cairns. Otherwise, the Tablelands are best explored using your own transport. There are four access roads from the coast: from the south via Palmerston Highway (north of Innisfail) through the scenic tropical rainforests of Wooroonooran National Park and Millaa Millaa; from Cairns, south via Gordonvale and the steeply climbing Gillies Highway; north via Smithfield, the Kuranda Range Road and Kuranda; and from Port Douglas via the Rex Range Road and Kennedy Highway. **Trans North**, T4095 8644, www.transnorthbus.com, provides daily services to Atherton, Yungaburra, Mareeba and Kuranda. To arrive via Kuranda Scenic Railway or Skyrail Gondola, see page 114. ▸▸ *See Transport, page 137.*

Tourist information Research the region from the VIC in Cairns. **Tropical Tableland Promotion Bureau** ① *corner of Silo Rd and Main St, Atherton, T4091 4222, www. athertontableland.com*, is the principal accredited regional body. For parks information contact the QPWS office in Cairns. **Kuranda VIC** ① *Centenary Park, Therwine St, T4093 9311, www.kuranda.org, 1000-1600*, has maps and accommodation, tours and activities details.

Around Cairns & the Atherton Tablelands

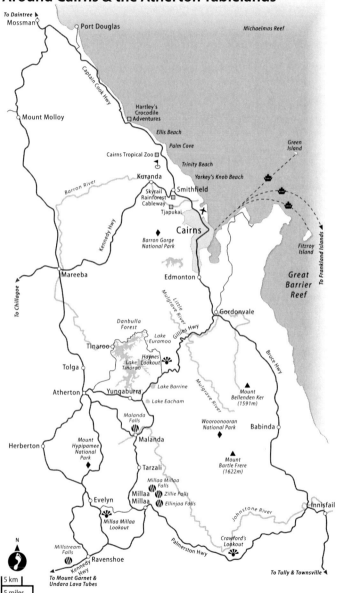

To Daintree
Mossman
Port Douglas
Michaelmas Reef
Captain Cook Hwy
Mount Molloy
Hartley's Crocodile Adventures
Ellis Beach
Palm Cove
Green Island
Cairns Tropical Zoo
Trinity Beach
Yorkey's Knob Beach
Barron River
Kuranda
Skyrail Rainforest Cableway
Smithfield
Tjapukai
Cairns
Fitzroy Island
Kennedy Hwy
Barron Gorge National Park
To Frankland Islands
Great Barrier Reef
Mareeba
Edmonton
To Chillagoe
Little Mulgrave River
Gordonvale
Danbulla Forest
Gillies Hwy
Lake Euramoo
Tinaroo
Haynes Lookout
Lake Tinaroo
Mulgrave River
Bruce Hwy
Mount Bellenden Ker (1591m)
Tolga
Lake Barrine
Lake Eacham
Atherton
Yungaburra
Wooroonooran National Park
Babinda
Malanda Falls
Herberton
Mount Hypipamee National Park
Malanda
Mount Bartle Frere (1622m)
Tarzali
Millaa Millaa Falls
Zillie Falls
Millaa Millaa
Evelyn
Ellinjaa Falls
Johnstone River
Innisfail
Millaa Millaa Lookout
Crawford's Lookout
N
Millstream Falls
Ravenshoe
Kennedy Hwy
Palmerston Hwy
5 km
5 miles
To Mount Garnet & Undara Lava Tubes
To Tully & Townsville

Kuranda

The small, arty settlement of Kuranda has become the main tourist attraction in the Atherton Tablelands, thanks to its proximity to Cairns, a scenic railway and its markets. But while there's no doubting its appeal, particularly the spectacular means of access, Kuranda has, to a large extent, become a victim of its own popularity. The town was first put on the map in 1891 with the completion of the railway, providing a vital link between the Hodgkinson Gold Fields and the coast.

Kuranda's main attraction is its permanent markets: **Heritage Markets** ① *just off Veivers Drive, daily 0900-1500*, and the nearby **Original Markets** ① *Therwine St, daily 0900-1500*. Other stalls and permanent shops are also strung along the village's main drag, **Coondoo Street**. The emphasis is on souvenirs, with much of it being expensive and tacky, but there are some artists and craftspeople producing pieces that are both unusual and good quality, so shop around. In addition to the markets themselves, the **Australis Gallery** ① *26 Coondoo St*, is worth a look, showcasing some fine work by local artists.

Below the Heritage Markets is **Koala Gardens** ① *T4093 9953, www.koalagardens.com, 0900-1600, $16, children $8*, which offers the inevitable photo sessions for $16 on top of the admission price. Also next to the Heritage Markets is **Birdworld** ① *T4093 9188, www.birdworldkuranda.com, 0900-1600, $16, children $8*, which is a free-flight complex showcasing some of Australia's most colourful (and audible) avian species. There is much emphasis on the endangered cassowary, though the numerous parrots and lorikeets will provide the best photo opportunities.

Another wildlife attraction is the **Australian Butterfly Sanctuary** ① *8 Veivers Drive, T4093 7575, www.australianbutterflies.com, 1000-1600, $16, children $8*. It is reputedly the world's largest and houses about a dozen of the country's most brilliant and beautiful Lepidoptera in a huge free-flight enclosure, well landscaped like a rainforest complete with stream and waterfalls. A bright red or white hat is recommended.

To complete the tour of all things winged and wonderful you could also consider a visit to **Batreach** ① *T4093 8858, www.batreach.com.au, Tue-Fri and Sun 1030-1430, entry by donation*, an independent wild bat rescue and rehabilitation hospital at the far end of Barang Street. Here you will get close up and personal with a number of species, most notably, the huge flying fox – a sort of startled-looking dog on a hang-glider. Those who think bats are vicious creatures, invented by witches and horror movie makers, will have their ideas changed here. There is a large local colony of flying foxes in the **Jum Rum Creek Park**, off Thongon Street. Follow the noise – and the unmistakable musty smell.

The award-winning **Rainforestation Nature Park** ① *T4085 5008, www.rainforest. com. au, 0900-1600, attractions $40, children $20, transportation and tours extra*, is located a few kilometres east of Kuranda on the Kuranda Range Road. Set amidst a rainforest and orchard setting it offers yet another chance to experience aboriginal culture and mingle with captive native animals. There is also an exhilarating one-hour tour of the complex and rainforest in an amphibious army vehicle.

If you did not arrive in Kuranda via the Skyrail or railway and it is the wet season then take a look at the **Barron Falls**, which can be accessed via Barron Falls Road (Wrights Lookout) south of the town. In 'the Wet' the floodgates are opened above the falls and the results can be truly spectacular.

Chillagoe

Given its isolation, yet easy access, from Cairns, the former mining settlement of Chillagoe presents an ideal opportunity to experience the outback proper, without having to

Undara Lava Tubes

The Undara Lava Tubes, on the edge of the Undara Volcanic National Park, 150 km south of Ravenshoe via Mount Surprise, are an amazing 190,000-year-old volcanic feature and well worth the journey. The unusual volcanic feature was formed during a massive eruption around 200,000 years ago when lava flowed down a dry riverbed. As the top layer of lava gradually cooled and hardened, the bottom layer flowed on, forming the so-called tubes.

There are regular guided tours available, also available from Cairns, as well as a restaurant, pool and accommodation ranging from charming train carriages to a swag tent village and powered sites, YHA affiliated. **Undara Experience**, T4097 1900, www.undara.com.au, runs day trips and excellent package deals by coach, self-drive or rail to see the lava tubes, with activities and accommodation. Their Wildlife at Sunset tour (of the lava tubes) starts at $46.

embark on a long and difficult 4WD journey from the coast. It's a fascinating little place, somewhat out of character with the rest of the Atherton Tablelands, and combines mining history with natural limestone caves and Aboriginal rock paintings. Chillagoe was a cattle station before the discovery of gold in the late 1880s dramatically transformed both the settlement and the landscape. The establishment of a rail link in 1900 led to a sharp increase of incomers and for the next 40 years the area produced almost 10 tonnes of gold and 185 tonnes of silver, as well many more tonnes of copper and lead. Those boom days are long gone and the population has declined dramatically, but the town retains a hint of its former importance in the sun-baked mining relics that remain.

The **Hub Interpretative Centre** ⓘ *Queen St, T4094 7111, www.chillagoehub.com.au, 0800-1700*, is the best source of local information and introduction to the settlement's mining history and can provide directions to the most obvious mining relics. **QPWS** ⓘ *on the corner of Cathedral St and Queen St*, offers guided tours of three of the local limestone caves. There are more caves and old copper mines about 10 km west of the town at **Mungana**, also the location of some Aboriginal rock paintings.

Lake Tinaroo and Danbulla Forest

Barron River Tinaroo Dam was completed in 1958, creating a vast series of flooded valleys that now make up Lake Tinaroo and provide the region with essential irrigation. The lake itself has an astonishing 200 km of shoreline and is a popular spot for water sports, especially barramundi fishing. Indeed, some say the lake contains the biggest 'barra' in Australia. The Danbulla Forest that fringes its northern bank is bisected by 28 km of unsealed scenic road that winds its way from the dam slipway, at Tolga, to Boar Pocket Road, northeast of Yungaburra.

Other than the various campsites, viewpoints and walks on offer, highlights include **Lake Euramoo**, a picturesque double explosion crater lake, **Mobo Creek Crater**, something of a geological odyssey, and the unmissable **Cathedral Fig**. Signposted and reached by a 5-minute walk, this example of the strangler fig species is indeed a sight to behold. The tree – though it is hard to see it as such – is 500 years old, over 50 m tall and 40 m around the base and is worth visiting at dawn, when its many avian inhabitants are full of chatter. Several types of nocturnal possum also inhabit the tree and are best seen with a torch after dark.

From the Cathedral Fig you emerge from the forest onto Boar Pocket Road. The short diversion to the **Haynes Lookout**, left on Boar Pocket Road, heading from the forest towards Gillies Highway, is worthy of investigation. The track passes through beautiful woodland before emerging at the edge of the mountain and the memorable views across the **Mulgrave River Valley** and **Bellenden Ker Range**. When the winds are right the site is often used by hang-gliders. Check out the message written on the launch pad.

For more information on the Danbulla Forest scenic drive and self-registration campsites (\$2), contact the **QPWS** ① *83 Main St, Atherton, T4091 1844, or their Tinaroo Office, T4095 8459.* The area is best explored in your own vehicle or on a regional tour.

Yungaburra and around

While Kuranda may be the most visited and high profile town in the Atherton Tablelands, sleepy little Yungaburra is the main event. Formerly called Allumba, it has changed little in over a century and offers a wonderful combination of history, alternative lifestyle and a cool and tranquil retreat from the coast. As well as an impressive gathering of listed historical buildings, it has good places to stay, eat and shop and is surrounded by some of the best scenery in the Tablelands. Lakes Tinaroo, Barrine and Eacham, see below, are all within a short drive and provide the focal point for a number of walks, scenic drives and water-based activities. The most spectacular way to reach Yungaburra is via the Gillies Highway and Mulgrave River Valley just south of Cairns. From the valley floor the road climbs almost 800 m up to the top of the Gillies Range. There is currently no official visitor information centre in the village, but the locals are always glad to help. There is also a useful website, www.yungaburra.com. The local **QWPS** office ① *Lake Eacham, T4095 3768*, provides information about campsites and all things environmental.

Most of the listed historical buildings were built from local wood, between 1910 and 1920. Two of the finest examples are **St Mark's** and **St Patrick's churches**, on Eacham Road. Other fine examples are evident on Cedar Street, next to the Lake Eacham Hotel. Look out for the *Yungaburra Heritage Village* leaflet, available from the VICs in Cairns and Atherton, or from most local businesses. Just a few minutes southwest of the village, on Curtain Fig Tree Road, is the 800-year-old **Curtain Fig Tree**, another impressive and ancient example of the strangler species (*Yungaburra* is Aboriginal for fig tree).

Yungaburra is also one of the best, and most accessible, places in the country in which to see that surreal quirk of nature, the duck-billed platypus. **Peterson Creek**, which slides gently past the village, is home to several pairs. The best place to see them is from the bottom and north of Penda Street, at the end of Cedar Street, and the best time is around dawn or sometimes at dusk. Sit quietly beside the river and look for any activity in the grass that fringes the river or on its surface. They are generally well submerged but once spotted are fairly obvious. Provided you are quiet they will generally go about their business, since their eyesight is fairly poor.

A few kilometres east of the village are two volcanic lakes, **Lake Barrine** and **Lake Eacham**. Lake Barrine is the largest and has been a tourist attraction for over 80 years. It's fringed with rainforest and circled by a 6-km walking track. Two lofty and ancient kauri pines, amongst Australia's largest species, are located at the start of the track. The long-established **Lake Barrine Rainforest Cruise and Tea House** ① *T4095 3847, www.lakebarrine.com.au*, is nestled on the northern shore and offers 40-minute trips on the lake (\$15, children \$8). Just south of Lake Barrine and accessed off the Gillies Highway, or from the Malanda Road, is Lake Eacham. Once again it is surrounded by rainforest and a 3.5-km walking track and is a favourite spot for a picnic and a cool dip. The most southerly fingers of Lake Tinaroo can also be accessed northeast of the village via Barrine Road.

Malanda and Millaa Millaa

The little village of Malanda marks the start of the famous Tablelands waterfalls region. Malanda has its own set of falls but they are actually amongst the least impressive in the group and the village is more famous for milk than water. Dairying has always been the raison d'être in Malanda. The first herds of cattle were brought by foot from the north of NSW – a journey that took a gruelling 16 months. Today, there are over 190 farmers in the region producing enough milk to make lattes and shakes from here to Alice Springs. The main attraction, other than a cool dip in the swimming hole below the falls, is the neighbouring **Malanda Falls Environmental Centre and Visitors Information** ⓘ *T4096 6957, 0930-1630,* which has some interesting displays on the geology, climate and natural history of the Tablelands.

A further 24 km south of Malanda is the sleepy agricultural service town of Millaa Millaa, which also has waterfalls and is surrounded by fields of black and white Friesian cattle. The **Millaa Millaa Falls** are the first of a trio – the others being the **Zillie Falls** and **Ellinjaa Falls** – which can be explored on a 16-km circuit accessed (and signposted) just east of the town on the **Palmerston Highway**, which links with the Bruce Highway just north of Innisfail. There are a few lesser-known waterfalls on the way and Crawford's Lookout, on the left, with its dramatic view through the forest to the North Johnstone River – a favourite spot for rafting.

The **Millaa Millaa Lookout** (at 850 m) just to the west of Millaa Millaa on the recently upgraded East Evelyn Road, is said to offer the best view in North Queensland. On a clear day you can see 180 degrees from the Tablelands to the coast, interrupted only by the Bellenden Ker Range and the two highest peaks in Queensland, Mount Bartle Frere (1622 m) and Mount Bellenden Ker (1591 m).

South of here are the impressive volcanic Undara Lava Tubes, see box above.

Mount Hypipamee National Park

Mount Hypipamee National Park is a small pocket of dense rainforest with a volcanic crater lake, waterfalls and some very special wildlife. During the day the trees are alive with the sound of many exotic birds such as the tame Lewin's honeyeaters, but it is at night that it really comes into its own. Armed with a torch and a little patience (preferably after midnight) you can see several of the 13 species of possum that inhabit the forest, including the coppery brush tail, the green ringtail, and the squirrel glider who leaps and flies from branch to branch. If you are really lucky you may also encounter the park's most famous resident, the Lumholtz's tree kangaroo, one of only two species of kangaroo that live in trees.

The 95,000-year-old **Crater Lake** – which is, in fact, a long, water-filled volcanic pipe blasted through the granite – is a 10-minute walk from the car park. With its unimaginable depths, algae-covered surface and eerie echoes it is quite an unnerving spectacle, like some horrific natural dungeon. The park has picnic facilities but no camping.

Port Douglas and the Daintree → For listings, see pages 126-138.

Almost since their inception the coastal ports of Cairns and Port Douglas, just 70 km apart, have slugged it out as to which is the most important. Although Cairns has gone on to become a world-famous tourist heavyweight, lesser-known Port Douglas has always known been sure it is a classier option, with its boutiques, fine restaurants and upmarket accommodation. Given its proximity to the Barrier Reef, the Mossman Gorge, Daintree and

Cape Tribulation, Port Douglas has never had a problem attracting tourist dollars, though the building of massive developments and multimillion dollar resorts will result in it losing its village feel and much of its charm.

Ins and outs

Port Douglas Tourist Information Centre ① *23 Macrossan St, T4099 5599, www.pddt.com. au, 0830-1800.* Mossman has the nearest **QPWS office** ① *1 Front St, T4098 2188, www.epa. qld.gov.au.* **Daintree Tourist Information Centre** ① *Stewart St, T4098 6120, www.daintree village.asn.au.* For Daintree and local walks information contact the QPWS office in Cairns, see page 113, or visit www.port-douglas-daintree.com.

Port Douglas

Like Cairns, Port Douglas places great emphasis on reef and rainforest tours, with only a few attractions in the town itself pulling in the crowds. See page 132 for details of the activities available in the area. About 6 km from the centre of town, at the junction of Captain Cook Highway and Port Douglas Road, the **Rainforest Habitat Wildlife Sanctuary** ① *T4099 3235, www.rainforesthabitat.com.au, 0800-1730, $30, children $15*, is well worth a visit, offering a fine introduction to the region's rich biodiversity and natural habitats. There are over 180 species housed in three main habitat enclosures – wetlands, rainforest and grassland – with many of the tenants being tame and easily approachable. 'Breakfast with the Birds' (0800-1100, $44, children $22, see page 131) is an enjoyable way to start the day, while 'Habitat After Dark' offers a truly unique dining experience.

Port Douglas is rather proud of its lovely **Four Mile Beach**, which attracts cosmopolitan crowds of topless backpackers and the more conservative resort clients. Many water-based activities are on offer for those not satisfied with merely sunbathing or swimming. A net is placed just offshore to ward off box jellyfish and other stingers and lifeguards are usually in attendance (always swim between the flags). Before picking your spot on the sand you might like to enjoy the picture-postcard view of the beach from **Flagstaff Hill**: turn right at the bottom of Mossman Street, then follow Wharf Street on to Island point Road. **Anzac Park** hosts a market every Sunday. It is a colourful affair and offers everything from sarongs to freshly squeezed orange juice. More expensive permanent boutiques are housed in the delightfully cool **Marina Mirage Complex**, Wharf Street. For further information, see www. portdouglasmarina.com.au.

Mossman Gorge and the Daintree Wilderness National Park

Built on the back of the sugar cane industry in the 1880s, **Mossman** sits on the banks of the Mossman River and has one of the world's most exotic tropical gardens at its back door in the form of the Daintree Wilderness National Park. Although the 80-year-old, fern-covered tall raintrees that form a cosy canopy on its northern fringe are a sight in themselves, it is the Mossman Gorge, some 5 km west of the town, that is its greatest attraction. Here, the Mossman River falls towards the town, fringed with rainforest and networked with a series of short walks. Many combine a walk with another big attraction – the cool swimming holes. Although the walks are excellent, you should also try following the river upstream for about 2 km – if you are fit. This will give you an ideal opportunity to see the region's most famous mascot – the huge Ulysses blue butterfly.

The tiny, former timber town of **Daintree** sits at the end of the Mossman–Daintree Road, sandwiched between the western and eastern blocks of the Daintree National Park. The village exudes a quaint and original charm and consists of an enormous model barramundi fish, a general store, a small timber museum, a couple of restaurants, a school and a caravan park. At the edge of the village is the biggest local attraction – the croc-infested **Daintree River**. Visitors can embark on a cruise on the river in search of these gargantuan saltwater crocodiles. There are several cruise operators to choose from, all of whom ply the river from Daintree village to the coast several times a day. You can either pick up the cruise near the village itself or at various points south to the Daintree/Cape Tribulation ferry crossing, but most people arrive on pre-organized tours. For independent choice and bookings call in at the general store (T4098 6146).

Cape Tribulation → *For listings, see pages 126-138.*

Although Cape Tribulation is the name attributed to a small settlement and headland that forms the main tourist focus of the region, the term itself is loosely used to describe a 40-km stretch of coastline within Daintree National Park and the start of the Bloomfield Track to Cooktown. It was Captain Cook who bestowed the name 'Tribulation', just before his ship *Endeavour* ran aground here in 1770. This and other names, such as Mount Sorrow, Mount Misery and Darkie's Downfall, are indeed fitting for a place of such wild and, at times, inhospitable beauty. People come to this remote wilderness not only to witness a rainforest rich in flora and fauna, but also to experience nature in the raw.

Ins and outs
Tourist information   Detailed information can be obtained from the VICs in Port Douglas or Cairns. Local information is available from Daintree Discovery Centre or Bat House (see page 125). For walks information contact the **QPWS** office in Cairns, see page 113. The **Australian Rainforest Foundation** website, www.wettropics.com.au, is also useful.

Sights
Five kilometres beyond the ferry crossing, the Cape Tribulation Road climbs steadily over the densely forested Waluwurriga Range to reach **Mount Alexandra Lookout**, offering the first glimpse of the coast and the mouth of the Daintree River. Turning back inland and 2 km past the lookout, is the turn-off (east) to the **Daintree Discovery Centre** ① *T4098 9171, www.daintree-rec.com.au, 0830-1700, $28, children $14*, with excellent displays on the local flora and fauna, and the added attraction of a 400-m boardwalk where guided walks are available as well as a 25-m canopy tower offering a bird's-eye view of the forest canopy. There's also a pleasant café from which to sit back and let the forest wildlife pervade the senses. Back on Cape Tribulation Road and just beyond the centre is the settlement of **Cow Bay** with its attractive bay and beach that can be reached by road 6 km to the east on Buchanan Creek Road.

Continuing north you are then given another interesting reminder that you are in the tropics by passing a well-manicured tea plantation before crossing Cooper Creek and hitting the coast below Mount Emmett. Oliver Creek then sees the first of a duo of excellent boardwalks, which provide insight into the botanical delights of the forest and mangrove swamps. **Marrdja boardwalk** takes about 45 minutes and is well worth a look. From here it is about 9 km to the settlement of Cape Tribulation. Here, too, is the second and equally interesting 1.2-km **Dubuji boardwalk**, taking about 45 minutes.

The headland at Cape Tribulation is also well worthy of investigation, as are its two beautiful beaches – **Emmagen** and **Myall** – that sit either side like two golden bookends. The Kulki picnic area and lookout is at the southern end of Emmagen Beach and is signposted just beyond the village. Just beyond that, the Kulki turn-off – 150 m – is the start of the **Mount Sorrow track**, a challenging 3.5-km ascent rewarded with spectacular views from the 650-m summit.

While in Cape Tribulation be sure to visit the **Bat House** ① *T4098 0063, Tue-Sun, 1030-1530, $4 donation at least,* opposite PK's Backpackers. Although you won't encounter the saviour of Gotham City, you will find the saviours of the local bat population, in the form of volunteers who tend the needs of injured and orphaned flying foxes. A range of interesting wildlife displays are also on view.

Beyond Cape Tribulation the road gradually degenerates to form the notorious, controversial blot on the landscape known as **Bloomfield Track**. From here you are entering real 'Tiger Country' and a 4WD is essential. A 2WD will get you only as far as Emmagen Creek, which offers a limited incursion into the fringes of the dense rainforest and some good swimming holes – thankfully, too clear and shallow for local crocodiles.

Cooktown → *For listings, see pages 126-138.*

Like Cairns and Port Douglas, Cooktown has grown in stature as an attractive lifestyle proposition and a popular tourist destination. There is plenty to see and do here, with the James Cook Museum the undeniable highlight. **Cookshire Council** ① *T4069 5444,* and **Nature's Powerhouse** ① *Finch Bay Road, T4069 6004, www.cooktowns.com,* cover visitor information services.

A good place to start is from the **Grassy Hill Lighthouse**, which is reached after a short climb at the end of Hope Street, north of the town centre. Here you can take in the views of the coast and town from the same spot Captain Cook reputedly worked out his safe passage back through the reef to the open sea. The old corrugated iron lighthouse that dominates the hill was built in England and shipped to Cooktown in 1885. For decades it served local and international shipping before being automated in 1927 and becoming obsolete in the 1980s. From Hope Street it is a short walk to the **James Cook Museum** ① *corner of Furneaux St and Helen St, T4069 5386, Apr-Jan 0930-1600 (reduced hours Feb-Mar), $8, children $3,* housed in a former convent built in 1889 and touted as one of the most significant museums in Australia. The museum is not dedicated solely to Cook; it also houses interesting displays covering the town's colourful and cosmopolitan history. Other sites of historical interest include the Cooktown Cemetery, at the southern edge of town along Endeavour Valley Road, where many former pioneers are buried.

Lizard Island is home to Australia's most northerly, and most exclusive, reef island resort (see page 130). The island lies 27 km off Cooktown and is almost 1000 ha, with the vast majority of that being national park. Tranquil and pristine with fantastic diving and snorkelling, it makes for a great trip. All the delights of the other popular islands are on offer without the hordes of tourists. There are over 24 tranquil beaches, backed by lush forests, mangroves and bush, all abundant in wildlife, while just offshore, immaculate, clear water reefs offer superb diving and snorkelling. The famous Cod Hole is considered one of the best dive sites on the reef and the island is also a popular base for big game fishermen in search of the elusive black marlin. A delightful walking track leads to Cook's Look, which at 359 m is the highest point on the island and the place where Captain Cook stood in 1770 trying to find passage through the reef. The island was named by Joseph Banks, the ship's naturalist, who must have kept himself busy searching for lizards as Cook struggled to find a way back out to the ocean.

Far North Queensland listings

😑 Sleeping

Cairns p111, map p112

There is plenty of choice and something to suit all budgets. Most of the major hotels and countless backpackers are in the heart of the city, especially along the Esplanade, while most motels are located on the main highways in and out of town. If you are willing to splash out, want access to a proper beach and wish to escape the city, ask at the VIC about the numerous apartment and resort options at Palm Beach and other northern beach resorts (about 20 mins north of the city). Prices fluctuate according to season, with some going through the roof at peak times (May-Sep). Prices are often reduced and special deals are offered through 'the Wet' (Jan-Mar). Despite the wealth of accommodation pre-booking is still advised. Cairns and TNQ Accommodation Centre, corner of Sheridan St and Alpin St, T4051 4066, www.accomcentre.com.au, can also be of assistance.

B&Bs

$$$ Fig Tree Lodge, 253 Sheridan St, T4041 0000, www.figtreelodge.com.au. More like a motel than a lodge, but fine facilities, a warm welcome and a bar.

$$$ Kookas B&B, 40 Hutchinson St, Edge Hill, T4053 3231, www.kookas-bnb.com. Some 10 km from city centre, a traditional modern home in an elevated position, 3 en suites tastefully decorated, friendly owners and lots of visiting kookaburras.

Backpackers

There is plenty of choice of backpackers with over 30 establishments, almost all within easy reach of the city centre. Most people gravitate towards the Esplanade where a string of places sit, virtually side by side, but you are advised to look into other options too.

Another small cluster of quieter hostels lies just west of the railway station. All offer the usual facilities and range of dorms, twins and doubles. Look for rooms with a/c or at least a powerful fan and windows that open, and check for approved fire safety regulations.

$$ Bohemia Resort, 231 McLeod St, T4041 7290, www.bohemiaresort.com.au. A little further out of the centre is this modern, excellent option. It is more like a tidy modern motel with great doubles and a pool. Regular shuttles to town.

$$ Caravella Hostels, at 77 the Esplanade, T4051 2159, and 149 the Esplanade, T4051 2431, www.caravella.com.au. Both are modern, with good facilities, a/c doubles and free meals.

$$ Dreamtime Travellers Rest, 4 Terminus St, T4031 6753, www.dreamtimetravel.com.au. Homely and friendly with a great atmosphere, well equipped with good facilities and a great pool and spa, as well as proper beds, not bunks.

$$ Geckos, 187 Bunda St, T4031 1344, www.geckosbackpackers.com.au. Rambling and spacious Queenslander with good facilities and caring staff. Rooms are spacious, have fans rather than a/c but are well ventilated. Good for doubles.

$$ Gilligan's Backpackers Hotel and Resort, 57 Grafton St, T4041 6566, www.gilligansbackpackers.com.au. Causing something of a stir in backpacking circles, this is one of a new breed, pitched somewhere between a backpackers and modern 3-star hotel. There is no doubting its class or range of facilities. It has a large pool, internet café, chic bar with dance floor and big screen TV. Rooms vary from spacious doubles with TV and futon lounge to traditional dorms.

$$ Njoy, 141 Sheridan St, T4031 1088, www.innthetropics.com. A quality option with single rooms, good motel-style doubles. Good pool. Also suitable for families.

$$ Nomads Beach House, 239 Sheridan St, T4041 4116, www.cairnsbeachhouse.com.au. North of the centre is this popular option with all the usual facilities, especially noted for its pool, beer/bistro garden and party atmosphere. Courtesy coach into town.

$$ Travellers Oasis, 8 Scott St, T4052 1377, www.travoasis.com.au. A large place that still maintains a pleasant quiet atmosphere, offering a good range of a/c rooms including value doubles ($64) and pool.

Motels, motor parks and apartments

There are endless motel and apartment options, with the vast majority offering the standard clean, spacious rooms and usual facilities, including the almost obligatory tropical flower paintings and palm tree-fringed swimming pools. Most motels are located on the main drag in and out of town (Sheridan St). If you are looking for a caravan park you are advised to base yourself in the northern beaches.

$$$$ Cairns Coconut Caravan Resort, on the Bruce Highway (about 6 km south, corner of Anderson Rd), T4054 6644, www.coconut.com.au. Offering sheer class and with all mod cons, this is one of the best in the country.

$$$ Cairns Rainbow Inn, 179 Sheridan St, T4051 1022, www.rainbowinn.com.au. A colourful good value motel with standard room options, restaurant, pool and spa.

$$$ Hides, 87 Lake St, T4051 1266, www.hideshotel.com.au. Historical and well-placed apartments offering budget options with shared facilities.

$$ Cairns Holiday Park, corner of James St and Little St, T4051 1467, www.cairnscamping.com.au. If you prefer to be in the city this is the best placed for sheer convenience and has been recently redeveloped to include a pool, TV and internet room and modern camp kitchen.

Atherton Tablelands p117, map p118

Although Kuranda attracts the tourist hordes like bees to honey, once the last train leaves and peace returns it can be a wonderful place to stay away from the usual coastal haunts. However, there aren't too many options and for something more luxurious you have to look further afield than Kuranda.

$$$$ Allumbah Pocket Cottages, 24-26 Gillies Highway, Yungaburra, T4095 3023, www.allumbahpocketcottages.com.au. A cluster of spacious and well-appointed, 1-bedroom and fully self-contained cottages complete with spa. The friendly and welcoming owners also offer 2 other exceptional 2-bedroom cottages, at 7/9 Pine St, ideal for romantic couples.

$$$$ Canopy Rainforest Tree Houses, between Malanda and Millaa Millaa (2.5 km on Hogan Rd east of Tarzali), T4096 5364, www.canopytreehouses.com.au. Five charming, fully self-contained pole houses set in wildife-rich bush offering real peace and quiet and all mod cons including a spa. There is also a fully self-contained 3-bedroom unit attached to the main building. Spa treatments and packages provide an added attraction.

$$$$ Kuranda Resort and Spa, 3 Greenhills Rd, Kuranda, T4093 7556, www.kurandaresortandspa.com. Just 2 km southwest of the village, this attractive new resort has a fine range of villas, a self-contained apartment and a multi-share budget option. Excellent facilities with a gym, spa, a spectacular pool, massage therapies and a fine restaurant. Recommended.

$$$ Curtain Fig Motel, 16 Gillies Highway, Yungaburra, T4095 3168, www.curtainfig.com. Good value, spacious self-contained units and a large fully self-contained apartment in the heart of the village.

$$$ Kuranda Rainforest Accommodation Park, 88 Kuranda Heights Rd, Kuranda, T4093 7316, www.kurandarainforest park.com.au. This 3-star place has cottages, cabins, powered and non-powered sites. Facilities include kitchen and pool.

$$ Kuranda Backpackers Hostel, 6 Arara St, Kuranda, T4093 7355, www.kuranda backpackershostel.com. Near the train station, this renovated 1907 traditional Queenslander is a fine if basic retreat with dorms, doubles, singles and good facilities. Pool, bike rental and pick-ups from Cairns.

$$ Lake Eacham Caravan Park, Lakes Drive, 1 km south of Lake Eacham, T4095 3730, www.lakeeachamtouristpark.com. The nearest motor park to Yungaburra. Basic but good value, it has cabins, powered and non-powered sites.

$$ Millaa Millaa Tourist Park, Malanda Rd, T4097 2290, www.millaapark.com. Closest park to the falls, 3-star, with cabins, powered and non-powered sites, pool, camp kitchen and café.

$$ On the Wallaby Backpackers, 34 Eacham Rd, Yungaburra, T4095 2031, www.onthewallaby.com. The best budget option is this excellent little backpackers offering dorms, doubles and camping for $10 (pair $15). The decor is all wood and stone, giving it a cosy ski lodge feel, very different to the bustling modern places in Cairns. Plenty of activities are on offer including an exciting range of wildlife and day/night canoeing tours on Lake Tinaroo from $30. Mountain bikes for hire. 2-day/1-night package with tour, canoeing and mountain biking for $169. Pick-ups from Cairns daily.

$$ Pteropus House B&B, corner of Carrington Rd and Hutton Rd, Atherton, T4091 2683, www.tolgabathospital.org. An excellent and unusual place to say (provided you love bats). Kind host Jenny Maclean runs not only a quality B&B with 2 tidy self-contained apartments, but a (separate) working fruit bat hospital. There is the opportunity to see some of the patients and sometimes assist in their care. Book ahead.

Port Douglas and the Daintree *p122*

There is plenty of choice in Port Douglas and though the emphasis is on 4-star resorts and apartments, budget travellers are also well catered for with a number of good backpackers, cheap motels and motor parks. Rates are naturally competitive and more expensive in the high season but at any time you are advised to shop around for special rates, especially in 'the Wet' (Dec-Mar).

Port Douglas

$$$ Glengarry Caravan Park, Mowbray River Rd, just short of Port Douglas, off the captain Cook Highway, T4098 5922, www.glengarry park.com.au. This motor park has fully self-contained en suite cabins, powered/non-powered sites, with a good camp kitchen and a pool.

$$$ Marae B&B, Lot 1, Ponzo Rd, Shannon-vale, T4098 4900, www.marae.com.au. This B&B provides an ideal sanctuary, yet is still within reach (15 km north) of Port Douglas. It is a beautiful eco-friendly place offering a cabana-style king room, close to the pool or another king within the house. Both have their own bathrooms.

$$$ Papillon B&B, 36 Coral Sea Drive, Mossman Gorge, T4098 2760, www.papillonstays.com.au. Contemporary wooden-pole house, set in a tropical garden near the Mossman Gorge. 2 well-appointed rooms with their own deck overlooking a heated pool. Both have a king-size double bed, en suite shower, a/c, fan, TV, DVD player, Wi-Fi and locally grown tea and coffee. Great hosts and excellent value.

$$ Dougie's Nomads Backpackers, 111 Davidson St, T4099 6200, www.dougies.com.au. The other good backpacker in town, this one has a/c doubles/twins, dorms and van/campsites, bar, bike hire and internet. Again, it offers free pick-ups from Cairns.

$$ Tropic Breeze Van Village, 24 Davidson St, closer to the centre of town, and only a short stroll from Four Mile Beach, T4099 5299. A 3-star motor park, it offers cabins, powered/ non-powered sites and a camp kitchen.

$$ YHA Port 'O' Call Eco Lodge, Port St, just off Davidson St, T4099 5422, www.portocall.com.au. One of 2 good backpackers in town. Motel-style with en suite doubles/twins, budget dorms and a fine restaurant/bar, pool and internet. Free pick-ups from Cairns.

Mossman Gorge and the Daintree Wilderness National Park p123

$$$$ Daintree Eco Lodge and Spa, 20 Daintree Rd, 3 km south of Daintree village, T4098 6100, www.daintree- ecolodge.com. au. This is an international multi-award winner and enjoys a good reputation, offering 15 luxury, serviced villas set in the rainforest, a specialist spa, Aboriginal and eco-based activities and a top-class restaurant. If you are looking to indulge for once – then this is it. Recommended.

$$$$ Silky Oaks Lodge, Finlayvale Road, north of Mossman, T4098 1666 www. silkyoakslodge.com.au. The most upmarket place in the immediate area. It offers de luxe designer 'riverhouses' fronting the Mossman River and superb 'treehouses' with spa. 5-star facilities including spa treatments and a fine restaurant. Complimentary activities and pick-ups are also available.

$$$ Red Mill House, Daintree village, T4098 6233, www.redmillhouse.com.au. One of a few good B&Bs in the heart of the village is this very pleasant and friendly option offering well-appointed rooms, some with shared facilities and some with en suites (separate from the main house). The place has a wonderfully peaceful atmosphere with lovely gardens and plenty of wildlife that you can watch from the deck. Good value.

$$ Daintree Riverview Caravan Park, 2 Stewart St, Daintree village, T4098 6119, www.daintreeriverview.com. En suite cabins, powered and non-powered sites right in the heart of the village. Modern amenities block.

Cape Tribulation p124

There is a wide range of accommodation in and around the Cape, though prices are well above the norm for north Queensland.

$$$ Cape Trib Beach House, Cape Tribulation Rd, T4098 0030, www. capetribbeach.com.au. At the top end of Cape Tribulation is this new and very congenial option. It offers a range of modern cabins (some en suite) from dorm to 'beachside'. The most attractive aspects

are the bush setting, its quiet atmosphere, the communal bar and bistro (with internet) all right next to the beach. A wide range of activities and tours are also available. The only drawback is the inability to park your vehicle near the cabins. This is definitely the best budget option for couples.

$$$ Lync Haven, T4098 9155, www.lync haven.com.au. Some 4 km north of Cow Bay Village, this park is very eco-friendly with plenty of wildlife around and also has a reputable restaurant.

$$$ PK's Jungle Village, Cape Tribulation Rd, in Cape Tribulation village, T4098 0040, www.pksjunglevillage.com.au. This is a well-established, mainstream hostel, popular with the social and party set. It has all the usual facilities including a lively bar, restaurant, pool and a host of activities.

$$ Crocodylus Village, near Cow Bay Village, along Buchanan Creek Rd, and the beach, T4098 9166, www.crocodylus capetrib.com. YHA-affiliated backpacker. By far the most ecologically in tune, this is essentially a glorified bush camp, with an interesting array of huts (some en suite) set around a large communal area and a landscaped pool. The only drawback is the 3-km distance from the beach. Regular shuttle buses are run, as are regular daily Cairns and Port Douglas transfers, tours and activities including local canoe trips.

$$ Ferntree Rainforest Resort, Camelot Close, T4041 6741, www.ferntreerainforest lodge.com.au. Just to the south of Cape Tribulation, this large complex has fine facilities and, for a resort, a pleasantly quiet and intimate feel. The wide range of rooms, villas and suites are well appointed, the bar/restaurant is a fine place to relax and the pool is truly memorable. Occasional good deals on offer and budget accommodation with full access to facilities.

Cooktown p125

$$$$ Sovereign Resort Hotel, on the corner of Charlotte St and Green St, T4043 0500, www.sovereign-resort.com.au. The most upmarket place in town offering 4-star rated modern 2-bedroom apartments, de luxe and standard units. It also has a reputable à la carte restaurant and a fine pool.

$$ Pam's Place YHA, on the corner of Charlotte St and Boundary St, T4069 5166, www.cooktownhostel.com.au. The main backpackers in town, with dorms, singles and en suite doubles and all the usual facilities including a pool, tour desk and bike hire.

Lizard Island

$$$$ Lizard Island Resort, T9413 6288, www.lizardisland.com.au. With some of the state's best views, the resort's accommodation is in lodges and chalets but the pick of the lot is the superb (and very expensive) Pavilion Suite, with its plunge pool and 4-poster daybed. The resort also boasts a 5-star restaurant and an exciting range of guest complimentary activities from windsurfing to guided nature walks.

🍴 Eating

Cairns *p111, map p112*
There's a huge choice. Many of the mid-range eateries best suited for day or early evening dining are found along the Esplanade. Don't forget the options on offer in the major hotels and in the Pier Complex. Seafood or Australian cuisine is generally recommended. The **International Food Court** on the Esplanade has a number of cheap outlets. See also under Bars and clubs below for cheap pub grub.

$$$ Red Ochre Restaurant, 43 Shields St, T4051 0100. Mon-Fri lunch and Mon-Sun dinner. An award-winning Australian restaurant, offering the best of Australian game fare including kangaroo, crocodile and local seafood favourites.

$$ Adelphi's Greek Taverna, 16 Aplin St, T4041 1500. Good Greek place offering both modern and traditional.

$$ Barnacle Bill's, 103 the Esplanade, T4051 2241. Another well-established seafood favourite.

$$ Café China, Rydges Plaza Hotel, corner of Spence St and Grafton St, T4041 2828. Daily from 1030. Considered the best of all the Chinese restaurants.

$$ Dundee's, Harbour Lights, 1 Marlin Parade, T4051 0399. Daily from 1130 and 0900 Sunday. Well-established favourite offering good value Australian cuisine in a relaxed atmosphere and with views over the harbour. Meat lovers will love the buffalo, roo, croc and barramundi combos. The seafood platters are also excellent.

$$ Fish D'Vine Café and Rum Bar, 17 Abbott St, T4031 6688. Daily from 1700. A new and very relaxed restaurant offering quality affordable seafood, budget cocktails and specifically rums from around the world.

$ Fusion Organics, corner of Grafton St and Aplin St, T4051 1388. Mon-Fri 0700-1700, Sat 0700-1400. Popular organic café serving up a good healthy breakfast and light lunches for about $15.

$ Gaura Nitai's Vegetarian, 55 Spence St, T4031 2255. Mon-Fri 1100-1430, 1800-2100, Sat 1800-2100. A lively place that offers great-value vegetarian selections.

$ Mudslide Café, Shop 5a Aplin St, T4041 6592. Daily 0730-late, Fri-Sat till 0200. Look no further for good coffee and to escape the hype.

$ Willie McBride's, in Fig Tree Lodge, corner of Sheridan St and Thomas St, T4041 0000. Daily from 1800. For value pub grub in a quieter Irish atmosphere.

Atherton Tablelands *p117, map p118*
Kuranda is awash with affordable cafés and eateries and Yungabarra also has a fair selection. Elsewhere the choice is limited.

$$ Nick's Swiss-Italian, on Gillies Highway, Yungaburra, T4095 3355, www.nicksrestaurant.com.au. Wed-Sun for lunch and Tue-Sun dinner 1130-2300. Passionately managed with good food, service and live music at the weekends.

$$ Rainforest View, 28 Coondoo St, Kuranda, T4093 9939. Wide range of dishes and views of the rainforest but it does get packed with tour groups.

$$-$ Kuranda Hotel, corner of Coondoo St and Arara St, Kuranda, T4093 7206. Another option with generous pub meals and a pleasant laid-back atmosphere.
$ Frogs, Kuranda, T4093 7405, in the heart of Coondoo St. Daily 0900-1600. The most popular café with the locals.
$ Whistlestop Café, 36 Cedar St, Yungaburra, T4095 3913. Breakfasts from 0700.

Port Douglas and The Daintree *p122*
There are plenty of options in Port Douglas, mostly along Macrossan St.
$$$ Rainforest Habitat Wildlife Sanctuary, 6 km south of Port Douglas centre, T4099 3235, www.rainforesthabitat.com.au. Jul-Oct. For something different consider breakfast or lunch here. It offers both a 'Breakfast with the Birds' or 'Lunch with the Lorikeets, both from $44, which includes park entry. Bookings essential.
$$ 2 Fish, 18 Wharf St, T4099 6350, and
$$ Table 41, 41 Macrossan St, T4099 4244, are both excellent for atmosphere and seafood.
$ Zinc, in prime location on the corner of Macrossan St and Davidson St, T4099 6260, www.zincportdouglas.com. Given the location it draws the crowds and is a good all-rounder. Relaxed alfresco breakfast or lunch and a lively dinner venue with quality Mod Oz cuisine and a fine cocktail list.
$ Beaches Café, on the Esplanade, overlooking Four Mile Beach, T4099 4998. Daily from 0700. For a good value breakfast and lots of tropical atmosphere.
$ Café Ecco, Shop 1, 43 Macrossan St, T4099 4056. Excellent for healthy lunches and a good breakfast.
$ Combined Club, Wharf St, T4099 5553. This place is unbeatable for the waterfront view and for value.
$ Iron Bar, 5 Macrossan St, T4099 4776. Well known for its imaginatively named and generous Australian dishes.

Cape Tribulation *p124*
See also Sleeping, page 129. Most resorts and backpackers listed have their own

restaurants or bistros, for breakfast, lunch and dinner.
$ Cassowary Café in the **Ferntree Resort**, is licensed and serves tasty breakfast, lunch and dinner with gourmet pizza a speciality.

🎇 Bars and clubs

Cairns *p111, map p112*
With so many backpackers descending on the city the nightlife is very much geared to the 'get dressed up (or down), get drunk and fall over' mentality. Finding somewhere to have a few good beers and a good conversation can be more difficult.
There is a wide range of pubs in the town from the traditional Aussie corner hotels to sports bars and, of course, the ubiquitous pseudo-Irish joints.
Cairns Rhino Bar and Bistro, corner of Spence St and Lake St, T4031 5305. Laid-back atmosphere, with live music, a bistro and a good balcony overlooking the main street.
Courthouse Hotel, in the former courthouse on Abbott St, T4031 4166. Daily until late. For something a little classier try the cool (as in temperature) atmosphere here. It is great during the heat of the day or for a little more decorum and offers live jazz on Sun nights and alfresco dining.
Gilligan's, 57 Grafton St, T4041 6566. Arguably the most popular backpacker bar and entertainment venue in Cairns, attached to one of its best backpackers. The poolside beer garden hosts live bands and DJs most nights of the week, with star performers and events staged at the weekends. If it all gets too much the Attic Lounge can provide some solace.
PJ O'Brien's, 87 Lake St, T4031 5333. Daily 1000-0300. The best of the Irish pubs is this popular spot. It has live music most nights and is not too shabby in the food department either.
Toybox, 53 Spence St, T4051 8223. Essentially a gay bar, but it welcomes both straight and gay and has highly entertaining drag shows.

Tropos, corner of Lake and Spence St, T4031 2530. Until 0500. Well established, this venue has regular theme nights.

Woolshed, 24 Shields St, T4031 6304. Very much backpacker-oriented, serving cheap drinks and generally going off well into the wee hours.

O Shopping

Cairns *p111, map p112*
Cairns has excellent shopping. The **Pier** has everything from opals to art works.

Aussie Bush Hats and Oilskins, Bellview Centre, 85 the Esplanade, T4037 0011. Australiana and traditional attire.

Cairns Night Markets, 54-60 Abbott St, T4051 7666. Daily 1630-2300. Over 100 stalls selling a rather predictable array of arts, crafts, clothing, food and souvenirs.

Rays Outdoors, 96 Mulgrave Rd. One of several outlets selling camping equipment.

Rusty's Bazaar, between Grafton St and Sheridan St. Fri evening and Sat-Sun morning. An eclectic conglomerate of colourful consumables.

Atherton Tablelands *p117, map p118*
Yungaburra markets, on the 4th Sat of the month, T4095 2111, www.yungaburra markets.com. 0700-1200. Good reputation for home-made arts, home-grown produce and the odd farm animal.

⚠ Activities and tours

Cairns *p111, map p112*
With hundreds of operators in the city vying (sometimes quite aggressively) for your tourist dollar, you are advised to seek unbiased information at the official and accredited VIC. Then shop around before choosing a specific activity, trip, or tour (or combination thereof) to suit your desires, your courage and your wallet. If you are looking to combine activities and save a few dollars try **Raging Thunder**, T4030 7990, www.ragingthunder.com.au.

Aerial tours
Cairns Heli Scenic, T4031 5999, www. cairns- heliscenic.com.au. 10 mins from $150.

Champagne Balloon Flights, T4039 9955, www.champagne balloons.com, **Raging Thunder**, T4030 7990, www.raging thunder. com.au, and **Hot Air**, T4039 2900, www. hotair.com.au, all offer similar hot air balloon trips from $225.

Daintree Air Services, T4034 9300, www. daintreeair.com.au. 60 mins fixed wing flight from $220.

Reefwatch Air Tours, T4035 9808, www. reefwatch.com. Fixed wing tours to Cooktown and the Undara Lava Tubes/ outback from $1150.

Sunlover Helicopters, T4035 9669, www. sunloverheli.com.au. 30mins ($295) to reef or rainforest with fly/cruise options from $389.

Bungee jumping
AJ Hackett, McGregor Rd, Smithfield, T4057 7188, www.ajhackett.com.au. Daily 1000-1700. Kiwi bungee jumping guru AJ Hackett has created an attractive jump complex in Smithfield, 15 mins north of Cairns. It offers a 50-m jump and also the popular jungle swing, a sort of half free-fall/ half swing that makes what you did when you were a toddler in the park seem awfully tame. Standard bungee $139, swing $89, combo $194. Pick-ups.

Cruises
There are many companies offering half, full or multi-day cruise options that concentrate on sailing, diving or just plain relaxing, with various island stopovers, reef pontoon visits and all manner of water-based activities thrown in. In general, for a basic Inner Reef Island trip without extras, expect to pay anywhere between $85-125. For an Outer Reef Cruise with snorkelling, anything from $125-250. For an Outer Reef Cruise with introductory dive from $135-250 and for a luxury 3-day cruise with accommodation,

meals and all activities included, about $500-1200. It all boils down to the type of vessel, its facilities, numbers, optional extras and the actual time allowed on the reef. Generally speaking, the smaller sailing companies do offer the most attractive rates and perhaps more peace and quiet, but lack the speed, convenience and razzmatazz of the fast, modern catamarans.

Big-Cat Green Island Reef Cruises, Reef St Terminal, 1 Spence St, T4051 0444, www. bigcat-cruises.com.au; **Great Adventures**, Reef St Terminal, T4044 9944, www.great adventures.com.au; **Reef Magic**, T4031 1588, www.reefmagic cruises.com.au; and **Sunlover Cruises**, T1800 810512, www. sunlover.com.au, are the main cruise operators in Cairns and like all the main operators are based at the new Reef Fleet Terminal on Spence St. They offer a range of tour options to Green Island, and beyond that, including certified dives, introductory dives, snorkelling, sightseeing and other water-based activities.

Compass, T4031 7217, www.reeftrip.com. An attractive alternative with a good value trip on board a modern vessel to Michaelmas and Hastings Reef, both on the outer reef. Also offered is free snorkelling, boom netting and optional dive extras, from $90. 2-day, 1-night trips are good value at $359.

Ecstasea, T4041 5588, www.divecairns .com.au. A 60-ft luxury yacht that also visits Upolo Cay with free snorkelling, from $115 (introductory dive $180).

Falla, T4041 2001, www.fallacruises.com.au. A charming, former pearl lugger that allows 4 hrs on Upolo Reef 30 km from Cairns, with free snorkelling. Departs 0900, returns 1730, $89, children $59 (introductory dives available).

Great Adventures, based in Cairns, and **Quicksilver**, based in Port Douglas, T4087 2100, www.quick silver-cruises.com.au. Both have huge floating pontoons moored on the outer reef where you can dive, snorkel, view the reef from a glass-bottom boat or with a very fetching-looking goldfish bowl on your head (you had better believe it), or simply sunbathe or watch the underwater world go by, from $199.

Ocean Spirit, T4031 2920, www.oceanspirit. com.au. An even more luxurious trip to Michaelmas Cay on the outer reef is offered on this beautiful vessel. All mod cons at $189, (introductory dive from $75).

Passions of Paradise, T4051 9505, www. passions.com.au. Large, modern catamaran that goes to Upolo Cay and Paradise Reef. From $129 (introductory dive $70). Departs daily 0800, returns 1800.

Diving

Cairns is an internationally renowned base for diving and there are dozens of dive shops, operators and schools. It is also an ideal place to learn, though certainly not the cheapest, costing from $325 for the most basic courses with no accommodation up to $470-1500 for an all-inclusive liveaboard course. Shop around and choose a reputable company with qualified instructors. The best diving is on the outer reef where the water is generally clearer and the fish species bigger. The following are just a sample and are not necessarily recommended above the many other operators. Almost all offer competitive rates and options for certified divers and snorkellers. Also see www.divingcairns. com.au.

Cairns Dive Centre, 121 Abbott St, T4051 0294, www.cairnsdive.com.au. Certification from $440 and a day's snorkel only from $85.
Down Under Dive, 287 Draper St, T4052 8300, www.downunderdive.com.au. 4-day/2-night certification from $480.
ProDive, corner of Abbott St and Shields St, T4031 5255, www.prodive-cairns.com.au. A range of trips including a 3-day/2-night certification with 11 dives from $620.
Reef Encounter, 100 Abbott St, T4031 7217, www.reeftrip.com. A 3-day/2-night certification, twin share, from $699.

Fishing

Cairns has been a world-class big game fishing venue for many years and as a result there are many excellent charters with experienced guides. Black marlin are the biggest species, capable of reaching weights of over 450 kg, which must be a bit like landing a pair of irate sumo wrestlers. Another commonly caught species is the wahoo, whose name is surely derived from the noise you make while catching it.

Cairns Reef Charter Services, T4031 4742, www.ausfish.com.au/crcs. One of the best charter companies, it has a fleet of ocean-going vessels and also offers an exciting range of multi-day ocean and inland trips to catch game fish or the famed barramundi.

Fishing Cairns, T4041 1169, www.fishingcairns.com.au. This place has an informative website listing a wide range of charters.

Horse trekking and mountain biking

Most of these companies offer combination packages with other activities or attractions.

Blazing Saddles, T4085 0197, www.blazingsaddles.com.au. Runs a half-day trek suitable for beginners, from $105, children $75. It also offers entertaining half-day ATV safaris from $125.

Dan's Mountain Biking, T4032 0066, www.cairns.aust.com/mtb. Half-day trips to the rainforest in Mulgrave Valley from $85. Full-day Cape Tribulation $125.

Rafting

Fancy tackling a 'Double D-Cup,' opting for the 'Corkscrew,' or going headfirst into the 'Wet and Moisty'? Well, you can with various rafting companies who have christened various rapids with such 'exotic' names. Cairns is the base for some excellent rafting with a wide range of adrenaline-pumping trips down the Barron, North Johnstone and Tully Rivers. It is all mighty fun, but watch out for the 'Doors of Deception'. The minimum age for rafting is usually 13 years.

Foaming Fury, 19-21 Barry St, T4031 3460, www.foamingfury.com.au. Tackles the Barron, half day from $131 and also offers something a bit different with a full-day 2-person sports rafting experience on the Russell River, from $160. It's also recommended for families.

R'n'R, Abbott St, T4035 3555, www.raft.com.au. A similar outfit to Raging Thunder, offering full-day trips down the Tully for $195, half day on the Barron for $130.

Raging Thunder, T4030 7990, www.ragingthunder.com.au. Half-, full-, and multi-day trips, as well as heli trips and many other activity combos. Half day on the Barron River from $133, full day on Tully River, $195. Also offers a wide variety of activity combos.

Sightseeing tours

There are numerous trips on offer that combine the Scenic Railway and Skyrail Gondola (see page 114). Others include deductions for the major sights. Ask at the VIC. 1-day 4WD tours to the Daintree and Cape Tribulation generally leave Cairns at about 0700 and return about 1800 and cost $150-175.

Billy Tea Bush Safaris, T4032 0077, www.billytea.com.au. Friendly, entertaining guides, day tours to Cape Tribulation and Chillagoe from $170.

Cairns Discovery Tours, T4053 5259, www.cairnsdiscoverytours.com. Half-day tour of city sights including the Botanical Gardens, Flying Doctor Service Visitor Centre and Northern Beaches, from $65, children $32.

Jungle Tours, T4041 9440, www.jungletours.com.au. Good value day trips to Cape Tribulation via Mossman Gorge from $145 and overnight trips and combination adventure packages from $185, staying at the Cape's backpacker establishments.

Northern Experience Eco Tours, T4058 0268, www.northernexperience.com.au. Another good company offering a wildlife edge to their day tour, from $137, children $95.

Trek North, T4033 2600, www.treknorth.com.au. Takes small groups to Cape Tribulation via the Daintree and Mossman Gorge, including a cruise on the Daintree River, from $160.

Tropic Wings, 278 Hartley St, T4035 3555, www.tropicwings.com.au. Offers an excellent tour to Kuranda combining the Kuranda Scenic Railway and Skyline Gondola with the addition of many exciting diversions and activities, from $149, children $75.

Tropical Horizons, T4035 6445, www.tropicalhorizonstours.com.au. Very comfortable, quality, small group tours to Port Douglas, Kuranda and the Cape, of up to 11 hrs from $161.

Wooroonooran Rainforest Safaris, T4032 1140, www.wooroonooran-safaris.com.au. Sightseeing and trekking trips in the beautiful Wooroonooran National Park and Mamu Rainforest Canopy Walkway south of Cairns, from $169.

Northern Great Barrier Reef Islands *p116*

Big Cat Green Island Reef Cruises, Reef Fleet Terminal, T4051 0444, www.bigcatcruises.com.au. This is one of the 2 main operators to Green Island. It offers half- and full-day cruises with optional extras from $75, children $40. It includes a choice of glass-bottom boat tour or snorkelling gear ($10 extra for both).

Frankland Islands Cruise and Dive, T4031 6300, www.franklandislands.com. Full-day trip with activities from $129 and camp transfers from $199. Also on offer is certified/introductory diving (full package) from $109 and a range of combo multi sight/tour package deals. The ferry departs daily from Cairns.

Great Adventures, the Wharf, Cairns, T4044 9944, www.greatadventures.com.au. There are 2 main tour operators to Green Island. This one offers basic transfers from $75, children $38, and a wide range of tour options with activity inclusions and optional extras. Additionally, there is a Green Island and Outer Reef (pontoon) tour from $210, children $105. Added extras include snorkel tour from $36, introductory dive from $138.

Atherton Tablelands *p117, map p118*

On The Wallaby Tablelands Tours, T4050 0650, www.onthewallaby.com. Entertaining guided tours of the Tablelands sights with excellent wildlife canoeing trips as a further option. Their 2-day/1-night accommodation/activity package based at their backpackers hostel in Yungaburra (see page 128) is good value and recommended. It also offers excellent backpacker-oriented wildlife and day/night canoeing.

Port Douglas and The Daintree *p122*
Cultural tours

Kuku-Yalanji Tours, T4098 2595, www.yalanji.com.au. Just short of the Mossman gorge car park is this operation. It offers excellent 2- to 3-hr Aboriginal cultural awareness walks that will enlighten you on the use of certain plants for medicinal purposes and traditional hunting methods, from $35, children $20. There is also a shop and gallery, open daily 0830-1700.

Diving and snorkelling

All the major reef operators are based at the Marina Mirage Wharf, Wharf St. Almost all of the Cairns-based companies also provide transfers from Port Douglas. The vast majority combine cruising with snorkelling and/or diving, with others being dive specialists. Those listed below are recommended but this does not imply that those not listed are not reputable.

Quicksilver, T4087 2100, www.quicksilver-cruises.com. This is the main operator in Port Douglas. Long established and highly professional, it will shuttle tourists out to their own pontoon on the edge of Agincourt Reef, where you can spend the day (5 hrs) diving, snorkelling or sunbathing. A basic day cruise with a buffet lunch costs $199, children $100. Diving and snorkelling is an added option.

Tech Dive Academy, 1/18 Macrossan St, Port Douglas, T0422-016517, www.tech-dive-academy.com.

Fishing
There are a posse of charter boats available to take you fishing. The VIC has the most recent charter listings.

Horse trekking
Wonga Beach Equestrian Centre, T4099 1117, www.beachhorserides.com.au. Entertaining rides along Wonga Beach, 20 km north, including Port Douglas transfers from $115, 3 hr.

Spas
Daintree Eco Lodge and Spa , see page 129. Offers massage (1 hr from $130) plus numerous other attractive options. Book ahead.

Wildlife and sightseeing tours
Fine Feather Tours, T4094 1199, www. fine feathertours.com.au. Operated by enthusiastic locals Del and Pat, with full-day birding tours from $235.

Reef and Rainforest Connections, 8/40 Macrossan St, Port Douglas, T4035 5588, www.reefandrainforest.com.au. Offers a wide range to Kuranda, Mossman Gorge, Daintree/Cape Tribulation and Cooktown.

On the Daintree River The search for crocs has become something of a cruise fest and there are dozens of operators. Pick-ups and day tours from Cairns or Port Douglas are available.

Chris Dahlberg's River Tours, T4098 7997, www.daintreerivertours.com.au. Operates an excellent dawn cruise (departs 0600 Nov-Mar and 0630 Apr-Oct), with an emphasis on bird spotting, from $55.

Crocodile Express, T4098 6120. This is the largest and longest serving operator, with 2 cruises. The most popular is their 1½-hr river cruise departing from the village hourly 1030-1600, from $25, children $12. The second is a 2½-hr Estuary Cruise that explores the lower reaches and the mouth of river.

Cape Tribulation *p124*
There are many activities on offer in the region, including crocodile spotting, sea kayaking, horse riding, reef cruising with diving or snorkelling and even candlelit dinners deep in the rainforest. These are best arranged through the main backpackers such as **The Cape Trib Beach House** (see page 129). See also Cairns and Port Douglas-based tour operators. Some do not run in the wet season (Dec-Mar) when access can be severely affected. Also consult the VICs in Cairns or Port Douglas.

Jungle Surfing Canopy Tours, T4098 0043, www.junglesurfingcanopytours.com.au. Offers a spot of 'rainforest canopy surfing', essentially a series of flying fox cables allowing the opportunity to do the inevitable 'Tarzan', from $90. Night wildlife spotting from $40.

Mason's Tours, T4098 0070, www. masonstours.com.au. Its guided rainforest walks are recommended. Their night walk spotting the doe-eyed possums is well worthwhile, from $49. A 4WD day trip exploring the Bloomfield Track to Cooktown with **Mason's Tours** costs from $240.

Cooktown *p125*
Cooktown offers a number of activities from self-guided local walks and historic town tours to reef fishing, cruising and snorkelling. Many tour operators in Cairns and Port Douglas offer day or multi day trips to Cooktown, some combining road travel with a scenic return flight.

⊖ Transport

Cairns *p111, map p112*
Trans North, T4095 8644, www. transnorthbus.com services the **Atherton Tablelands** including **Kuranda**, daily.

Car
The wet road conditions around Cairns and far north Queensland can be, in a word, aquatic. For up-to-date conditions and flood warnings, T131111. For RACQ road conditions report T1300 130595.

Campervan rentals and purchase (second hand), **Travellers Auto Barn**, 123-

125 Bunda St, T4041 3722, www.travellers-autobarn.com.au. It offers guaranteed buy-backs in Sydney.

Car rental The airport and Abbott St and Lake St in the city have most outlets. **Avis**, 135 Lake St and airport, T4051 5911; **Budget**, 153 Lake St, T4051 9222; **All Day Rentals**, Shop 1/ 62 Abbott St, T4031 3348; **MiniCar Rentals**, 150 Sheridan St, T1300 735577; **4WD Hire**, 440 Sheridan St, T4032 3094. For a standard car and 7-day hire expect to pay from $70 a day. Some of the larger companies like Avis also offer 4WD hire from around $175 per day.

Train

The station is on Bunda St. Travel centre is open Mon-Fri 0900-1700, Sat 0800-1200, T4036 9250. For other long-distance enquiries, T1300 131722, 24 hr, www.traveltrain.qr.com.au. There are 3 coastal train services to/from **Brisbane** and beyond, ranging in standards of luxury and price. The most popular is the fast **Tilt Train** (departs Brisbane Mon and Fri, Cairns Sun and Wed); alternatively there is the **Sunlander** (departs Brisbane 0835, Tue, Sat, Sun and Thu). There is one outback service, the **Gulflander**, that shuttles between **Croydon** and **Normanton**. A local scenic service also operates to **Kuranda**, T4036 9333, www.ksr.com.au, from $45, children $23 ($68 return). Ask about the various holiday and discoverer passes, for price reductions and packages.

Northern Great Barrier Reef Islands *p116*

For **Green Island**, ferries leave the Reef Fleet Terminal on waterfront, Cairns, with additional transfers from Palm Beach (Northern Beaches) and Port Douglas. For **Fitzroy Island**, **Fitzroy Island Ferry**, T4030 7900, departs from Cairns, day-trip from $68, children $37, www.ragingthunder.com.au. For **Lizard Island**, see Cooktown page 138.

Atherton Tablelands *p117, map p118*

Most visitors to **Kuranda** make the village part

of a day-tour package from Cairns, with the highlight actually accessing it via the Barron Gorge and the Skyline Gondola, the Scenic Railway or both. See page 132 for operators in Cairns. Prices and schedules for the **Skyrail**, T4038 1555, and **Scenic Railway**, T4036 9333, are listed on page 114. **Kuranda Shuttle**, T0418-772953, and **Trans North**, T4095 8644, www.transnorthbus.com share services to Kuranda at the most competitive price. **Trans North** also runs daily services to **Yungaburra**.

Port Douglas *p122*
Air

Port Douglas is accessed from Cairns International Airport. **Airport Connections**, T4099 5950, www.tnqshuttle.com, offers services at least every hour daily from 0630-1630, $32, children $16.

Bus

Note many accommodation and activity operators offer free or low-cost transfers from Cairns. Ask at the VIC for details. **Coral Reef Coaches**, 35 Front St, Mossman, T4098 2800, www.coralreefcoaches.com.au, run regular local bus services to Cairns (and airport) via Mossman from $35. **Sun Palm Coaches**, 16 Teamsters Close, Port Douglas, T4087 2900, www.sunpalm transport.com, also connect Cairns with Port Douglas, Cairns Northern Beaches, Daintree, Cow Bay and Cape Tribulation. The main bus stops are on Grant St and at the Marina Mirage (Wharf) Complex.

Cycling/scooter
Holiday Bike and Hire, 6/40 Macrossan St, T4099 6144, hires out bikes.

Cape Tribulation *p124*
Bus
Coral Reef Coaches, 37 Front St, Mossman, T4098 2800, offers daily scheduled services and tour packages from **Cairns** and **Port Douglas**, from $35 one way (Cairns).

Car

Self drive is recommended but all roads in the area can be treacherous in the wet season (Dec-Mar). For road information, T131940, www.131940.qld.gov.au. **Daintree River Ferry**, 15 km southeast of Daintree village, runs daily from 0600-2400, pedestrian $2 return, vehicle $20 return. Beyond Cape Tribulation (36 km), the road degenerates into the strictly 4WD Bloomfield Track, which winds its precarious 120 km way to **Cooktown**. Fuel is available 4 km east of Cow Bay village and 6 km north at the Rainforest Village Store. In the event of breakdown contact the RACQ (Cow Bay), T4098 9037.

Cooktown p125

Skytrans Airlines, T4046 2462, www.skytrans.com.au, operates regular transfers to **Cairns** from $122 one way (with a 3-day advance purchase). If you are not joining a tour from Cairns or Port Douglas contact Cooktown VIC (see page 136) for the latest information on scheduled bus services. For **Lizard Island**, there are various regional air operators and vessel charter companies but prices and times vary. VIC in Cooktown is the best place to enquire for the most up-to-date options. **Daintree Air Services**, T4034 9300, www.daintreeair.com.au, offers a day package from $690, departing from Cairns. **Skytrans Airlines**, T4040 6700, www.skytrans. com.au, also offers air charters from Cairns or Cooktown.

● Directory

Cairns *p111, map p112*

Banks All the major banks have branches in the city centre, especially at the intersection of Shields St and Abbott St. **Internet and library** Cairns City Public Library, 151 Abbott St, T4044 3720. Free internet. **Medical services** Cairns Base Hospital, the Esplanade (north), T4050 6333. Cairns City 24-hr Medical centre, 120-124 Mulgrave Rd, T4051 2755. **Post** 13 Grafton St, T131318. Mon-Fri 0830-1700. Postcode 4870. **Useful numbers** Police, emergency T000, 5 Sheridan St, T4030 7000.

Port Douglas *p122*

Banks Macrossan St or Port Village Centre. **Internet** Port Douglas Video, corner Port Douglas Rd and Barrier St, T4098 5350. Daily 0900-2200. **Medical services** Mossman, T4098 1248. Port Village Medical Centre, Shop 17, shopping centre, Macrossan St, T4099 5043, 24 hrs. **Post** 5 Owen St, T4099 5210. Mon-Fri 0900-1700, Sat 0900-1400. Postcode 4877. **Pharmacy** Macrossan St Pharmacy, 13/14 Port Village Centre, T4099 5223. **Useful numbers** Police, 31 Wharf St, T4087 1999.

Contents

Footnotes

Index

Titles available in the Footprint *Focus* range

Latin America	UK RRP	US RRP
Bahia & Salvador	£7.99	$11.95
Buenos Aires & Pampas	£7.99	$11.95
Costa Rica	£8.99	$12.95
Cuzco, La Paz & Lake Titicaca	£8.99	$12.95
El Salvador	£5.99	$8.95
Guadalajara & Pacific Coast	£6.99	$9.95
Guatemala	£8.99	$12.95
Guyana, Guyane & Suriname	£5.99	$8.95
Havana	£6.99	$9.95
Honduras	£7.99	$11.95
Nicaragua	£7.99	$11.95
Paraguay	£5.99	$8.95
Quito & Galápagos Islands	£7.99	$11.95
Recife & Northeast Brazil	£7.99	$11.95
Rio de Janeiro	£8.99	$12.95
São Paulo	£5.99	$8.95
Uruguay	£6.99	$9.95
Venezuela	£8.99	$12.95
Yucatán Peninsula	£6.99	$9.95

Asia	UK RRP	US RRP
Angkor Wat	£5.99	$8.95
Bali & Lombok	£8.99	$12.95
Chennai & Tamil Nadu	£8.99	$12.95
Chiang Mai & Northern Thailand	£7.99	$11.95
Goa	£6.99	$9.95
Hanoi & Northern Vietnam	£8.99	$12.95
Ho Chi Minh City & Mekong Delta	£7.99	$11.95
Java	£7.99	$11.95
Kerala	£7.99	$11.95
Kolkata & West Bengal	£5.99	$8.95
Mumbai & Gujarat	£8.99	$12.95

Africa & Middle East	UK RRP	US RRP
Beirut	£6.99	$9.95
Damascus	£5.99	$8.95
Durban & KwaZulu Natal	£8.99	$12.95
Fès & Northern Morocco	£8.99	$12.95
Jerusalem	£8.99	$12.95
Johannesburg & Kruger National Park	£7.99	$11.95
Kenya's beaches	£8.99	$12.95
Kilimanjaro & Northern Tanzania	£8.99	$12.95
Zanzibar & Pemba	£7.99	$11.95

Europe	UK RRP	US RRP
Bilbao & Basque Region	£6.99	$9.95
Granada & Sierra Nevada	£6.99	$9.95
Málaga	£5.99	$8.95
Orkney & Shetland Islands	£5.99	$8.95
Skye & Outer Hebrides	£6.99	$9.95

North America	UK RRP	US RRP
Vancouver & Rockies	£8.99	$12.95

Australasia	UK RRP	US RRP
Brisbane & Queensland	£8.99	$12.95
Perth	£7.99	$11.95

For the latest books, e-books and smart phone app releases, and a wealth of travel information, visit us at: www.footprinttravelguides.com.

footprinttravelguides.com

Join us on facebook for the latest travel news, product releases, offers and amazing competitions: www.facebook. com/footprintbooks.com.